BAT[…]
TURNING […]

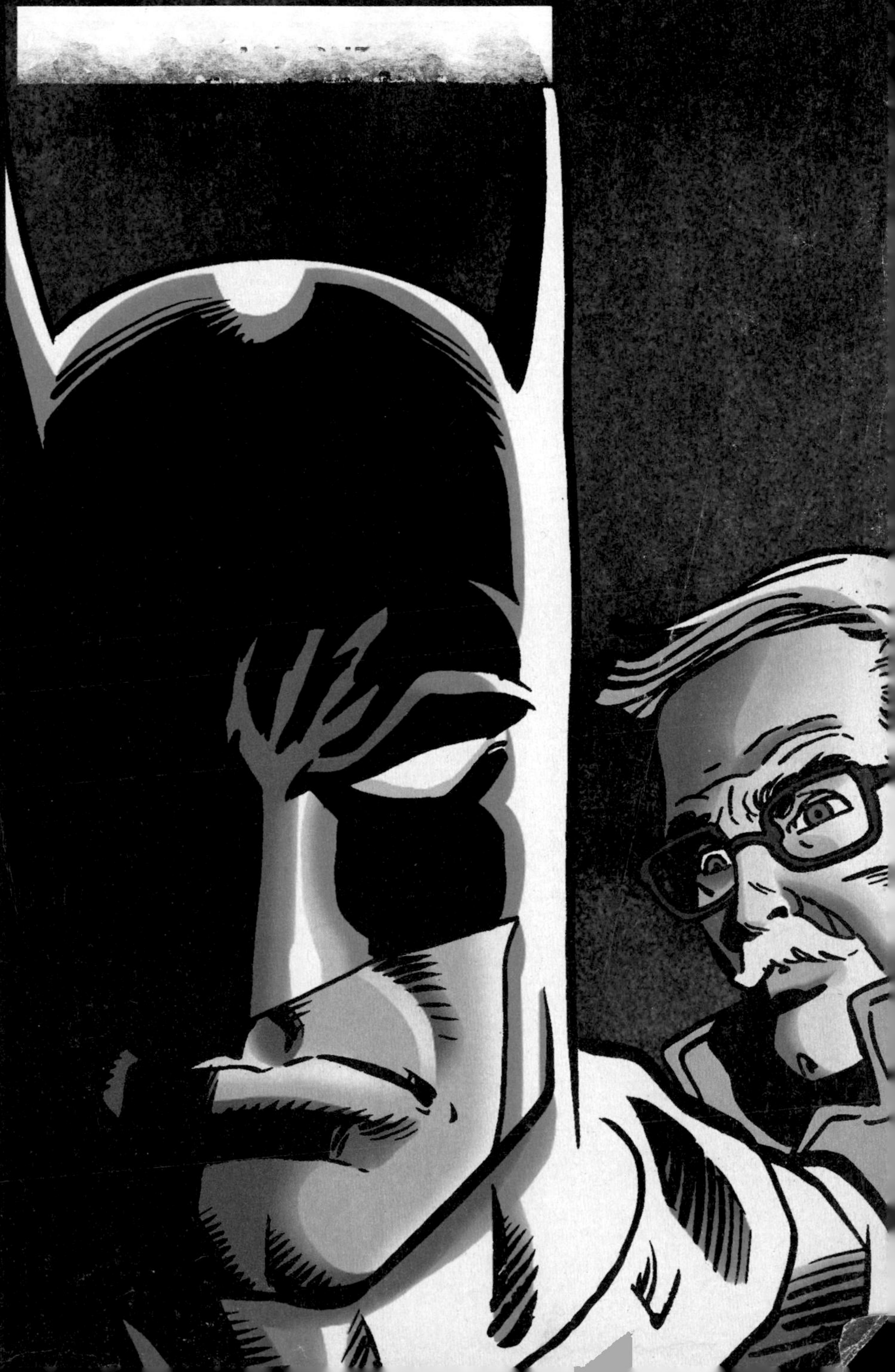

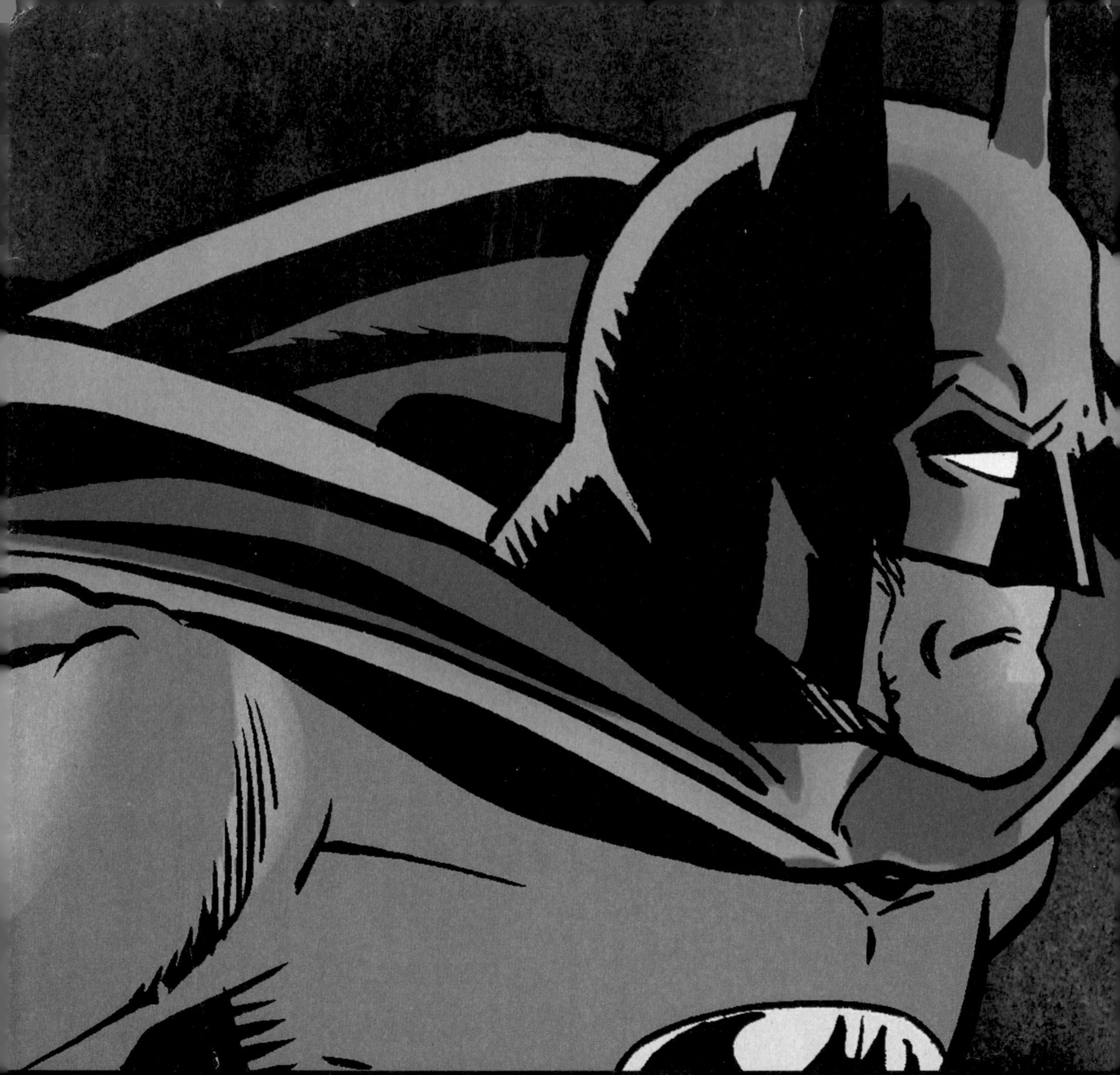

Greg Rucka · Ed Brubaker · Chuck Dixon WRITERS Steve Lieber · Joe Giella

Tom McCraw · Shannon Blanchard · Glenn Whitmore · John Kalisz · Patricia Mulvihill COLORISTS

BAT
TURNIN

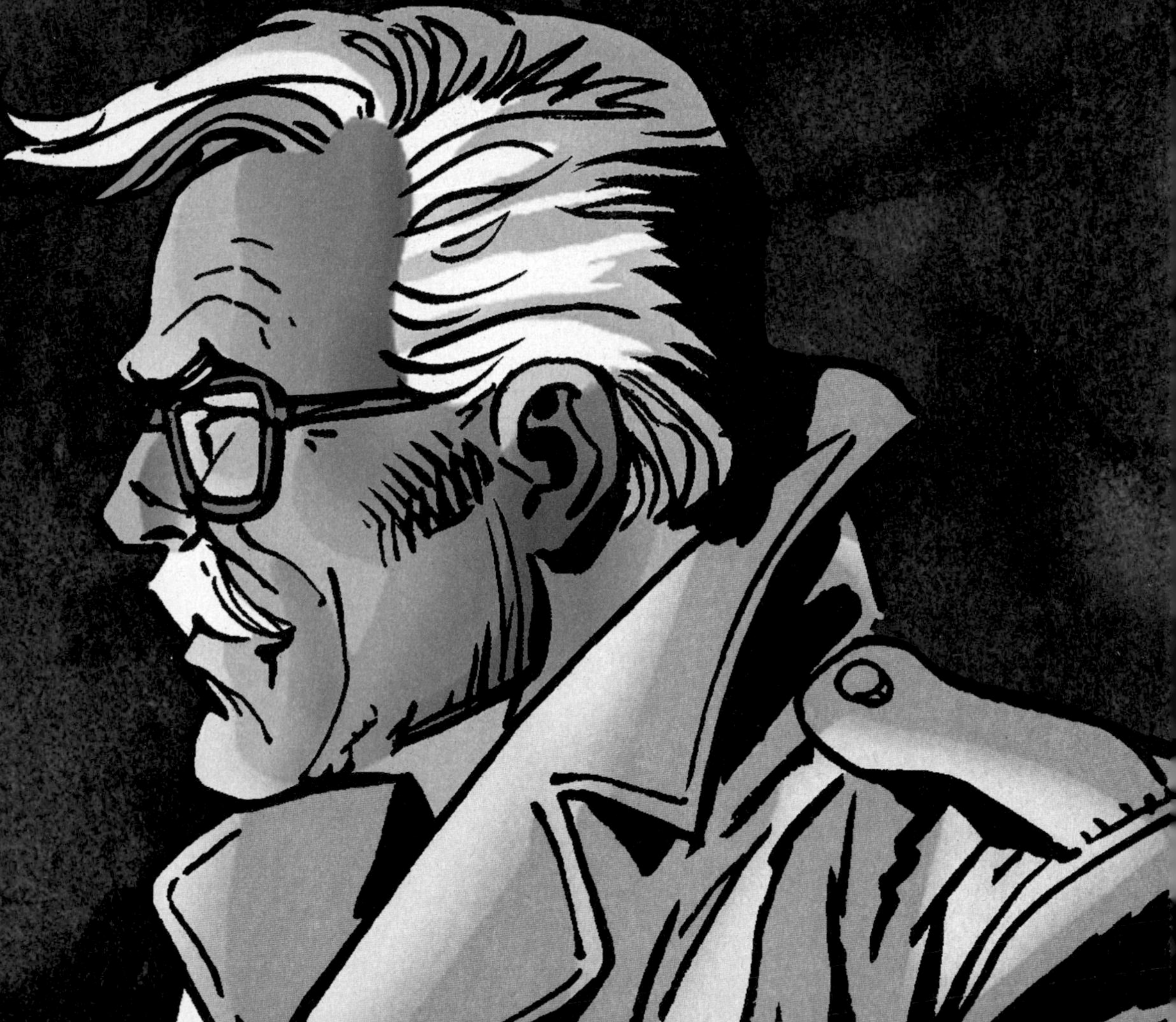

ick Giordano and Bob Smith · Brent Anderson · Paul Pope and Claude St. Aubin ARTISTS

Willie Shubert LETTERER

Batman created by Bob Kane

MAN

POINTS

DAN DIDIO
Senior VP-Executive Editor

MATT IDELSON
Editor-original series

MICHAEL WRIGHT
Associate Editor-original series

PETER HAMBOUSSI
Editor-collected edition

ROBBIN BROSTERMAN
Senior Art Director

PAUL LEVITZ
President & Publisher

GEORG BREWER
VP-Design & DC Direct Creative

RICHARD BRUNING
Senior VP-Creative Director

PATRICK CALDON
Executive VP-Finance & Operations

CHRIS CARAMALIS
VP-Finance

JOHN CUNNINGHAM
VP-Marketing

TERRI CUNNINGHAM
VP-Managing Editor

ALISON GILL
VP-Manufacturing

HANK KANALZ
VP-General Manager, WildStorm

JIM LEE
Editorial Director-WildStorm

PAULA LOWITT
Senior VP-Business & Legal Affairs

MARYELLEN MCLAUGHLIN
VP-Advertising & Custom Publishing

JOHN NEE
VP-Business Development

GREGORY NOVECK
Senior VP-Creative Affairs

SUE POHJA
VP-Book Trade Sales

CHERYL RUBIN
Senior VP-Brand Management

JEFF TROJAN
VP-Business Development, DC Direct

BOB WAYNE
VP-Sales

Cover illustration by Tim Sale
Publication design by Amelia Grohman

BATMAN: TURNING POINTS

DC Comics
1700 Broadway, New York, NY 10019
A Warner Bros. Entertainment Company.

Printed in Canada. First Printing.
ISBN: 1-4012-1360-X
ISBN 13: 978-1-4012-1360-2

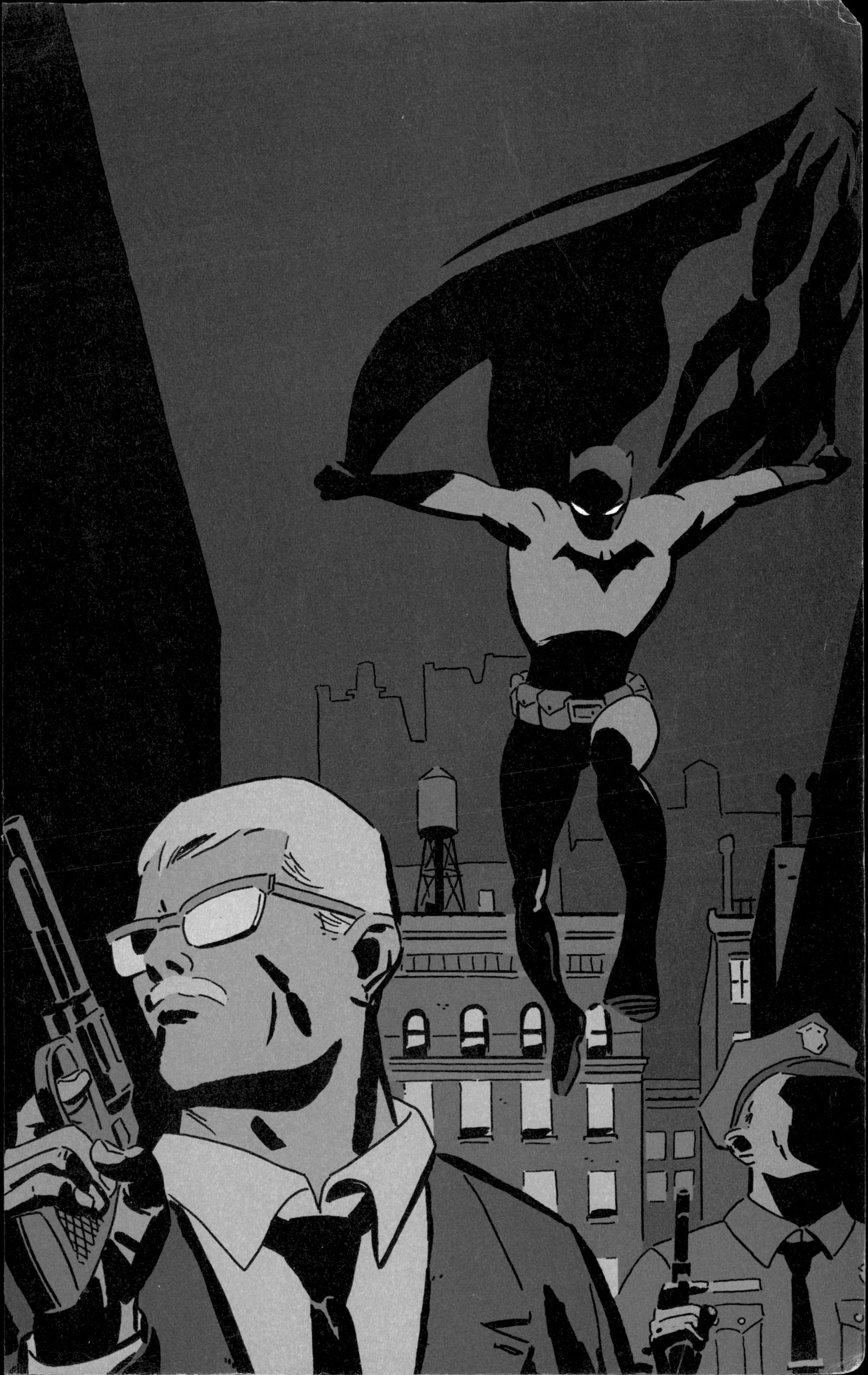

CHAPTER ONE

UNEASY ALLIES

Greg Rucka
writer

Steve Lieber
artist

Javier Pulido
cover artist

Tom McCraw
colorist

Willie Schubert
letterer

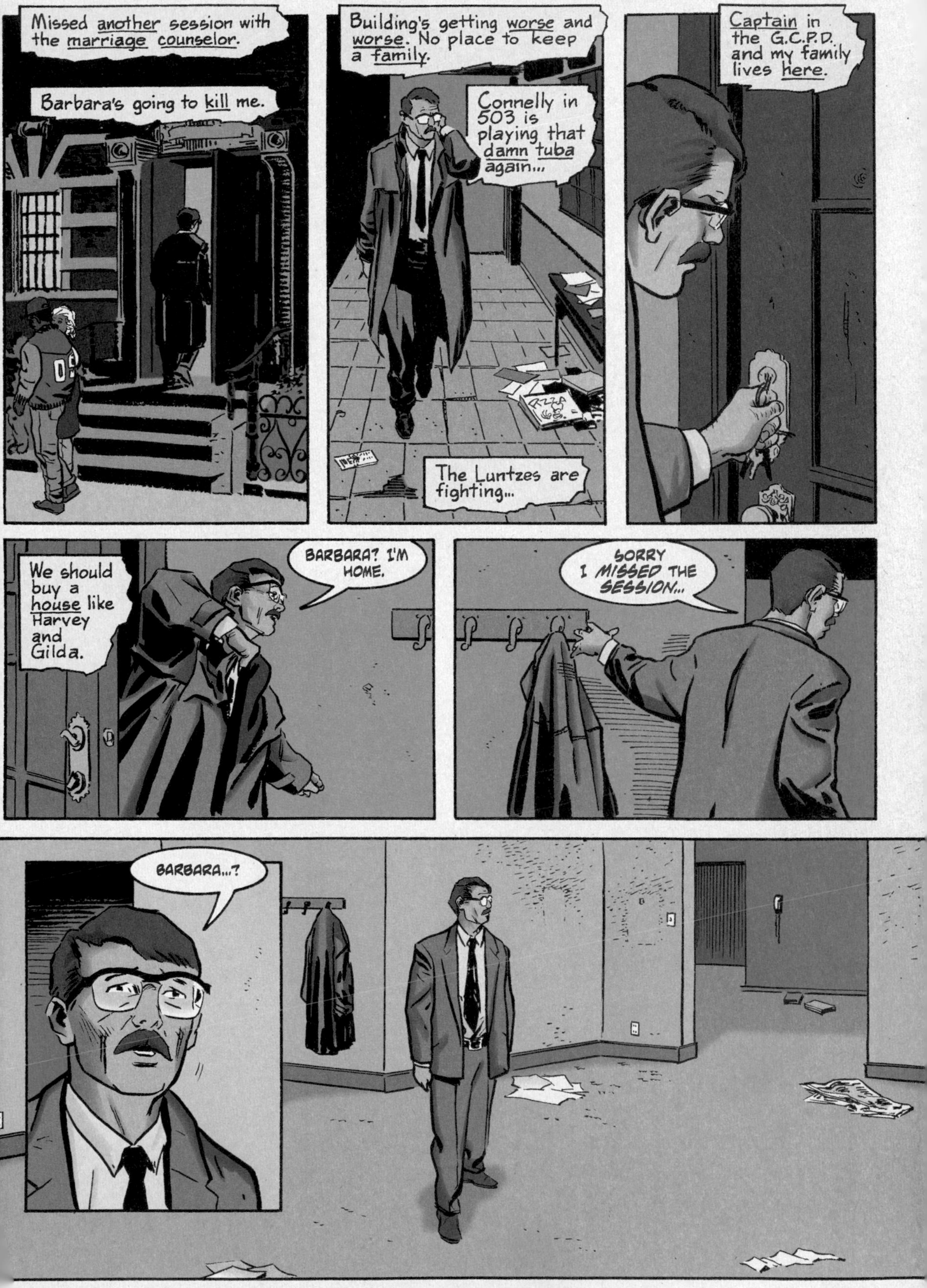
Missed another session with the marriage counselor.
Barbara's going to kill me.
Building's getting worse and worse. No place to keep a family.
Connelly in 503 is playing that damn tuba again...
The Luntzes are fighting...
Captain in the G.C.P.D. and my family lives here.
We should buy a house like Harvey and Gilda.
BARBARA? I'M HOME.
SORRY I MISSED THE SESSION...
BARBARA...?

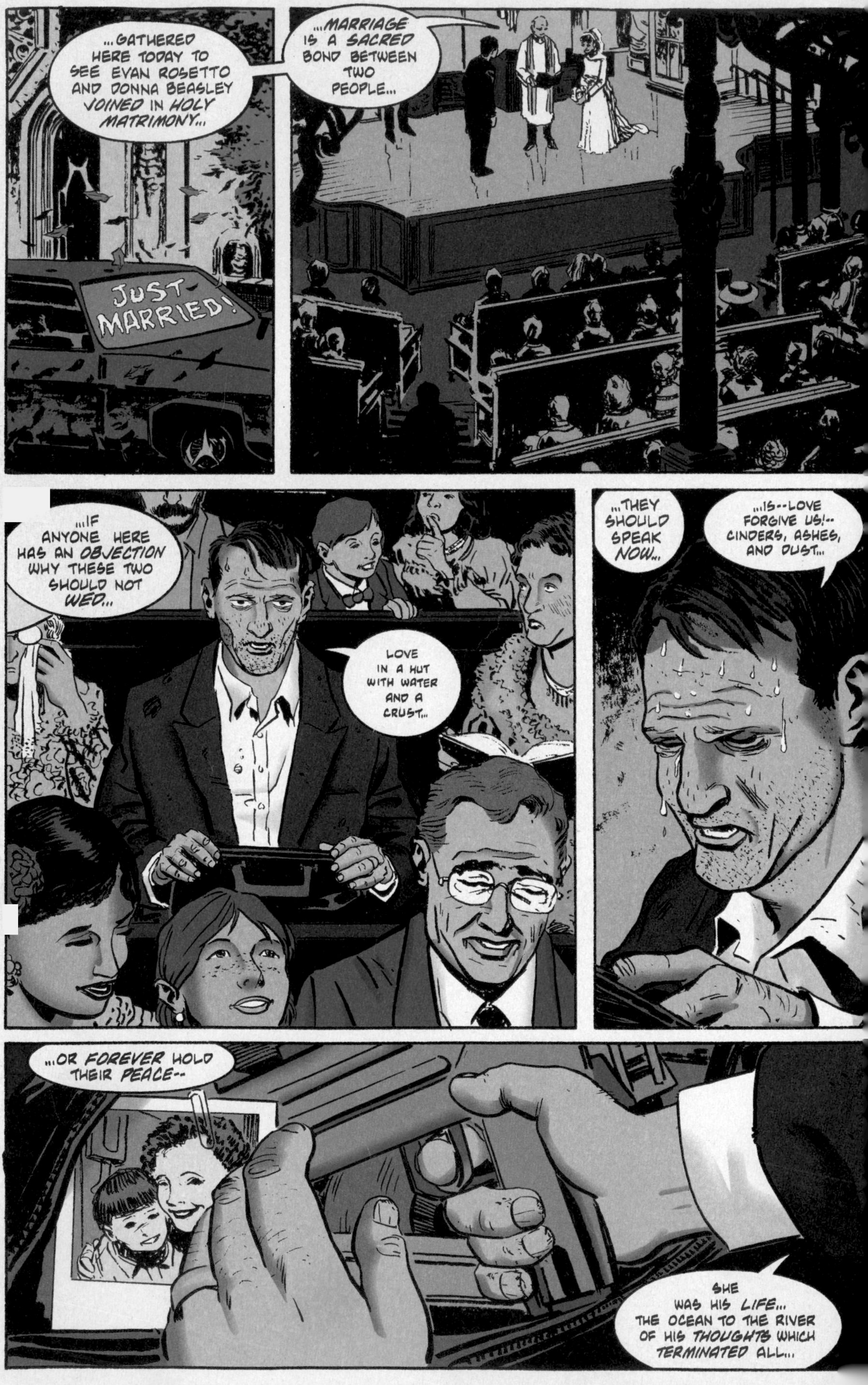
...GATHERED HERE TODAY TO SEE EVAN ROSETTO AND DONNA BEASLEY JOINED IN HOLY MATRIMONY...
JUST MARRIED!
...MARRIAGE IS A SACRED BOND BETWEEN TWO PEOPLE...
...IF ANYONE HERE HAS AN OBJECTION WHY THESE TWO SHOULD NOT WED...
LOVE IN A HUT WITH WATER AND A CRUST...
...THEY SHOULD SPEAK NOW...
...IS--LOVE FORGIVE US!--CINDERS, ASHES, AND DUST...
...OR FOREVER HOLD THEIR PEACE--
SHE WAS HIS LIFE... THE OCEAN TO THE RIVER OF HIS THOUGHTS WHICH TERMINATED ALL...

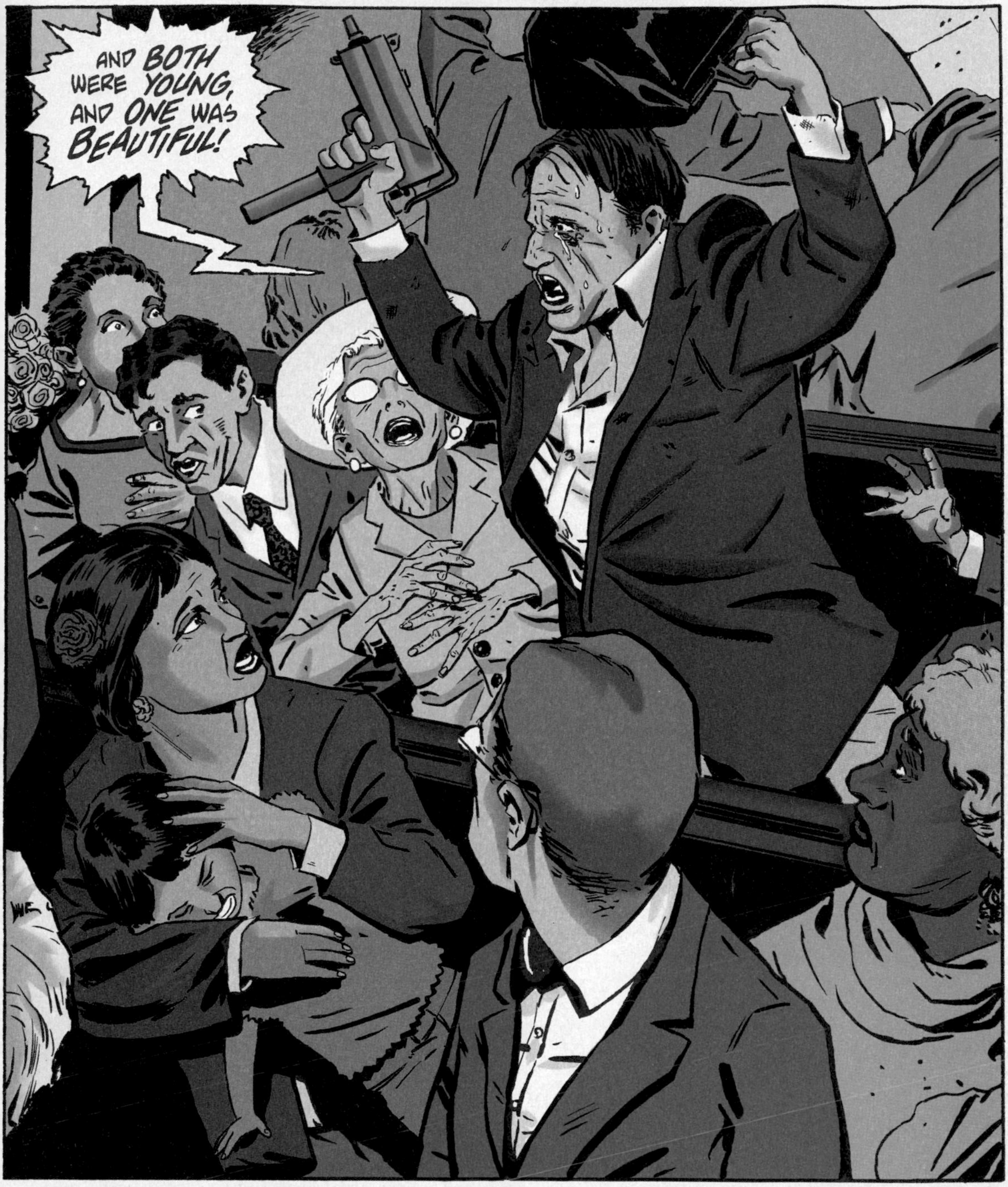
AND BOTH WERE YOUNG, AND ONE WAS BEAUTIFUL!

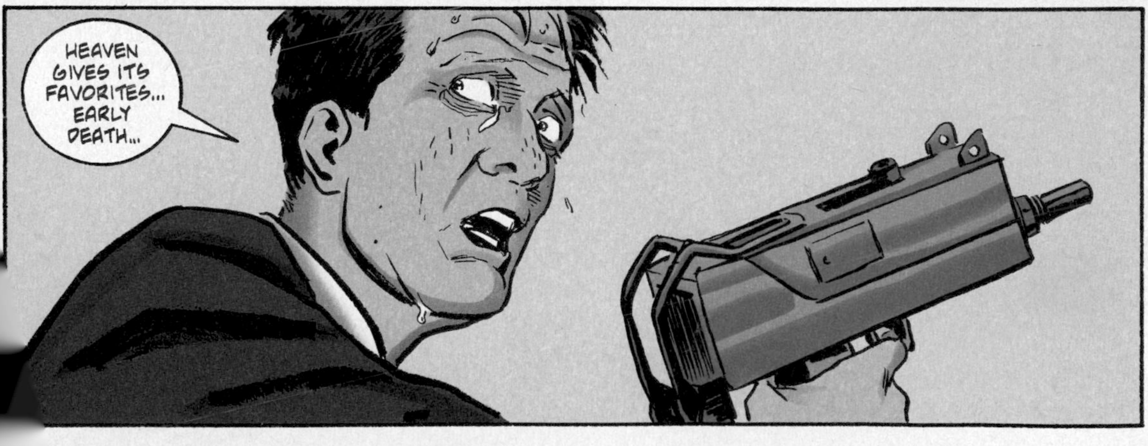
HEAVEN GIVES ITS FAVORITES... EARLY DEATH...

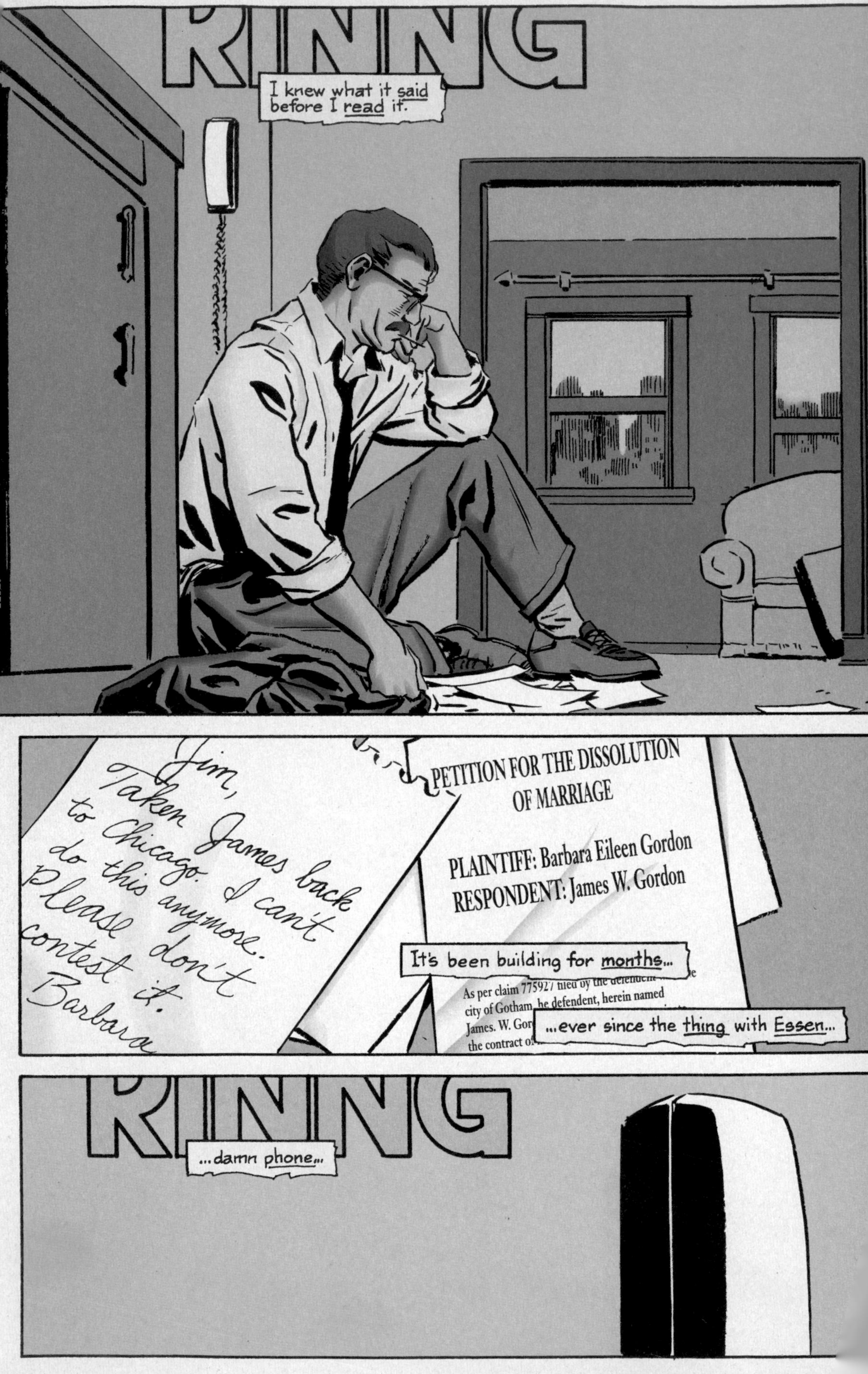
RINNG
I knew what it said before I read it.
Jim,
Taken James back to Chicago. I can't do this anymore. Please don't contest it.
Barbara
PETITION FOR THE DISSOLUTION OF MARRIAGE
PLAINTIFF: Barbara Eileen Gordon
RESPONDENT: James W. Gordon
It's been building for months...
As per claim 775927 filed by the defendent
city of Gotham, he defendent, herein named
James. W. Gor
the contract of
...ever since the thing with Essen...
RINNG
...damn phone...

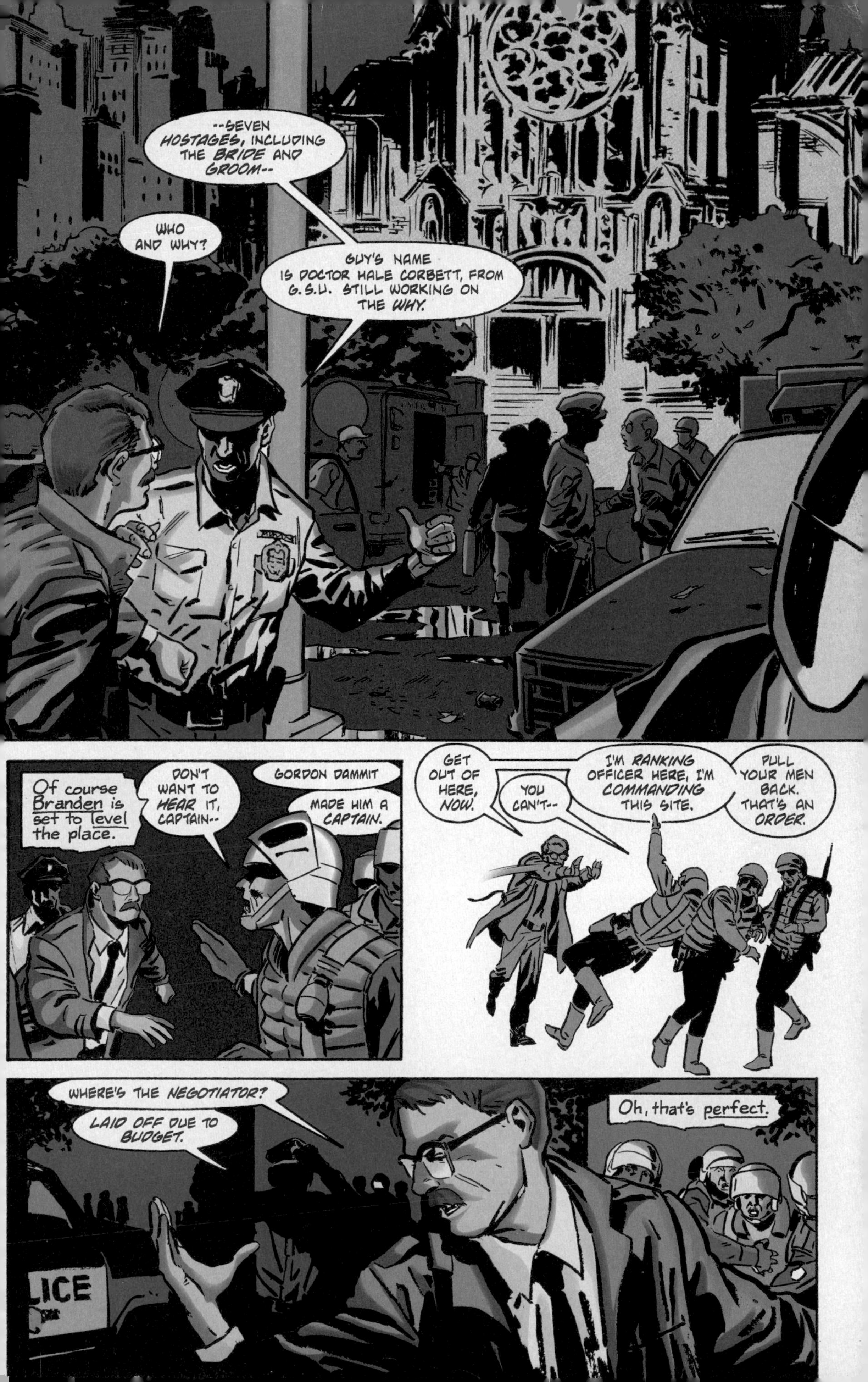
--SEVEN HOSTAGES, INCLUDING THE BRIDE AND GROOM--
WHO AND WHY?
GUY'S NAME IS DOCTOR HALE CORBETT, FROM G.S.U. STILL WORKING ON THE WHY.
Of course Branden is set to level the place.
DON'T WANT TO HEAR IT, CAPTAIN--
GORDON DAMMIT
MADE HIM A CAPTAIN.
GET OUT OF HERE, NOW.
YOU CAN'T--
I'M RANKING OFFICER HERE, I'M COMMANDING THIS SITE.
PULL YOUR MEN BACK. THAT'S AN ORDER.
WHERE'S THE NEGOTIATOR?
LAID OFF DUE TO BUDGET.
Oh, that's perfect.
LICE

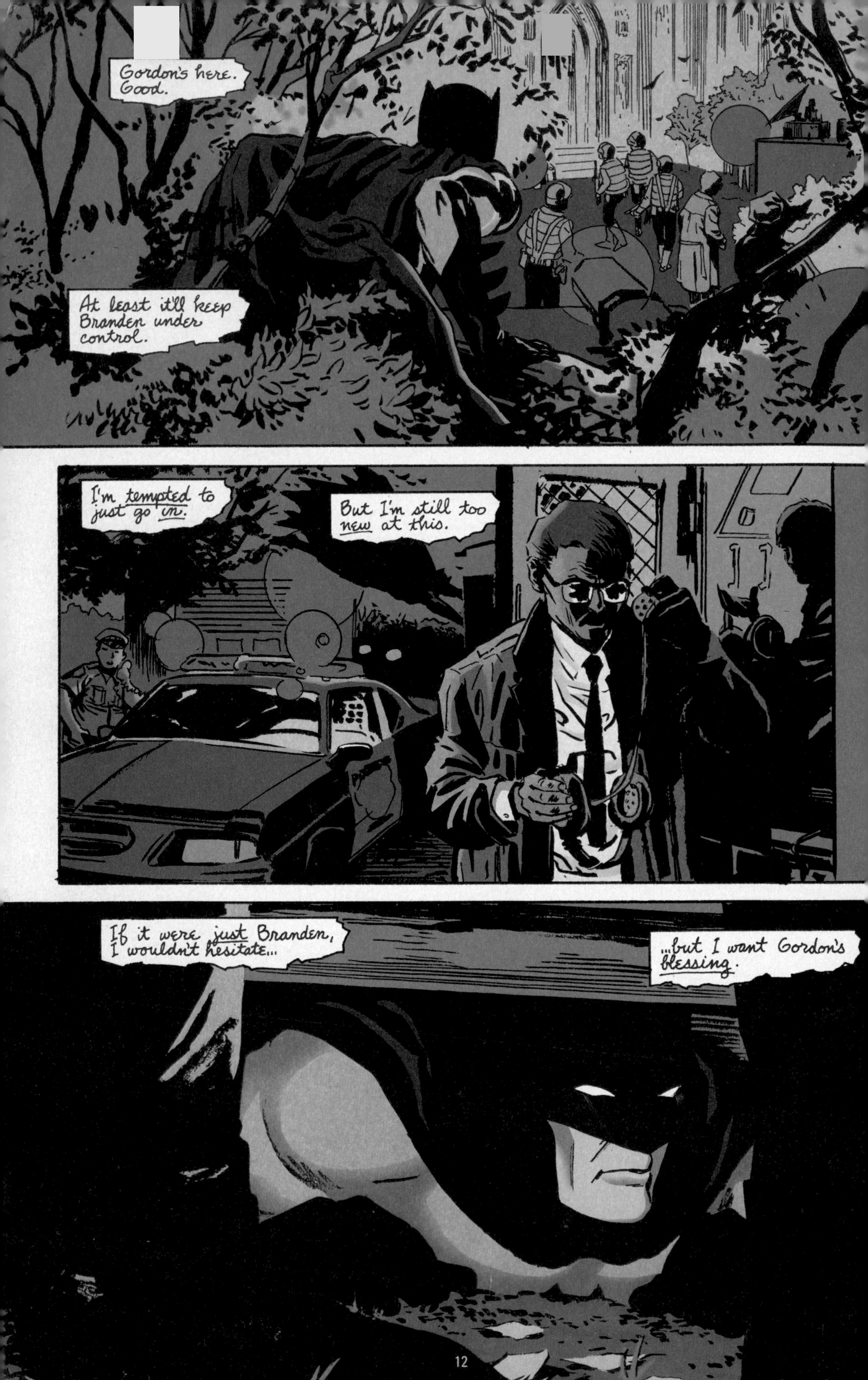
Gordon's here. Good.
At least it'll keep Branden under control.
I'm tempted to just go in.
But I'm still too new at this.
If it were just Branden, I wouldn't hesitate...
...but I want Gordon's blessing.

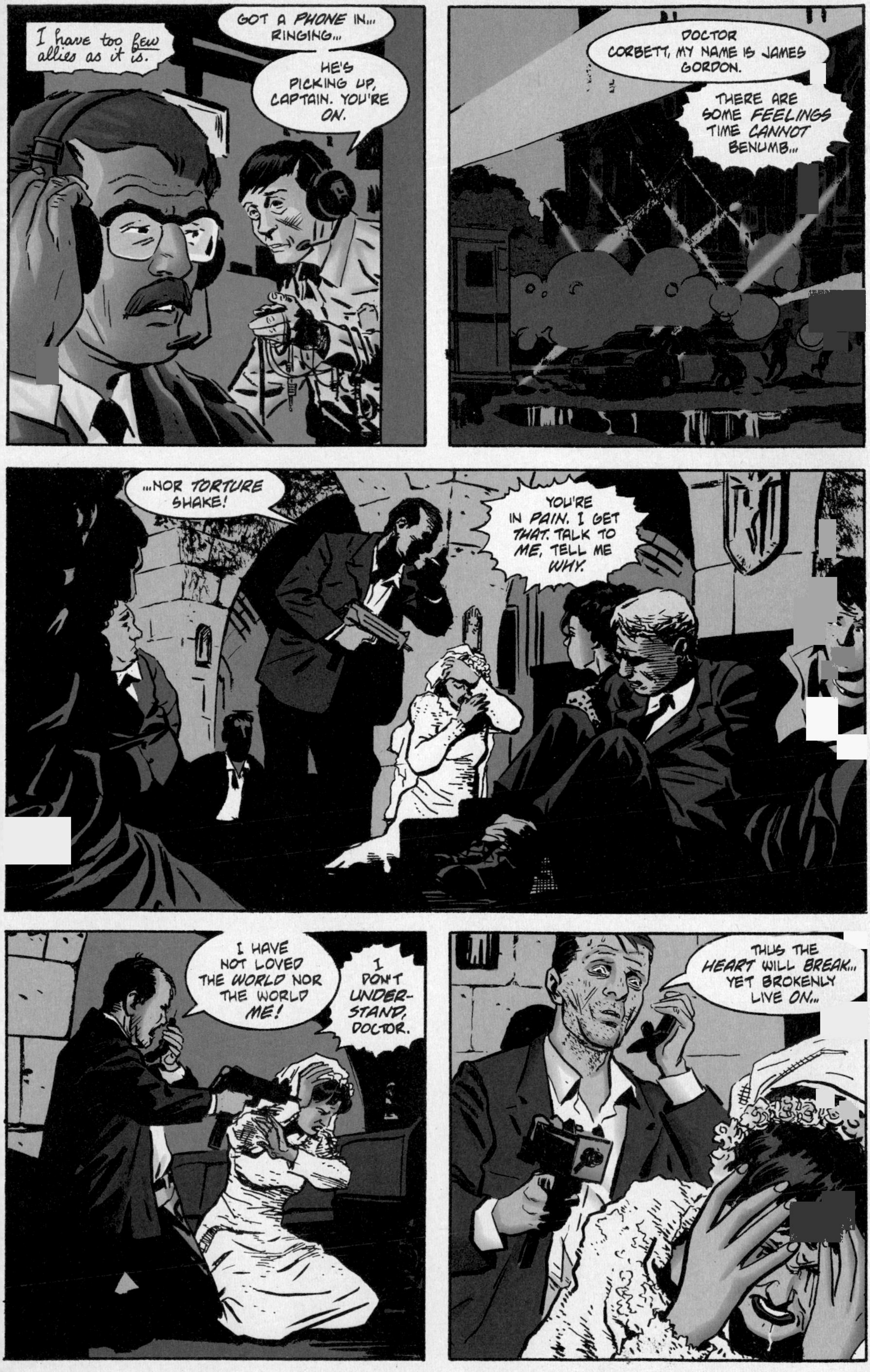
I have too few allies as it is.
GOT A PHONE IN... RINGING...
HE'S PICKING UP, CAPTAIN. YOU'RE ON.
DOCTOR CORBETT, MY NAME IS JAMES GORDON.
THERE ARE SOME FEELINGS TIME CANNOT BENUMB...
...NOR TORTURE SHAKE!
YOU'RE IN PAIN. I GET THAT. TALK TO ME, TELL ME WHY.
I HAVE NOT LOVED THE WORLD NOR THE WORLD ME!
I DON'T UNDERSTAND, DOCTOR.
THUS THE HEART WILL BREAK... YET BROKENLY LIVE ON...

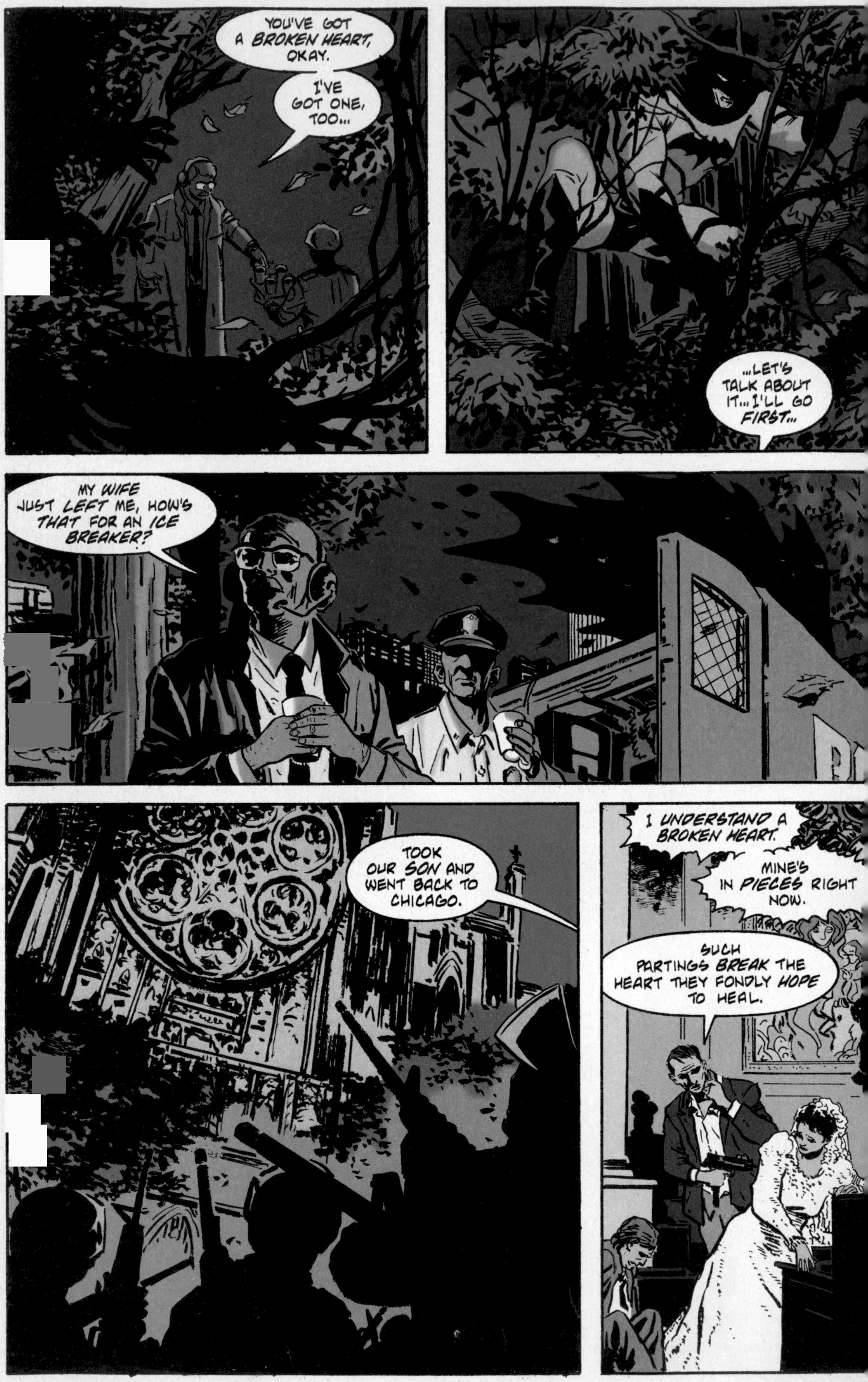
YOU'VE GOT A BROKEN HEART, OKAY.
I'VE GOT ONE, TOO...
...LET'S TALK ABOUT IT... I'LL GO FIRST...
MY WIFE JUST LEFT ME, HOW'S THAT FOR AN ICE BREAKER?
TOOK OUR SON AND WENT BACK TO CHICAGO.
I UNDERSTAND A BROKEN HEART.
MINE'S IN PIECES RIGHT NOW.
SUCH PARTINGS BREAK THE HEART THEY FONDLY HOPE TO HEAL.

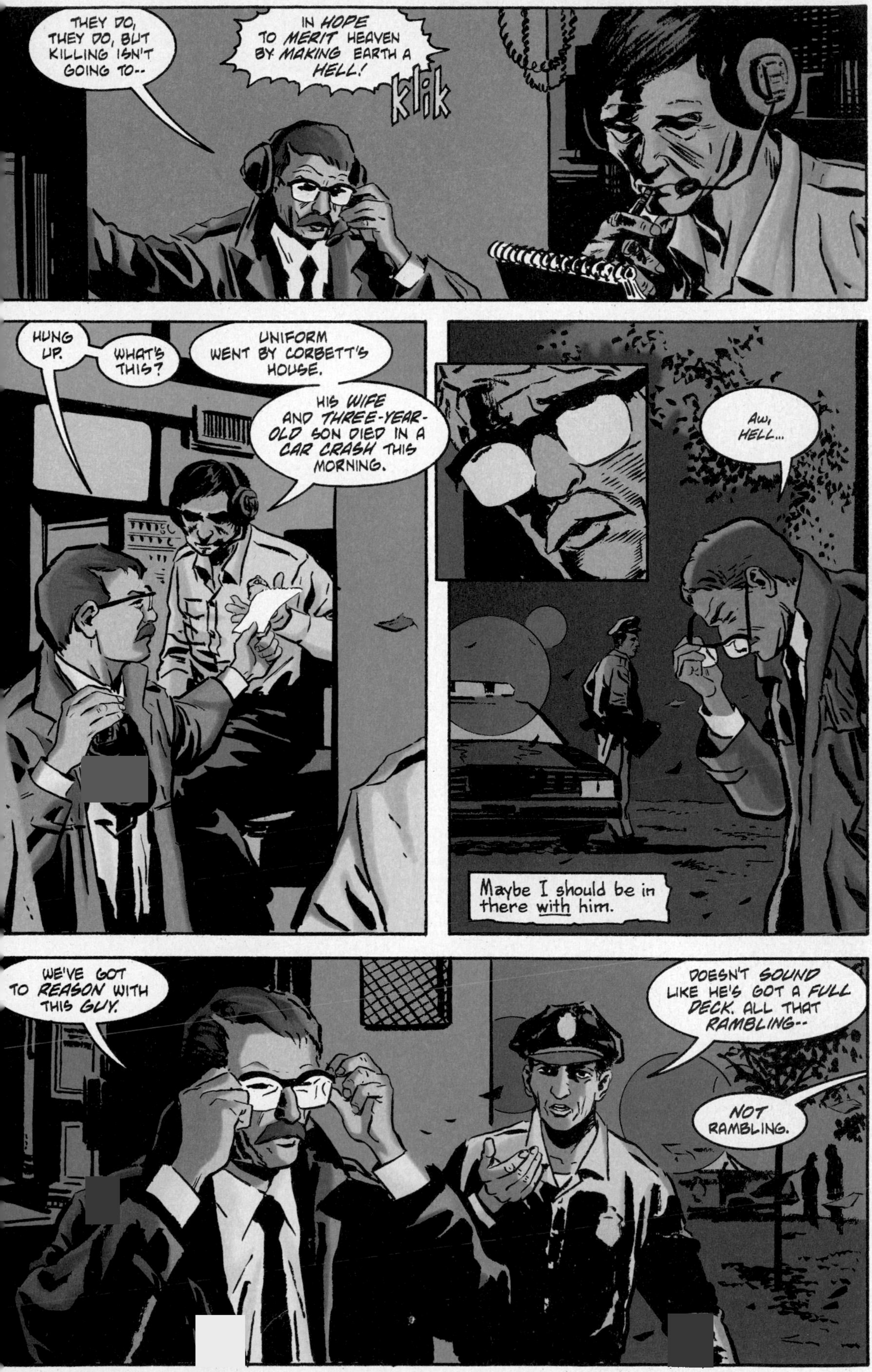
THEY DO, THEY DO, BUT KILLING ISN'T GOING TO--
IN HOPE TO MERIT HEAVEN BY MAKING EARTH A HELL!
klik
HUNG UP.
WHAT'S THIS?
UNIFORM WENT BY CORBETT'S HOUSE.
HIS WIFE AND THREE-YEAR-OLD SON DIED IN A CAR CRASH THIS MORNING.
AW, HELL...
Maybe I should be in there with him.
WE'VE GOT TO REASON WITH THIS GUY.
DOESN'T SOUND LIKE HE'S GOT A FULL DECK. ALL THAT RAMBLING--
NOT RAMBLING.

QUOTING.

QUOTING *LORD BYRON*, IN FACT.

HOW LONG WERE YOU *LISTENING?*

NOT *LONG.*

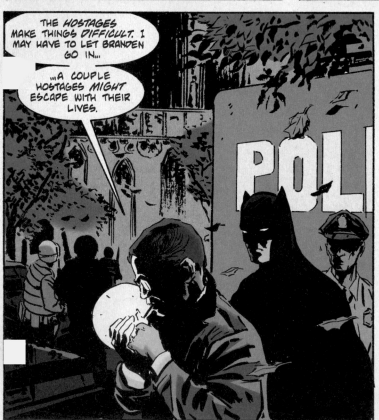

THE *HOSTAGES* MAKE THINGS *DIFFICULT.* I MAY HAVE TO LET BRANDEN GO IN...

...A COUPLE HOSTAGES *MIGHT* ESCAPE WITH THEIR LIVES.

POLI

UNLESS YOU HAVE AN *ALTERNATIVE?*

I *DO.*

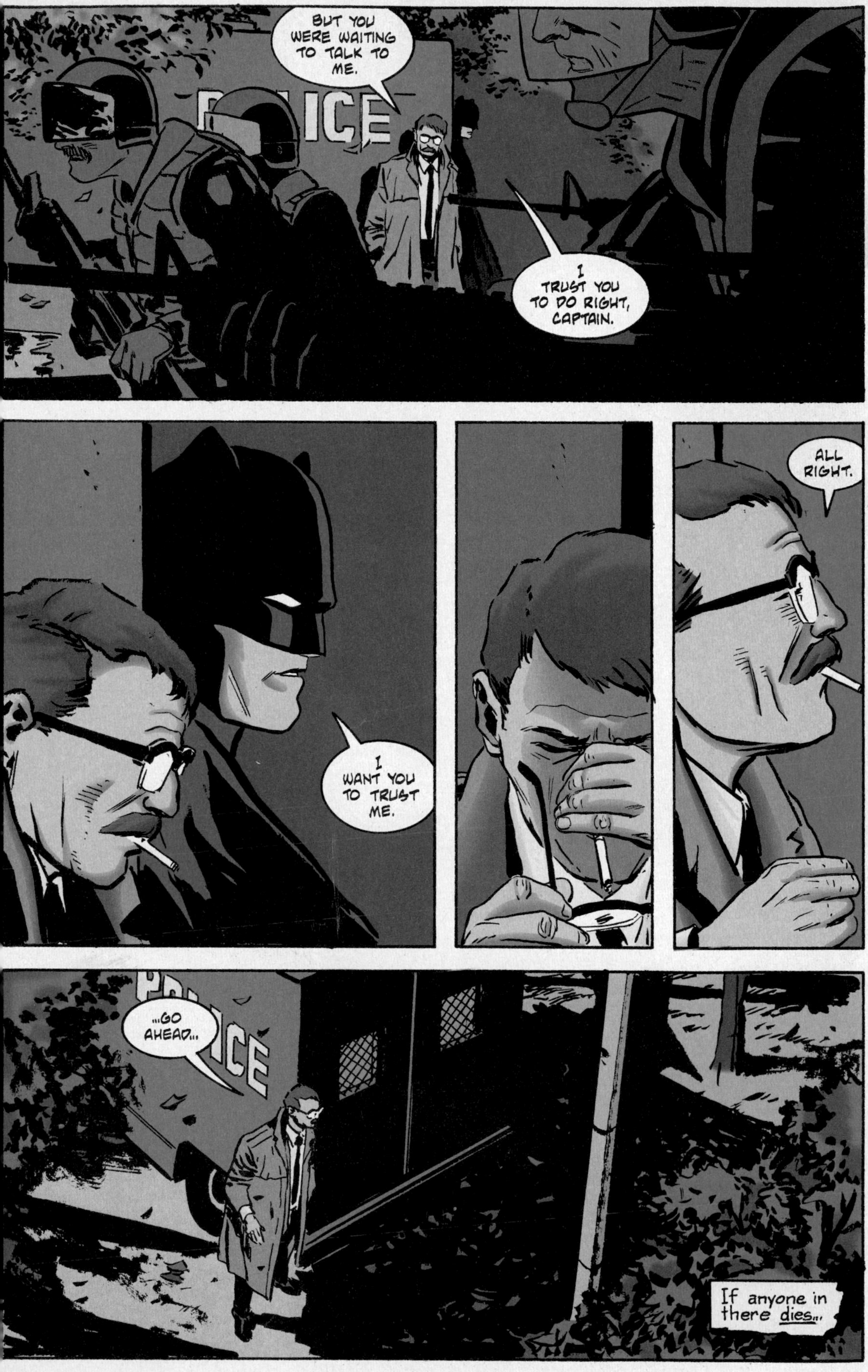
BUT YOU WERE WAITING TO TALK TO ME.
I TRUST YOU TO DO RIGHT, CAPTAIN.
I WANT YOU TO TRUST ME.
ALL RIGHT.
...GO AHEAD...
If anyone in there dies...

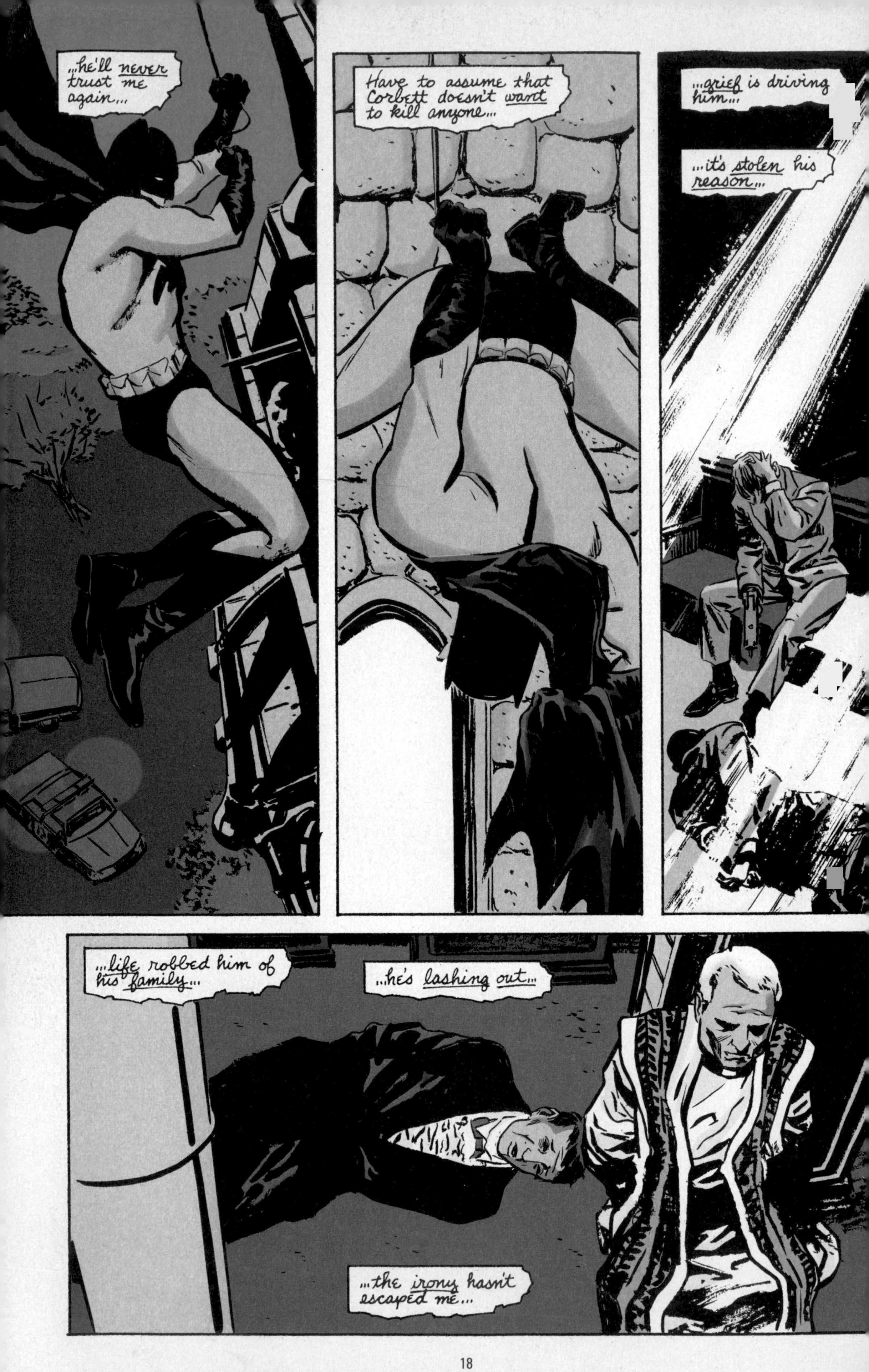
...he'll never trust me again...
Have to assume that Corbett doesn't want to kill anyone...
...grief is driving him...
...it's stolen his reason...
...life robbed him of his family...
...he's lashing out...
...the irony hasn't escaped me...

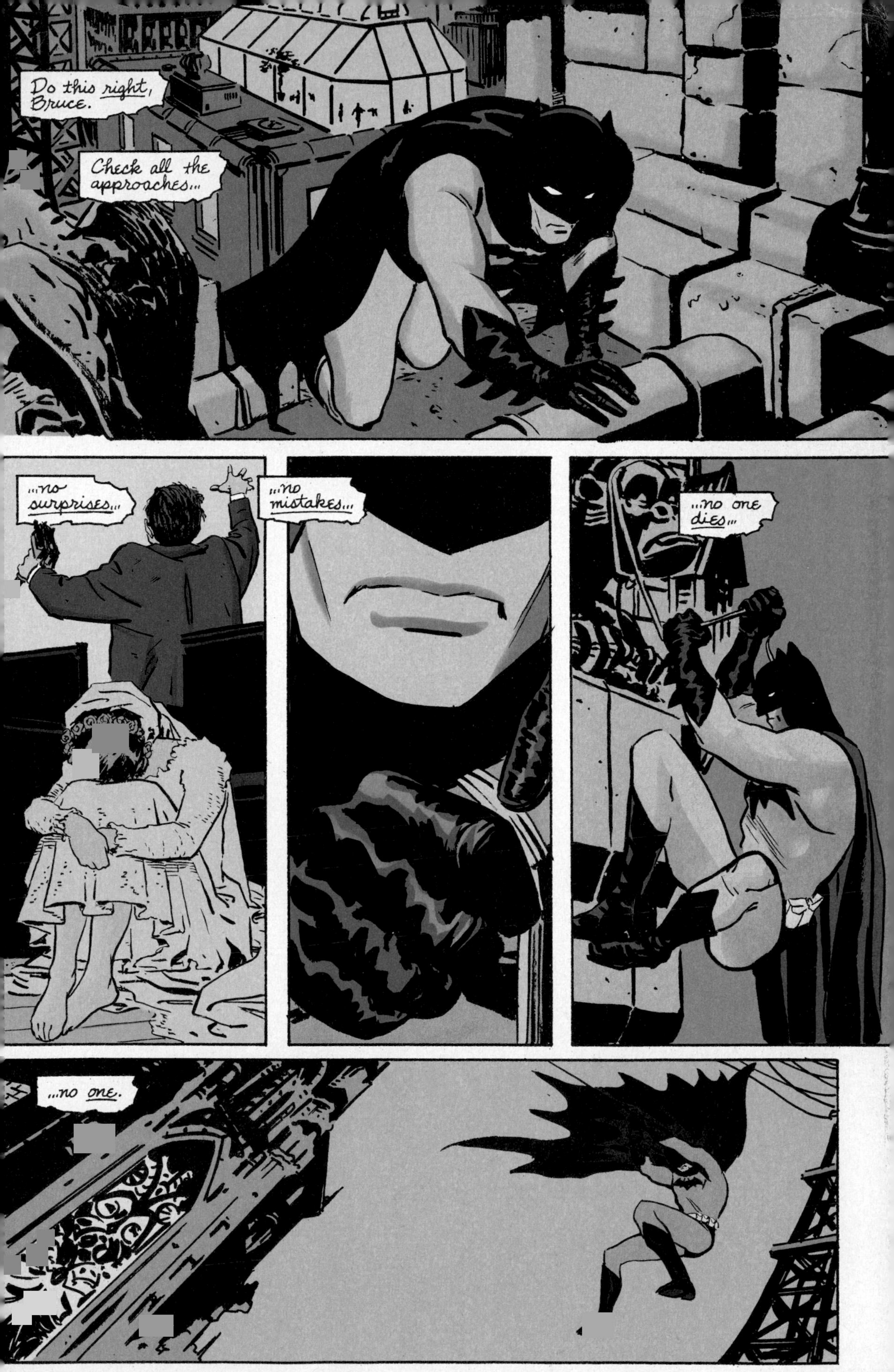
Do this right, Bruce.
Check all the approaches...
...no surprises...
...no mistakes...
...no one dies...
...no one.

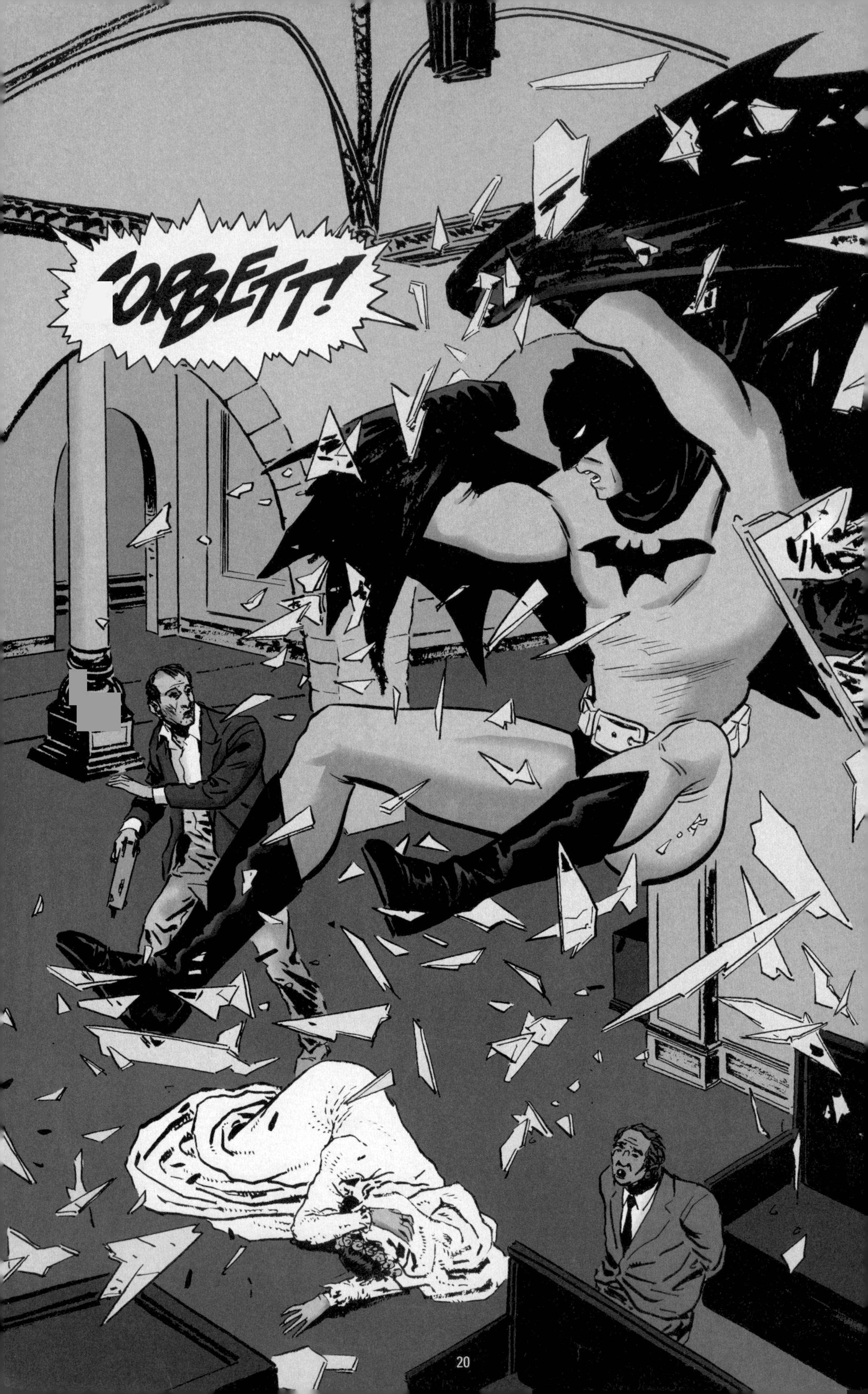
ORBETT!

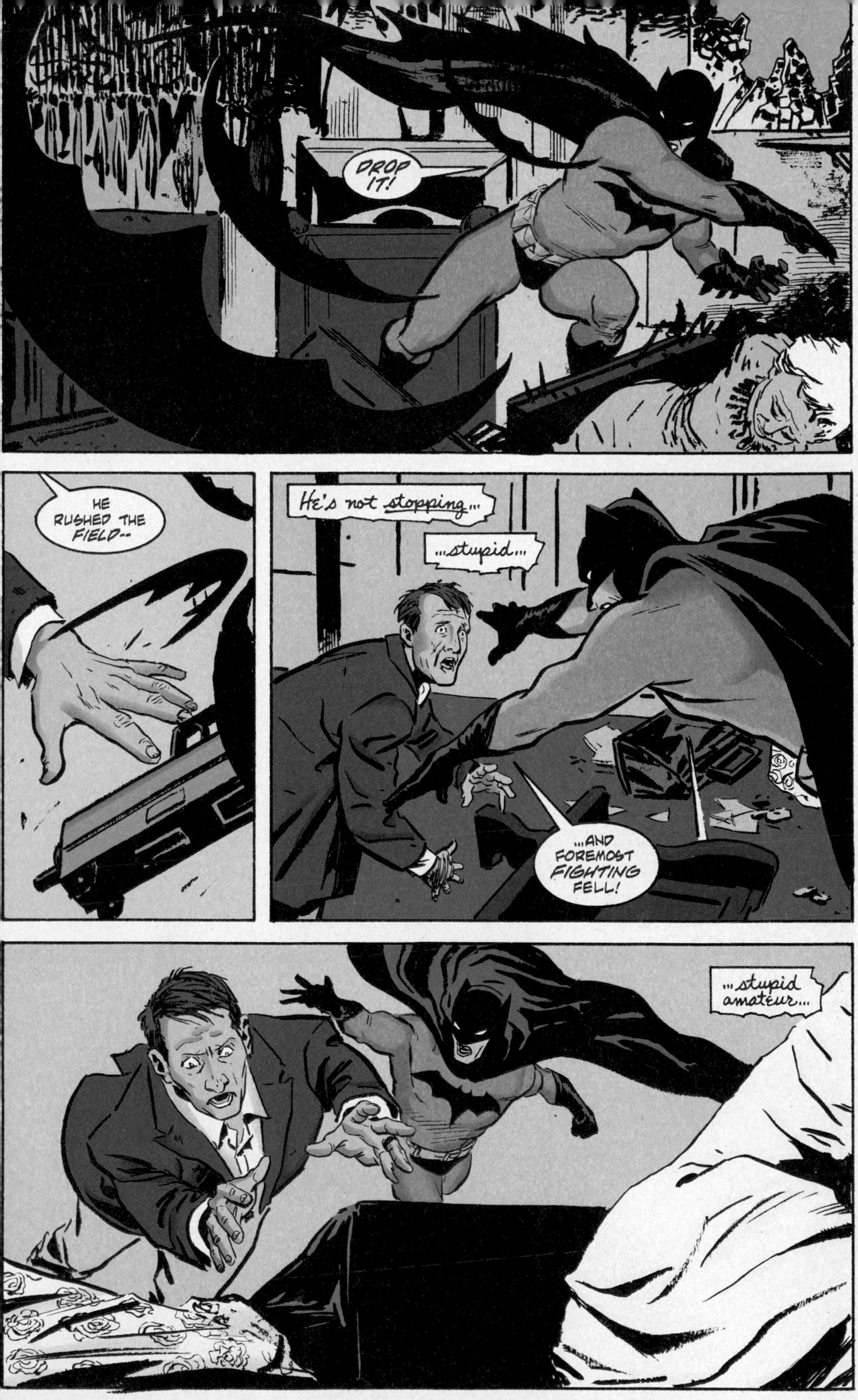
DROP IT!
HE RUSHED THE FIELD--
He's not stopping...
...stupid...
...AND FOREMOST FIGHTING FELL!
...stupid amateur...

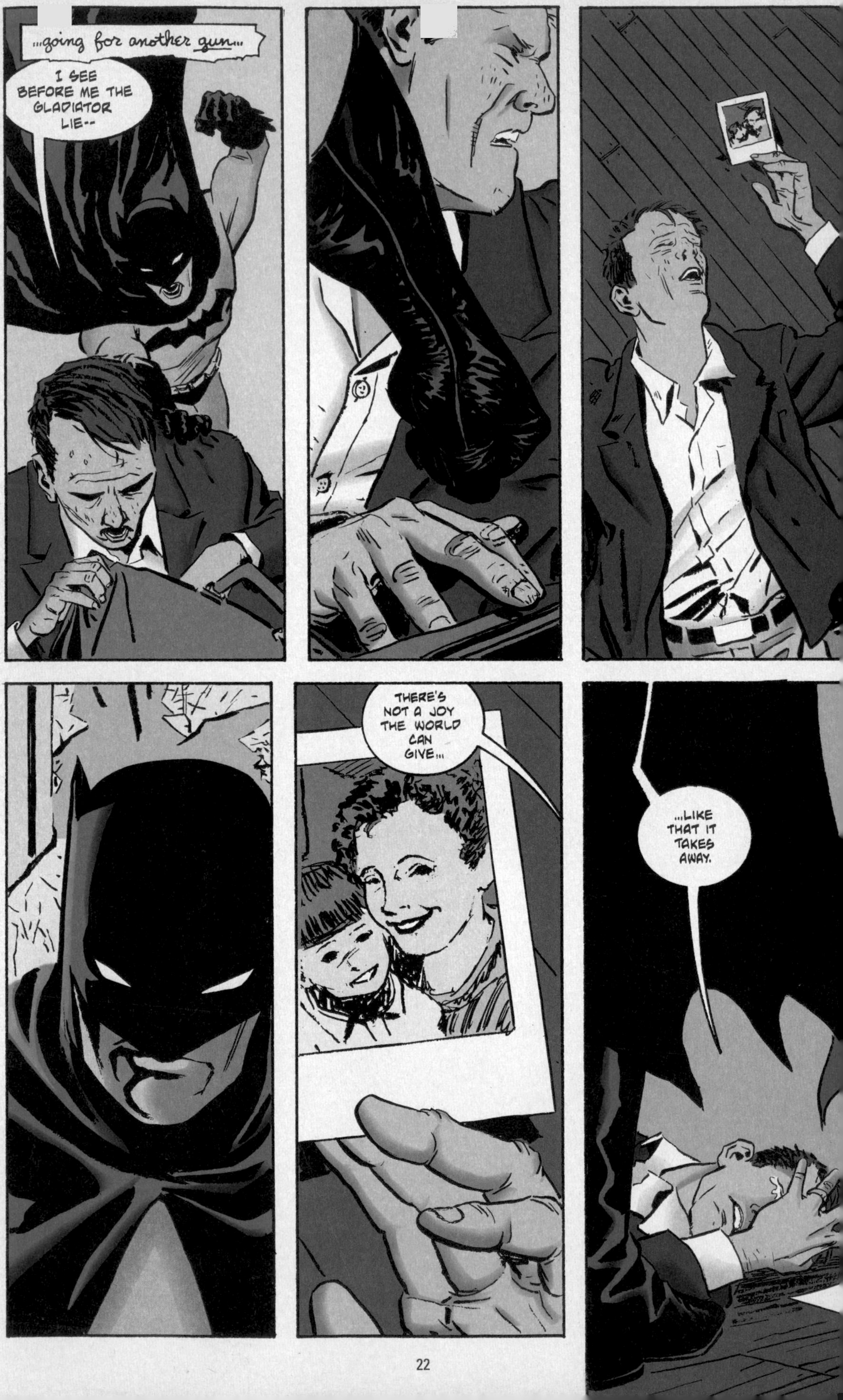
...going for another gun...
I SEE BEFORE ME THE GLADIATOR LIE--
THERE'S NOT A JOY THE WORLD CAN GIVE...
...LIKE THAT IT TAKES AWAY.

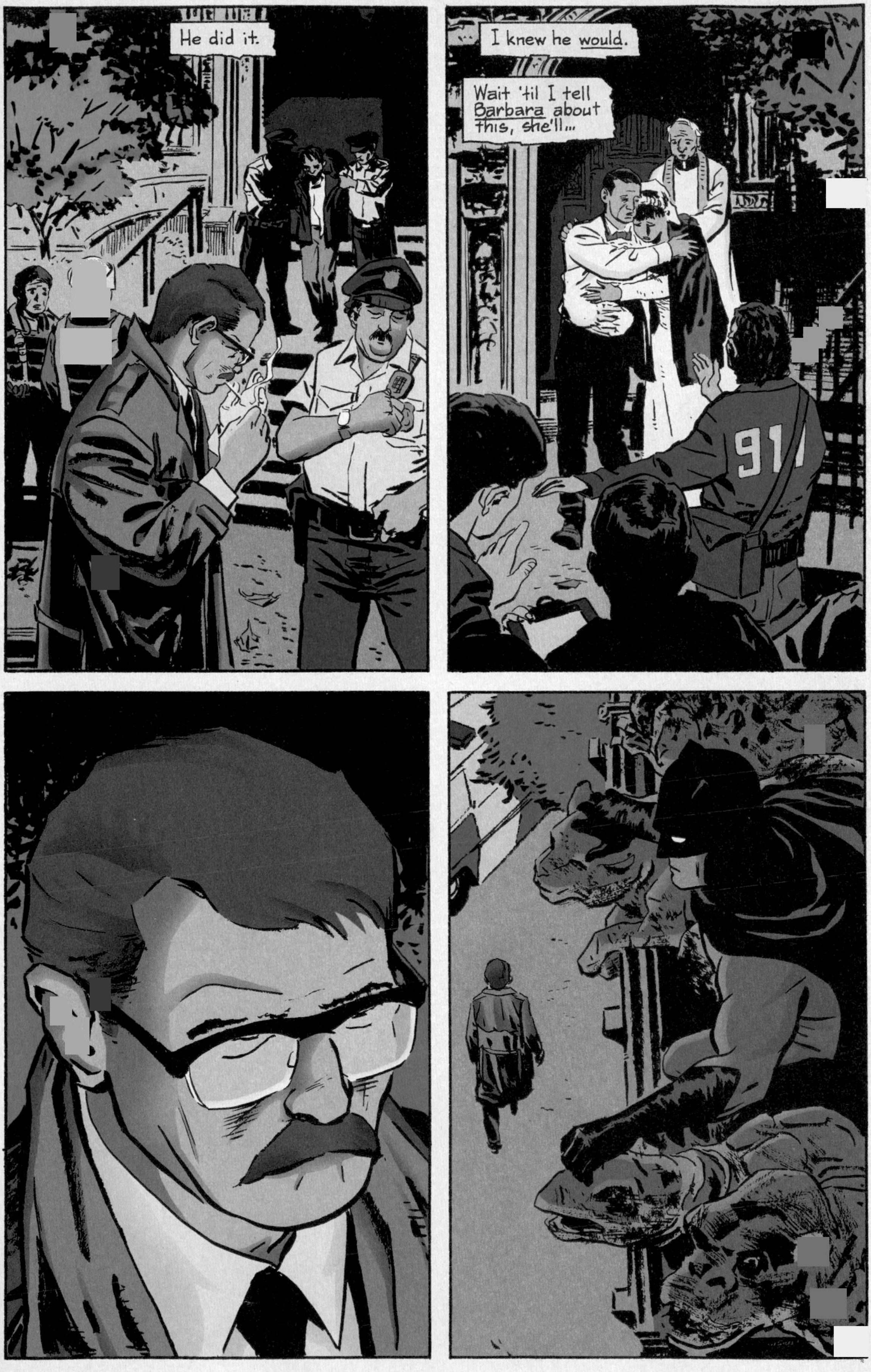
He did it.
I knew he would.
Wait 'til I tell Barbara about this, she'll...

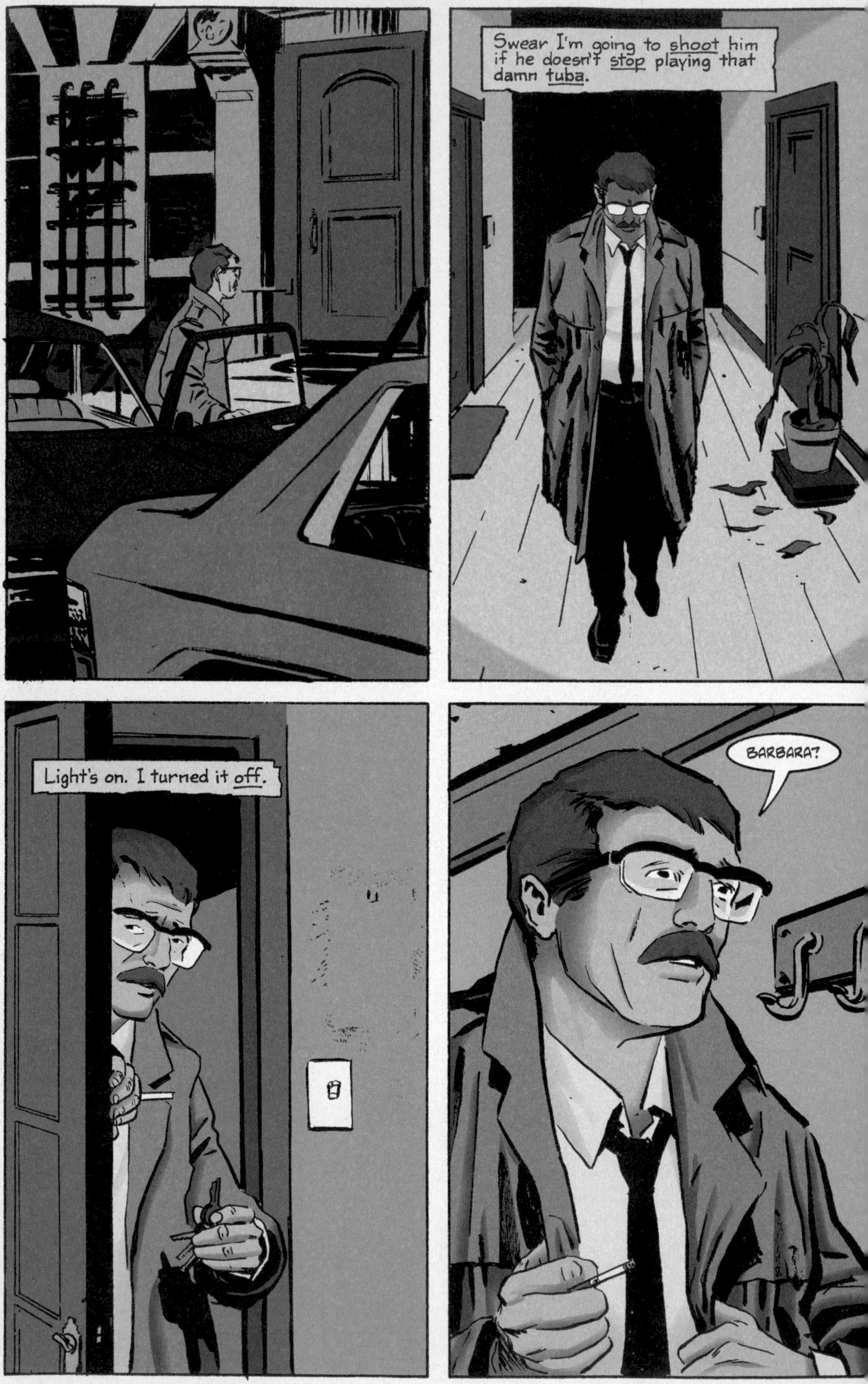
Swear I'm going to shoot him if he doesn't stop playing that damn tuba.
Light's on. I turned it off.
BARBARA?

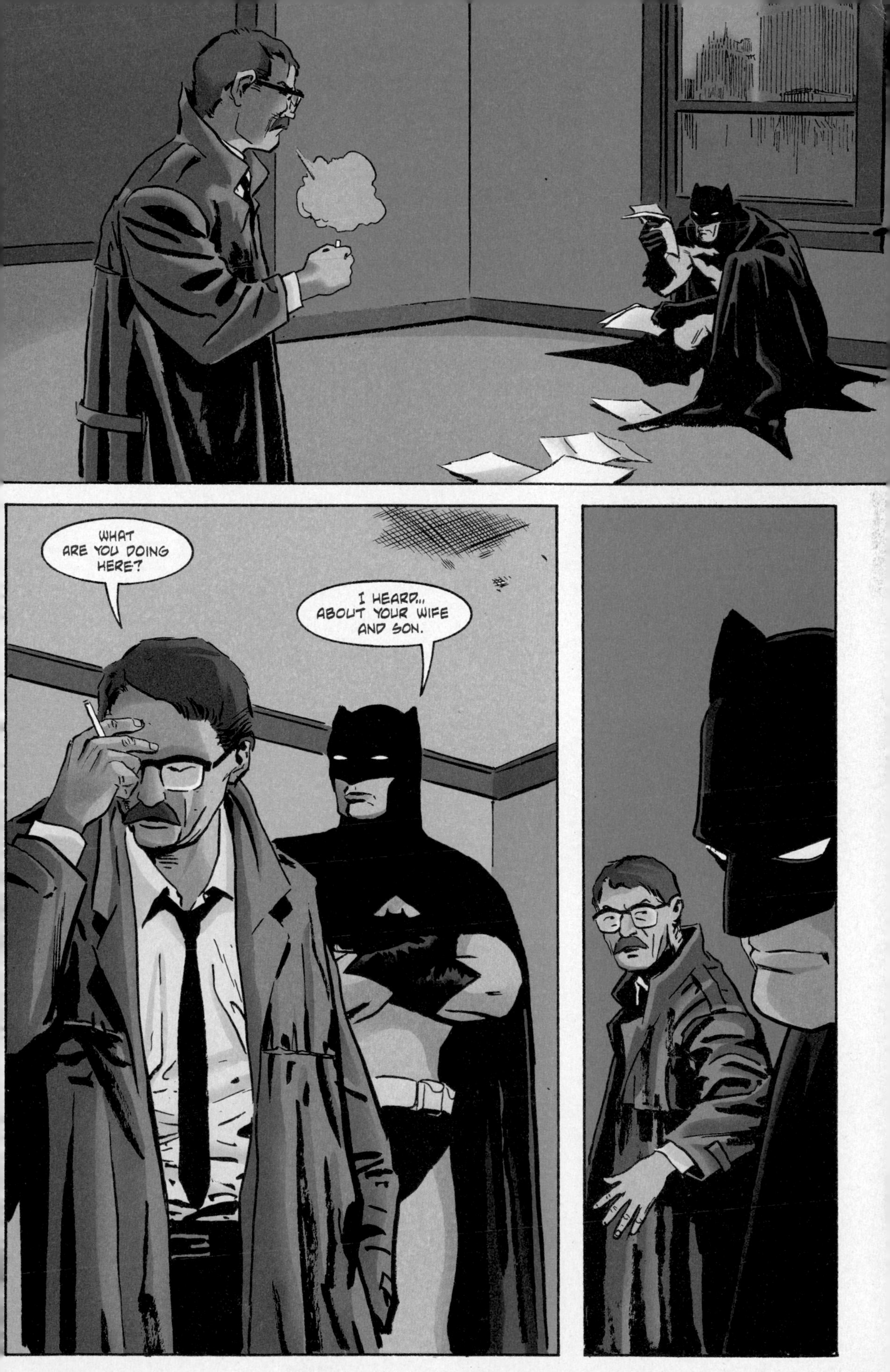
WHAT ARE YOU DOING HERE?
I HEARD... ABOUT YOUR WIFE AND SON.

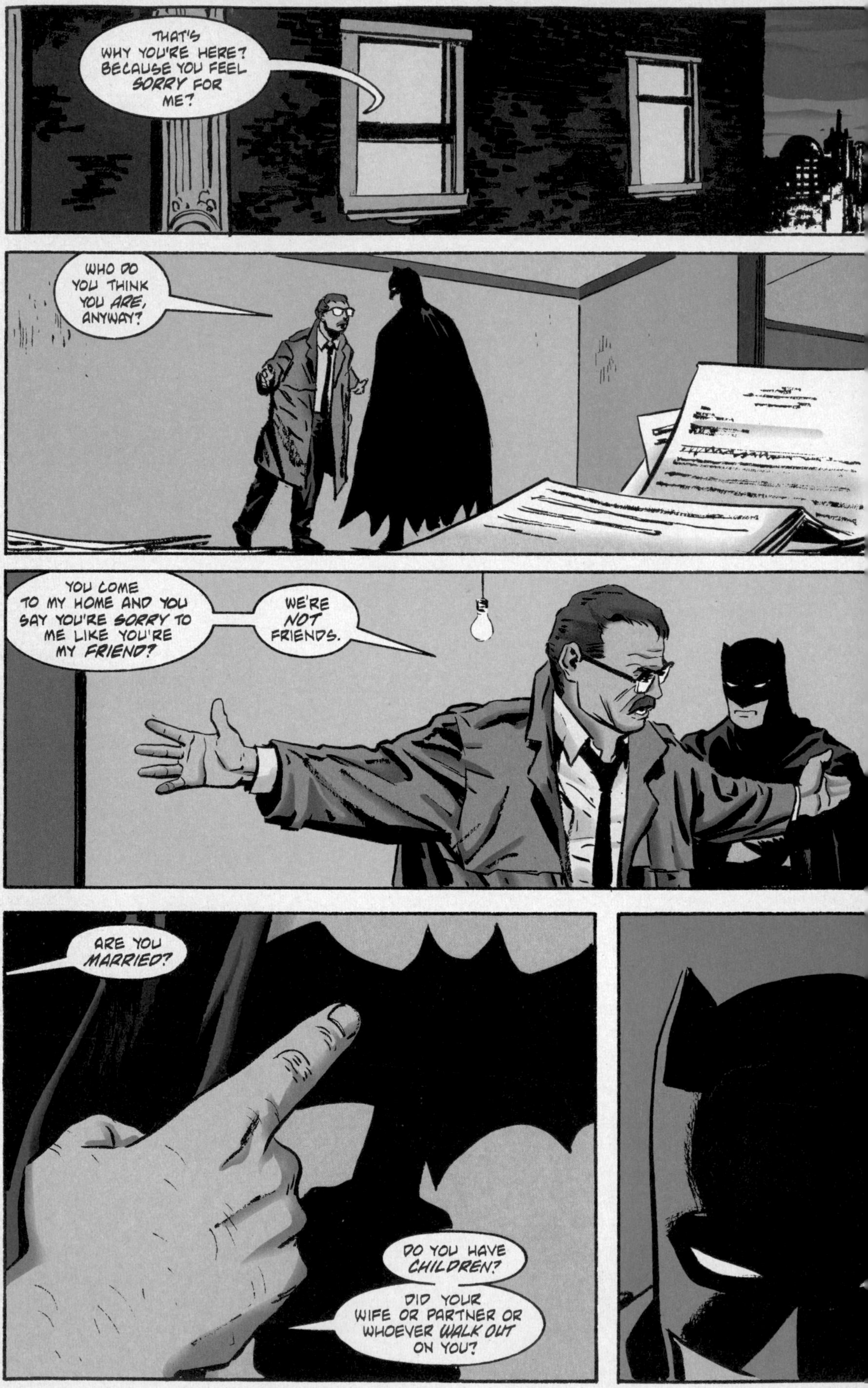

THAT'S WHY YOU'RE HERE? BECAUSE YOU FEEL SORRY FOR ME?
WHO DO YOU THINK YOU ARE, ANYWAY?
YOU COME TO MY HOME AND YOU SAY YOU'RE SORRY TO ME LIKE YOU'RE MY FRIEND?
WE'RE NOT FRIENDS.
ARE YOU MARRIED?
DO YOU HAVE CHILDREN?
DID YOUR WIFE OR PARTNER OR WHOEVER WALK OUT ON YOU?

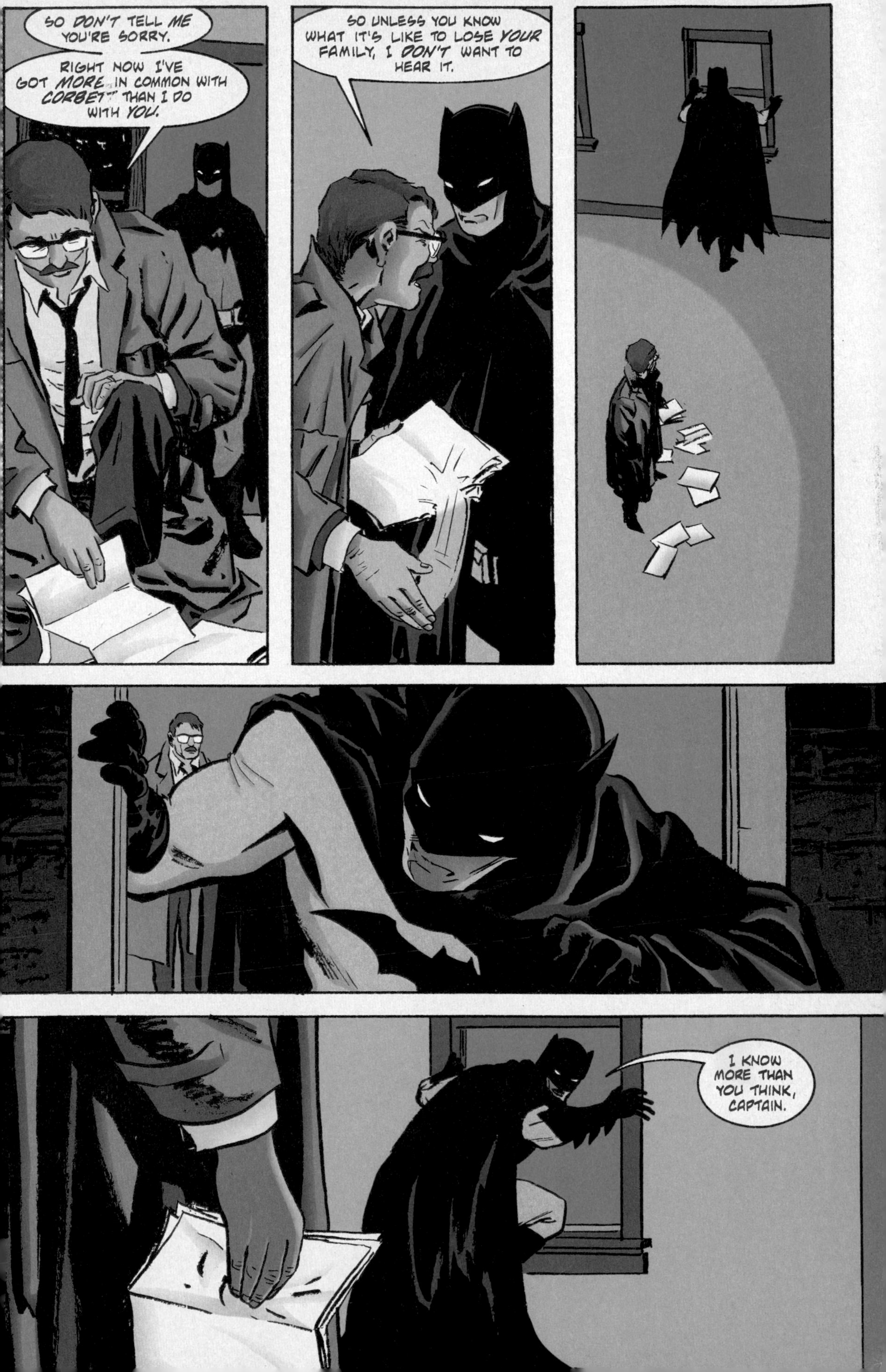
SO DON'T TELL ME YOU'RE SORRY.
RIGHT NOW I'VE GOT MORE IN COMMON WITH CORBETT THAN I DO WITH YOU.
SO UNLESS YOU KNOW WHAT IT'S LIKE TO LOSE YOUR FAMILY, I DON'T WANT TO HEAR IT.
I KNOW MORE THAN YOU THINK, CAPTAIN.

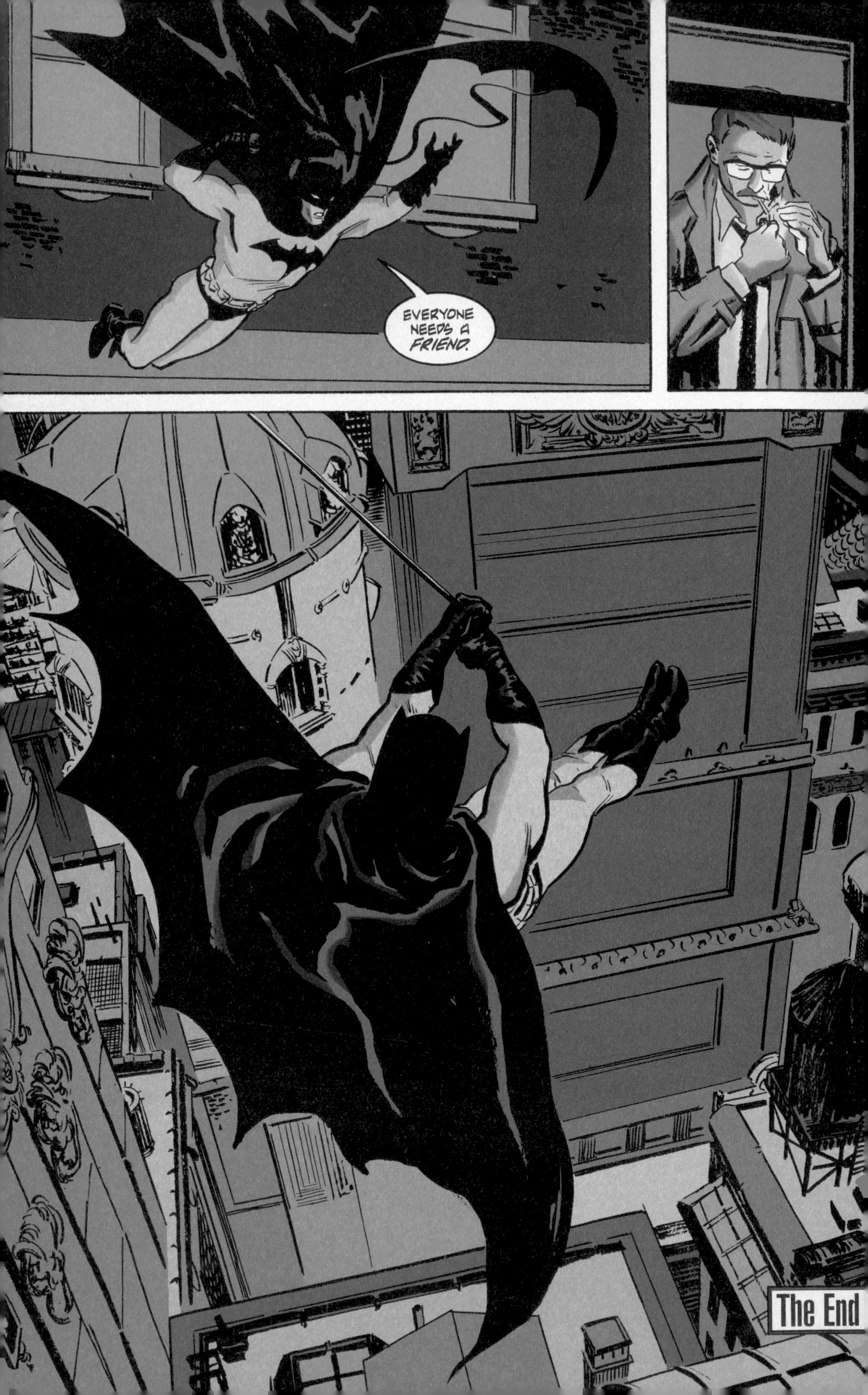
EVERYONE NEEDS A FRIEND.
The End

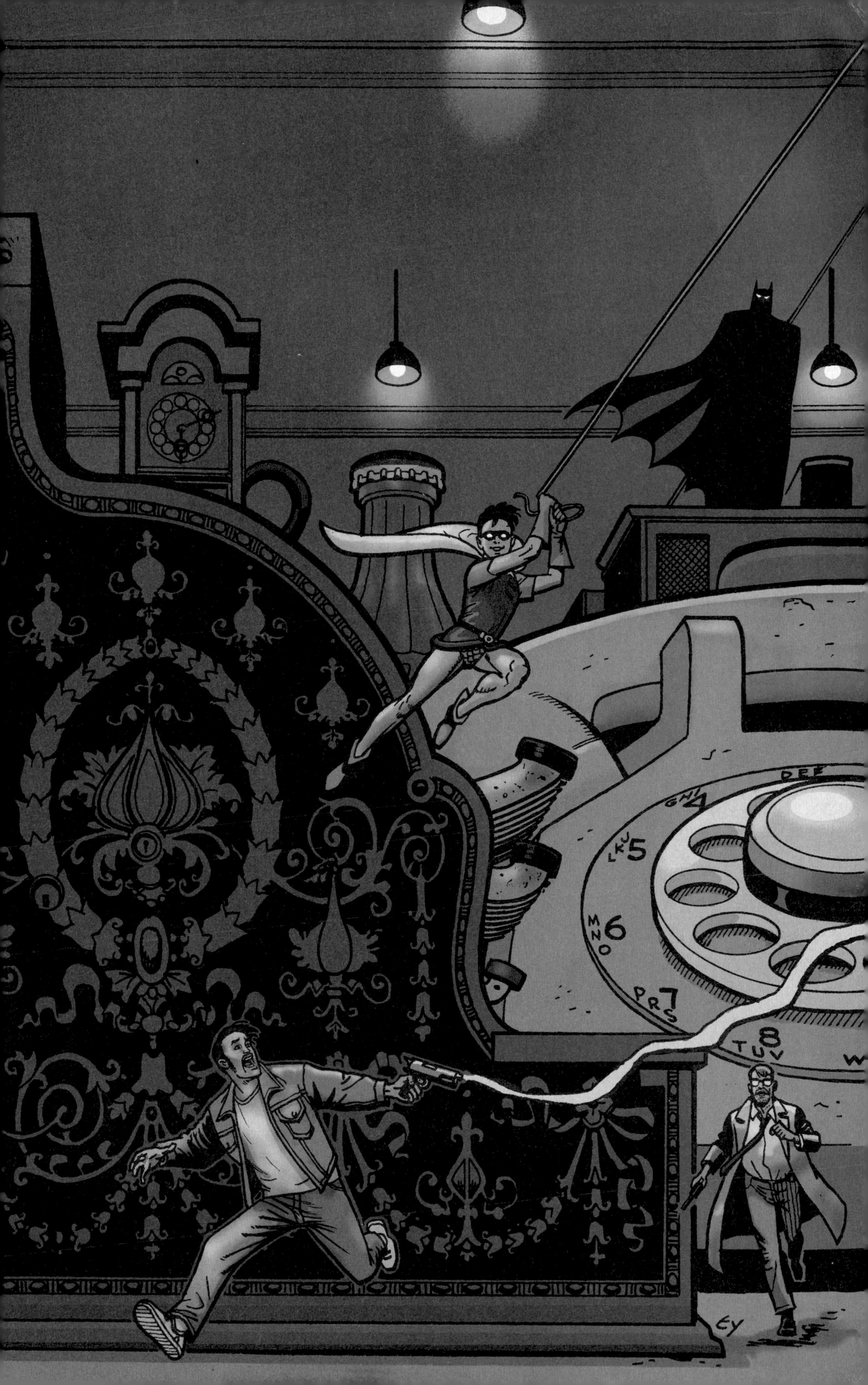
DEF
MNO 6
PRS 7
TUV 8

CHAPTER TWO

...AND THEN THERE WERE...THREE?

Ed Brubaker
writer

Joe Giella
artist

Ty Templeton
cover artist

Shannon Blanchard
colorist

Willie Schubert
letterer

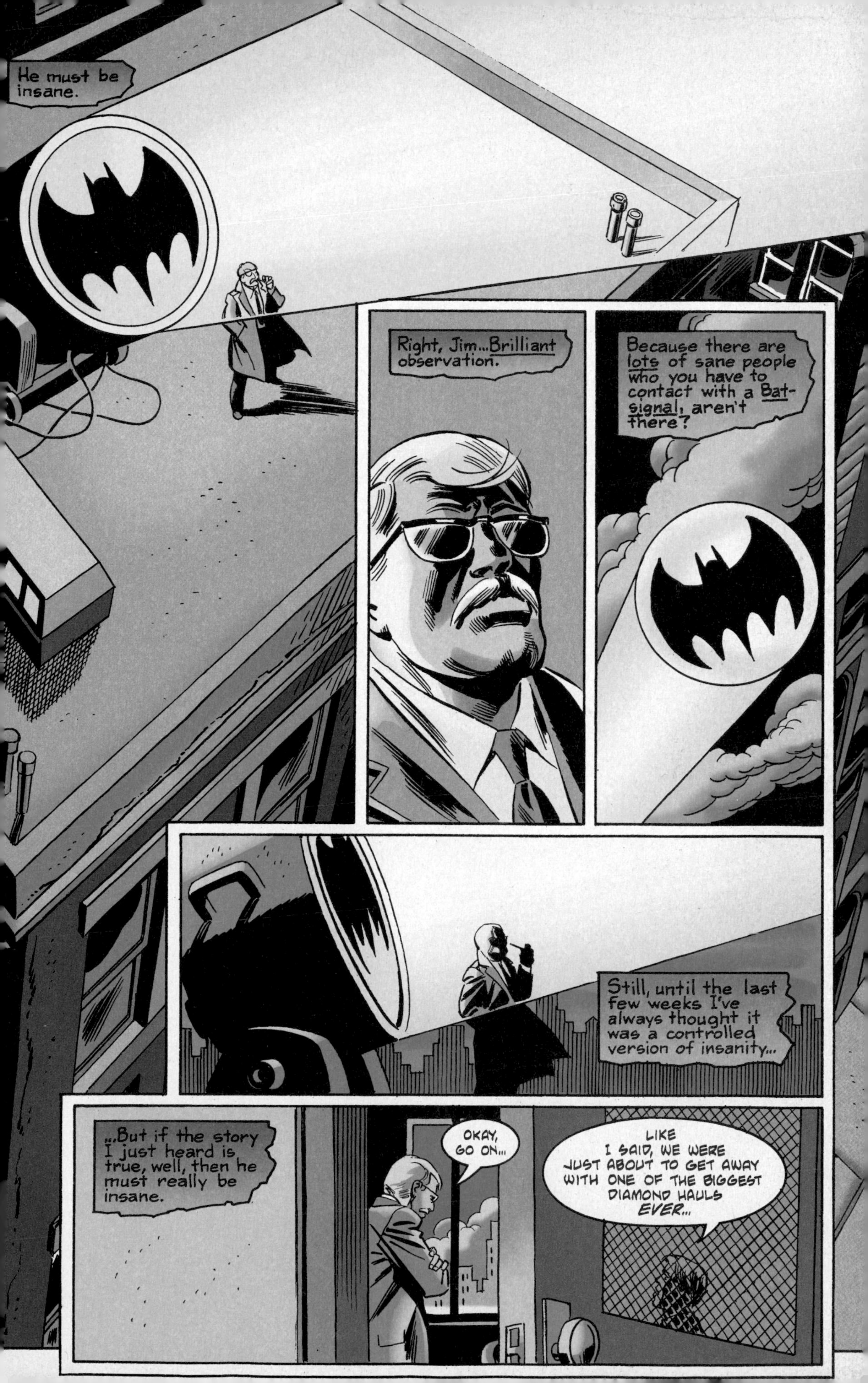
He must be insane.
Right, Jim...Brilliant observation.
Because there are lots of sane people who you have to contact with a Bat-signal, aren't there?
Still, until the last few weeks I've always thought it was a controlled version of insanity...
...But if the story I just heard is true, well, then he must really be insane.
OKAY, GO ON...
LIKE I SAID, WE WERE JUST ABOUT TO GET AWAY WITH ONE OF THE BIGGEST DIAMOND HAULS EVER...

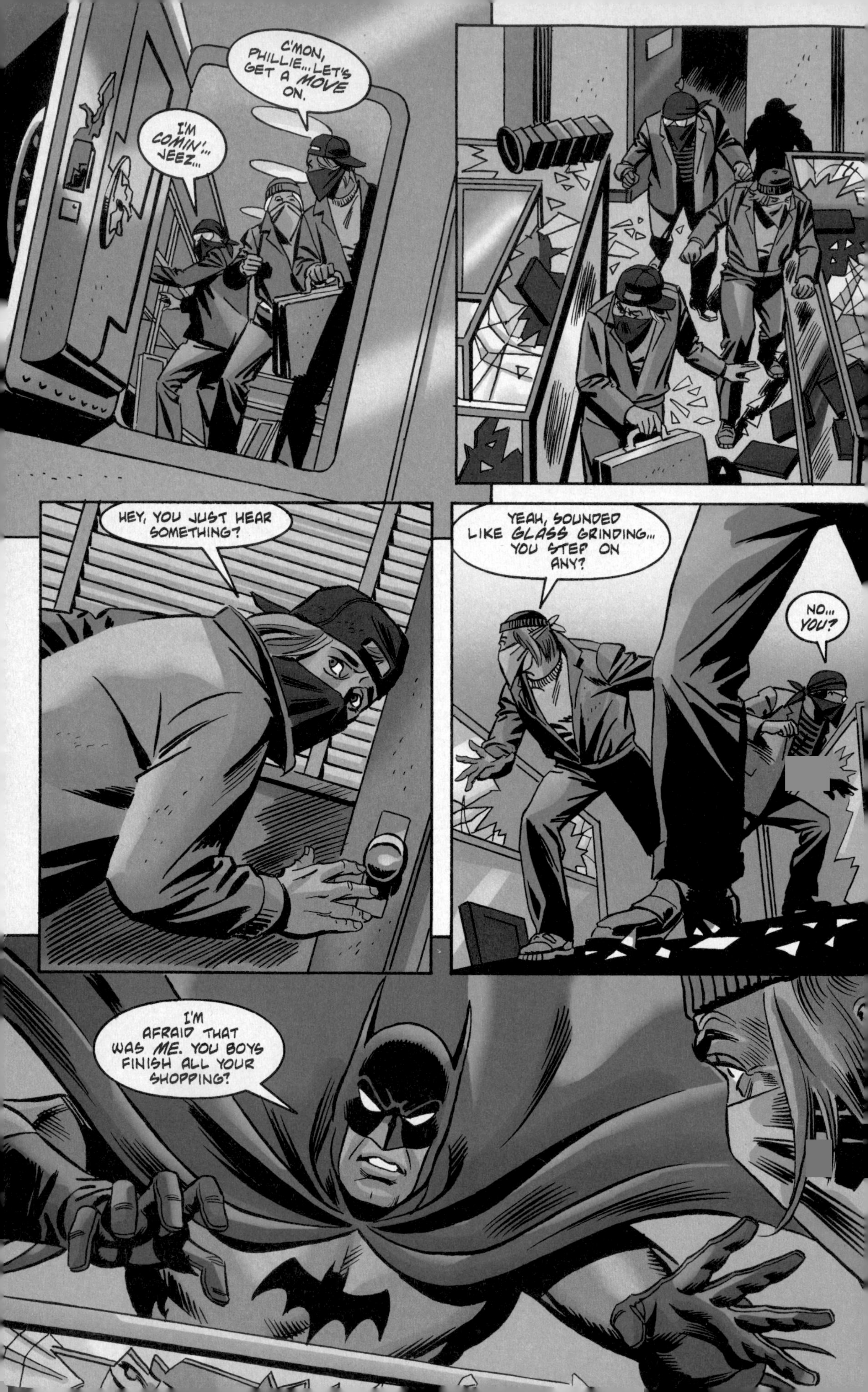
C'MON, PHILLIE... LET'S GET A MOVE ON.
I'M COMIN'... JEEZ...
HEY, YOU JUST HEAR SOMETHING?
YEAH, SOUNDED LIKE GLASS GRINDING... YOU STEP ON ANY?
NO... YOU?
I'M AFRAID THAT WAS ME. YOU BOYS FINISH ALL YOUR SHOPPING?

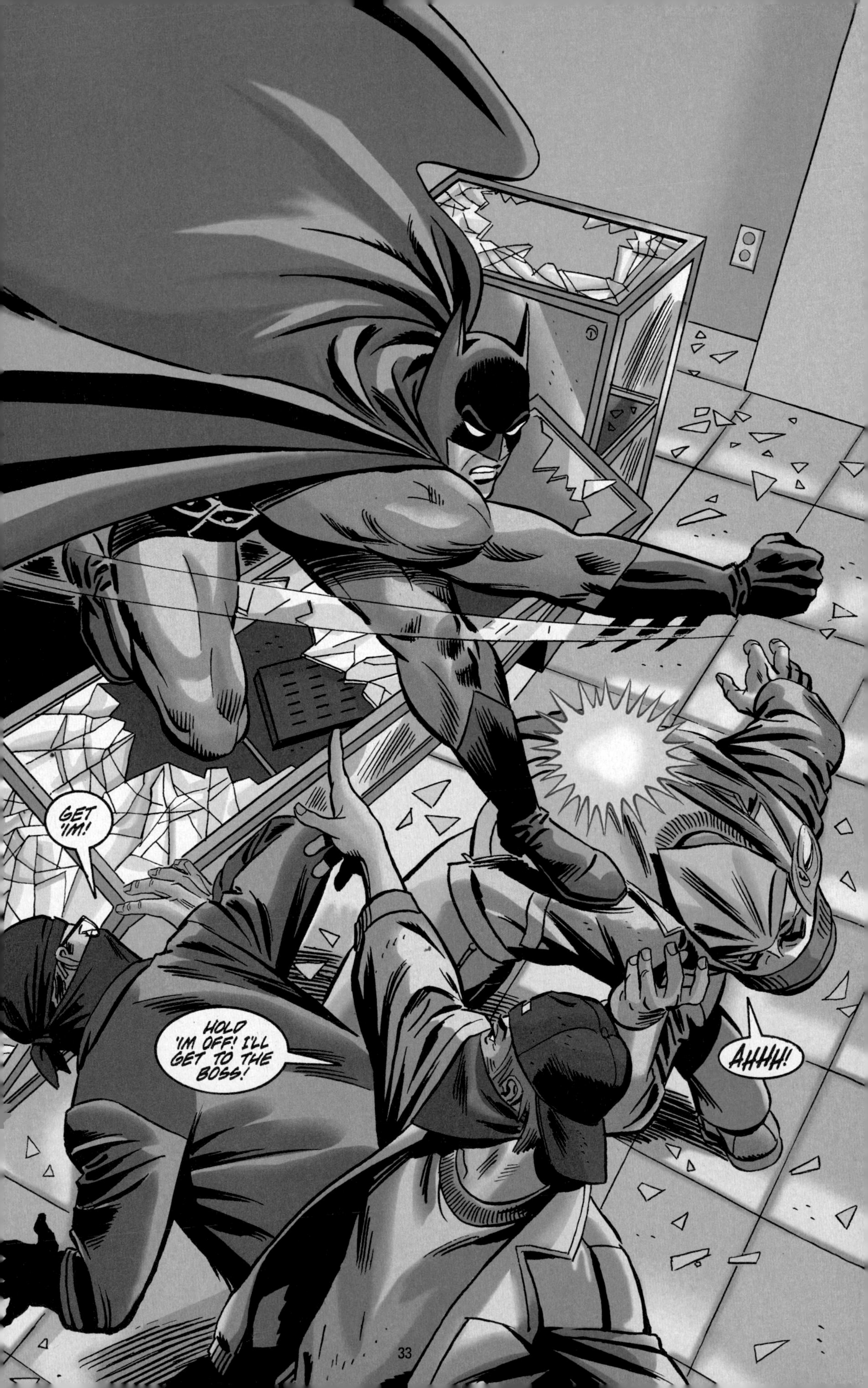
GET 'IM!
HOLD 'IM OFF! I'LL GET TO THE BOSS!
AHHH!

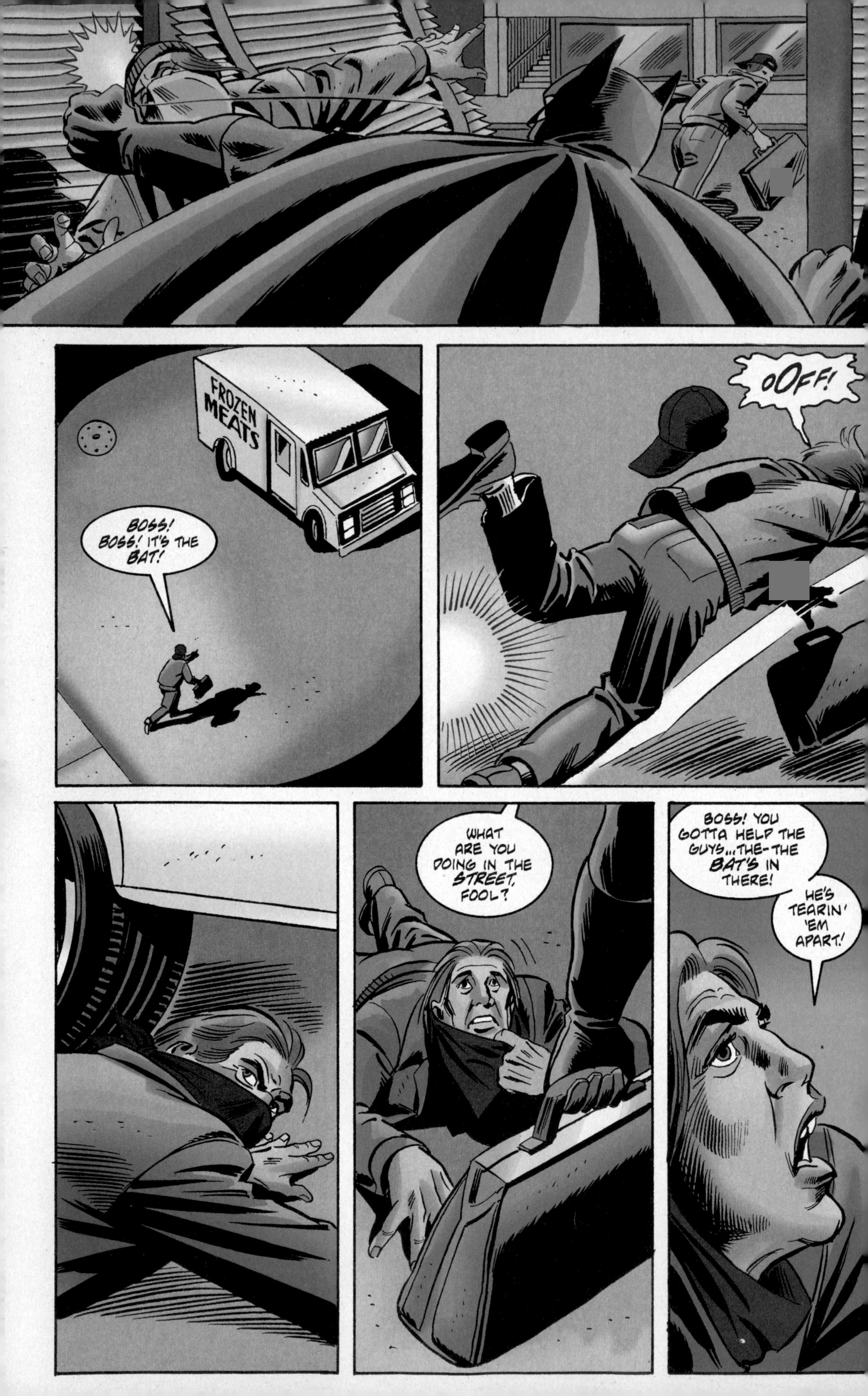
FROZEN MEATS
BOSS! BOSS! IT'S THE BAT!
OOFF!
WHAT ARE YOU DOING IN THE STREET, FOOL?
BOSS! YOU GOTTA HELP THE GUYS...THE- THE BAT'S IN THERE!
HE'S TEARIN' 'EM APART!

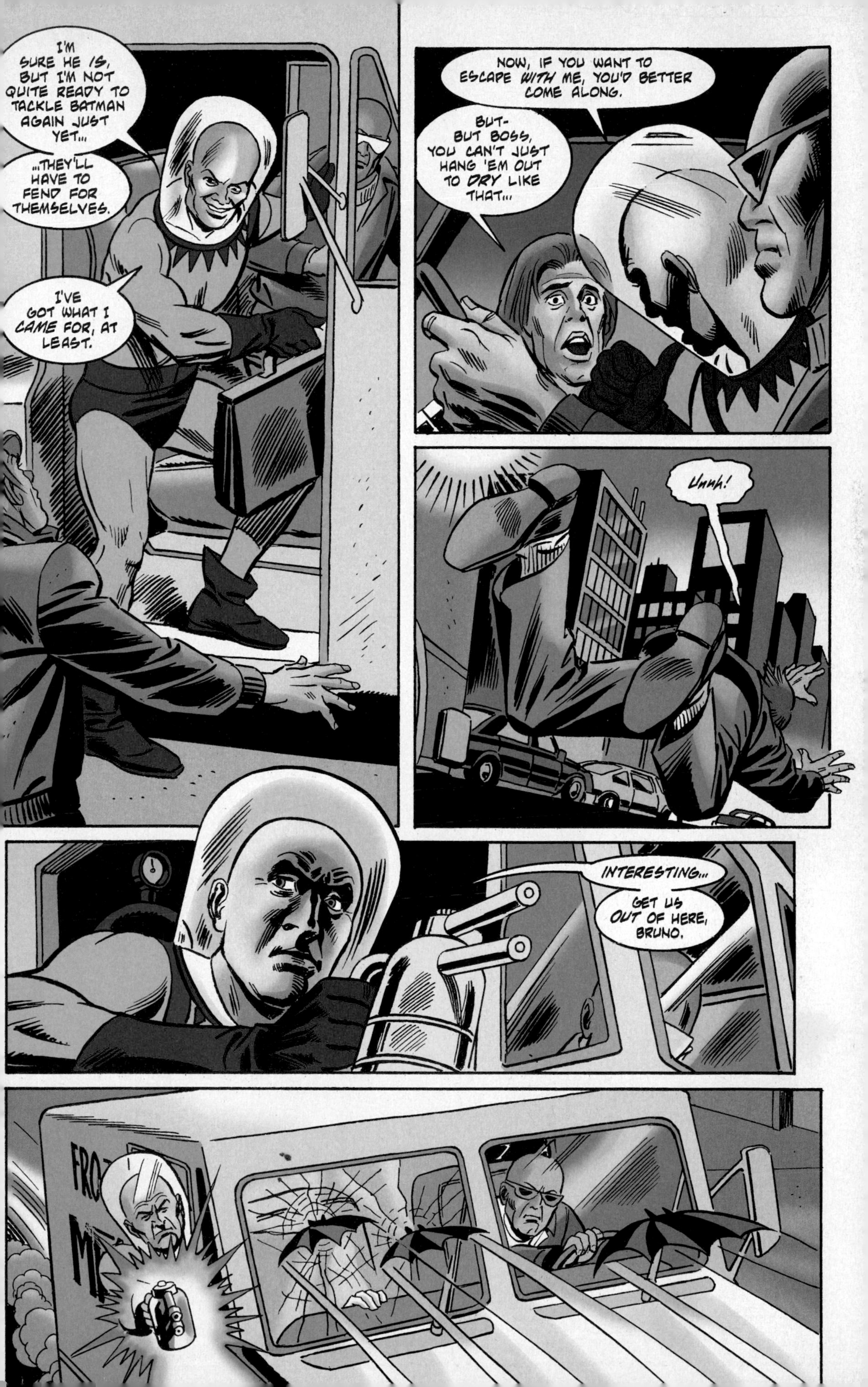
I'M SURE HE IS, BUT I'M NOT QUITE READY TO TACKLE BATMAN AGAIN JUST YET...
...THEY'LL HAVE TO FEND FOR THEMSELVES.
I'VE GOT WHAT I CAME FOR, AT LEAST.
NOW, IF YOU WANT TO ESCAPE WITH ME, YOU'D BETTER COME ALONG.
BUT-BUT BOSS, YOU CAN'T JUST HANG 'EM OUT TO DRY LIKE THAT...
Unnh!
INTERESTING...
GET US OUT OF HERE, BRUNO.

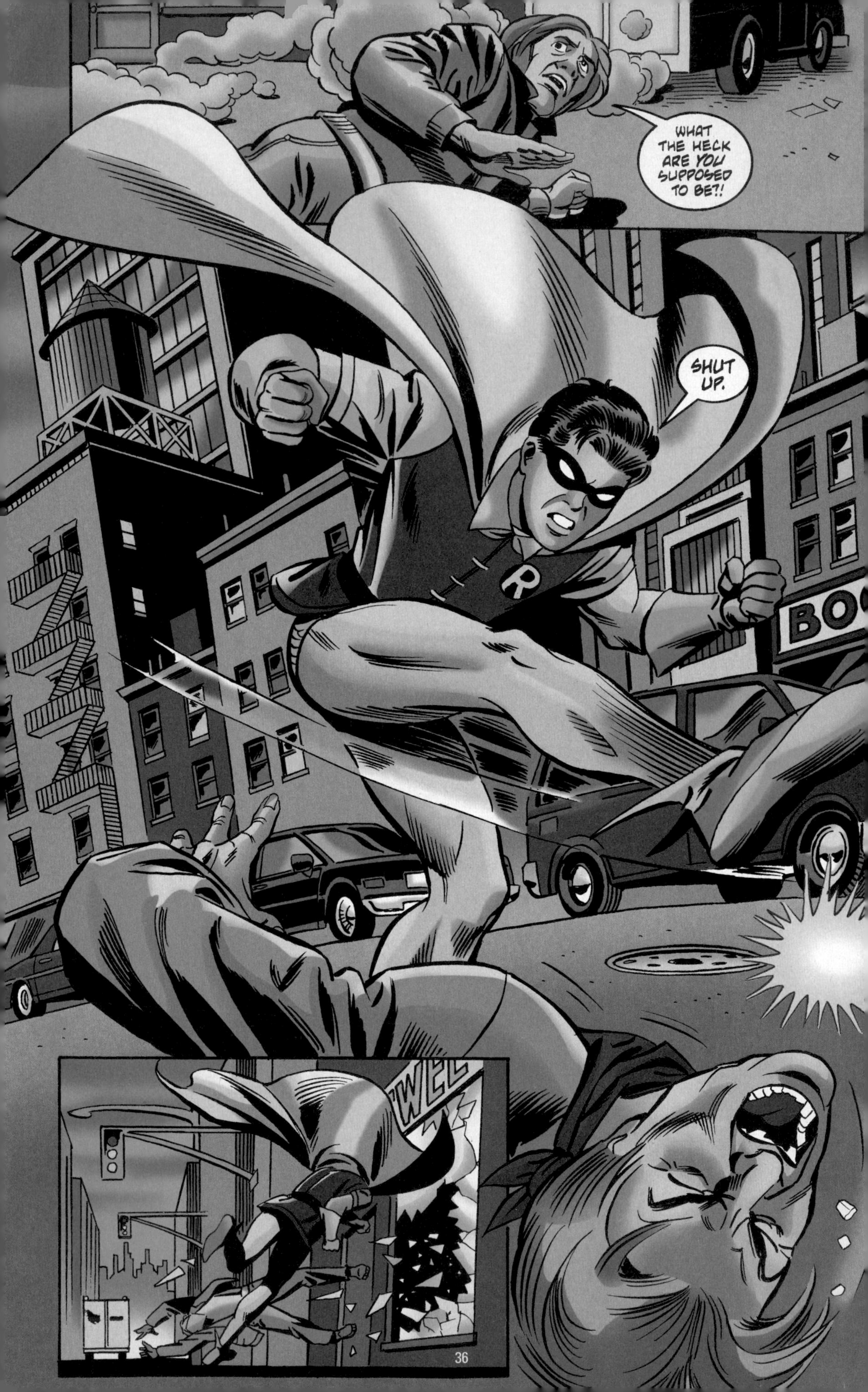
WHAT THE HECK ARE YOU SUPPOSED TO BE?!
SHUT UP.
BOO
WEL

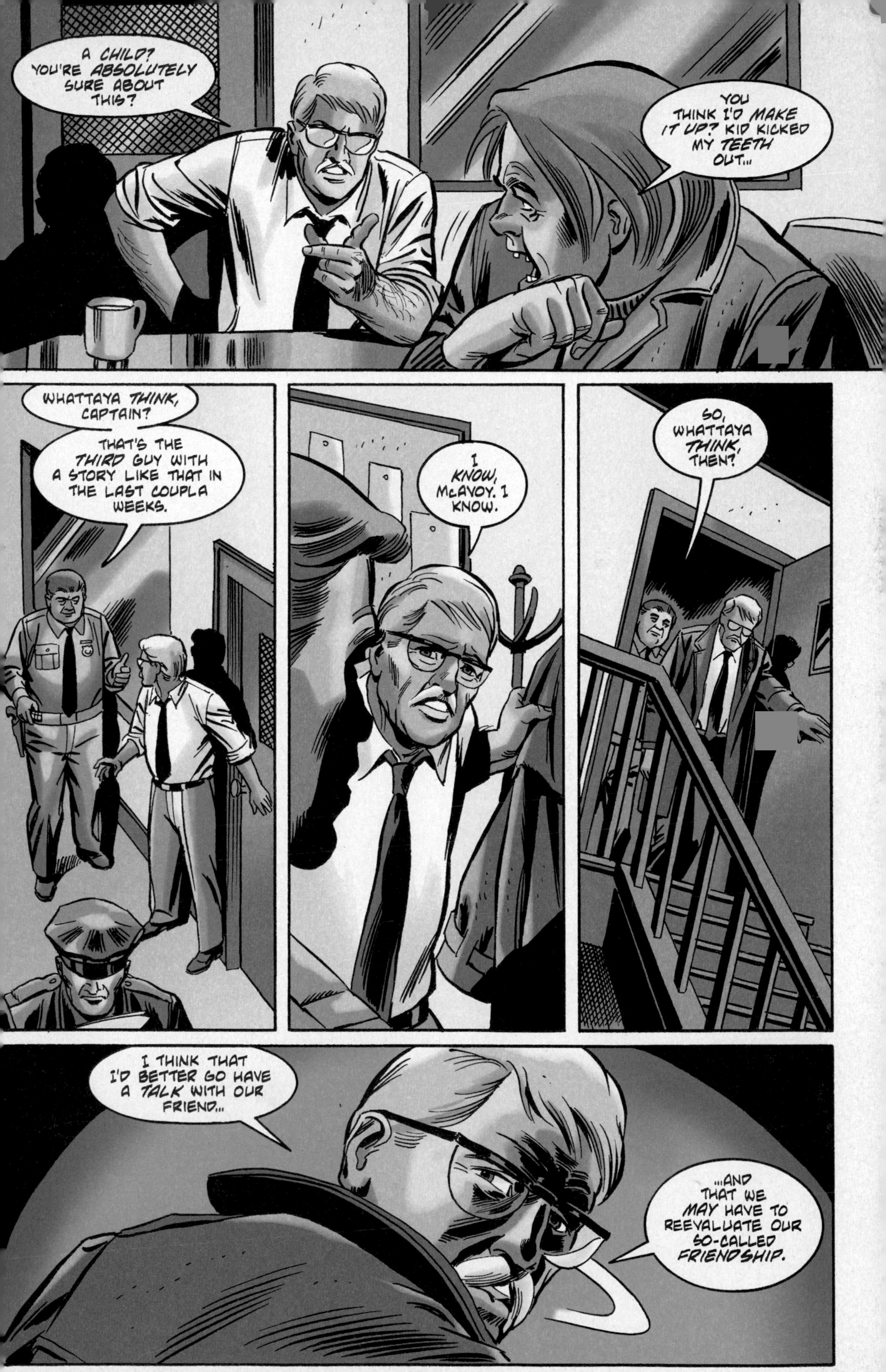
A CHILD? YOU'RE ABSOLUTELY SURE ABOUT THIS?
YOU THINK I'D MAKE IT UP? KID KICKED MY TEETH OUT...
WHATTAYA THINK, CAPTAIN?
THAT'S THE THIRD GUY WITH A STORY LIKE THAT IN THE LAST COUPLA WEEKS.
I KNOW, McAVOY. I KNOW.
SO, WHATTAYA THINK, THEN?
I THINK THAT I'D BETTER GO HAVE A TALK WITH OUR FRIEND...
...AND THAT WE MAY HAVE TO REEVALUATE OUR SO-CALLED FRIENDSHIP.

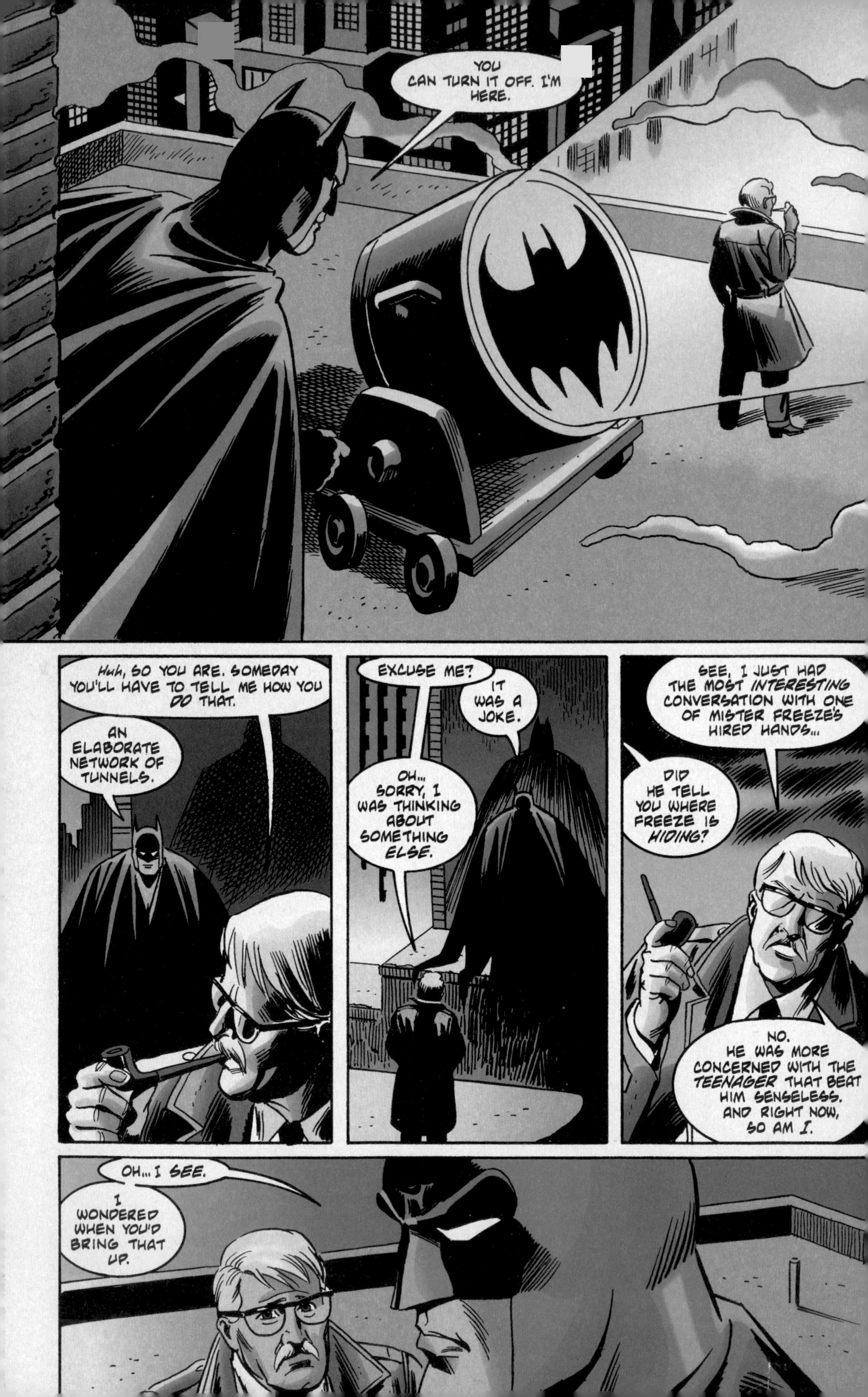
YOU CAN TURN IT OFF. I'M HERE.
Huh, SO YOU ARE. SOMEDAY YOU'LL HAVE TO TELL ME HOW YOU DO THAT.
AN ELABORATE NETWORK OF TUNNELS.
EXCUSE ME?
IT WAS A JOKE.
OH... SORRY, I WAS THINKING ABOUT SOMETHING ELSE.
SEE, I JUST HAD THE MOST INTERESTING CONVERSATION WITH ONE OF MISTER FREEZE'S HIRED HANDS...
DID HE TELL YOU WHERE FREEZE IS HIDING?
NO. HE WAS MORE CONCERNED WITH THE TEENAGER THAT BEAT HIM SENSELESS. AND RIGHT NOW, SO AM I.
OH... I SEE.
I WONDERED WHEN YOU'D BRING THAT UP.

THEN IT'S *TRUE?*

MY GOD, WHAT IS GOING ON INSIDE THAT COWL OF YOURS?!

YOU DON'T UNDERSTAND.

WHAT'S THERE TO *UNDERSTAND,* EXACTLY? YOU'RE TRAINING SOME KID TO FOLLOW IN YOUR FOOTSTEPS! PUTTING HIM IN THE PATH OF *BULLETS* AND *MADMEN!*

THAT'S *NOT* WHAT I'M DOING.

OH, REALLY? THEN *EXPLAIN* IT TO ME, PLEASE...

I'M *HELPING* HIM.

WHAT!? HELPING HIM GET *KILLED?*

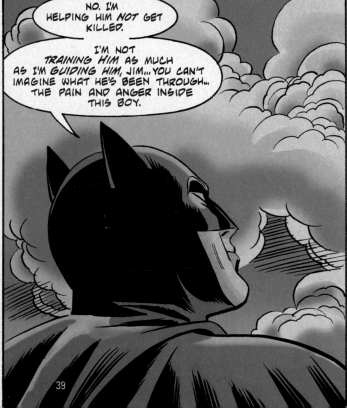

NO. I'M HELPING HIM *NOT* GET KILLED.

I'M NOT *TRAINING HIM* AS MUCH AS I'M *GUIDING HIM,* JIM.... YOU CAN'T IMAGINE WHAT HE'S BEEN THROUGH... THE PAIN AND ANGER INSIDE THIS BOY.

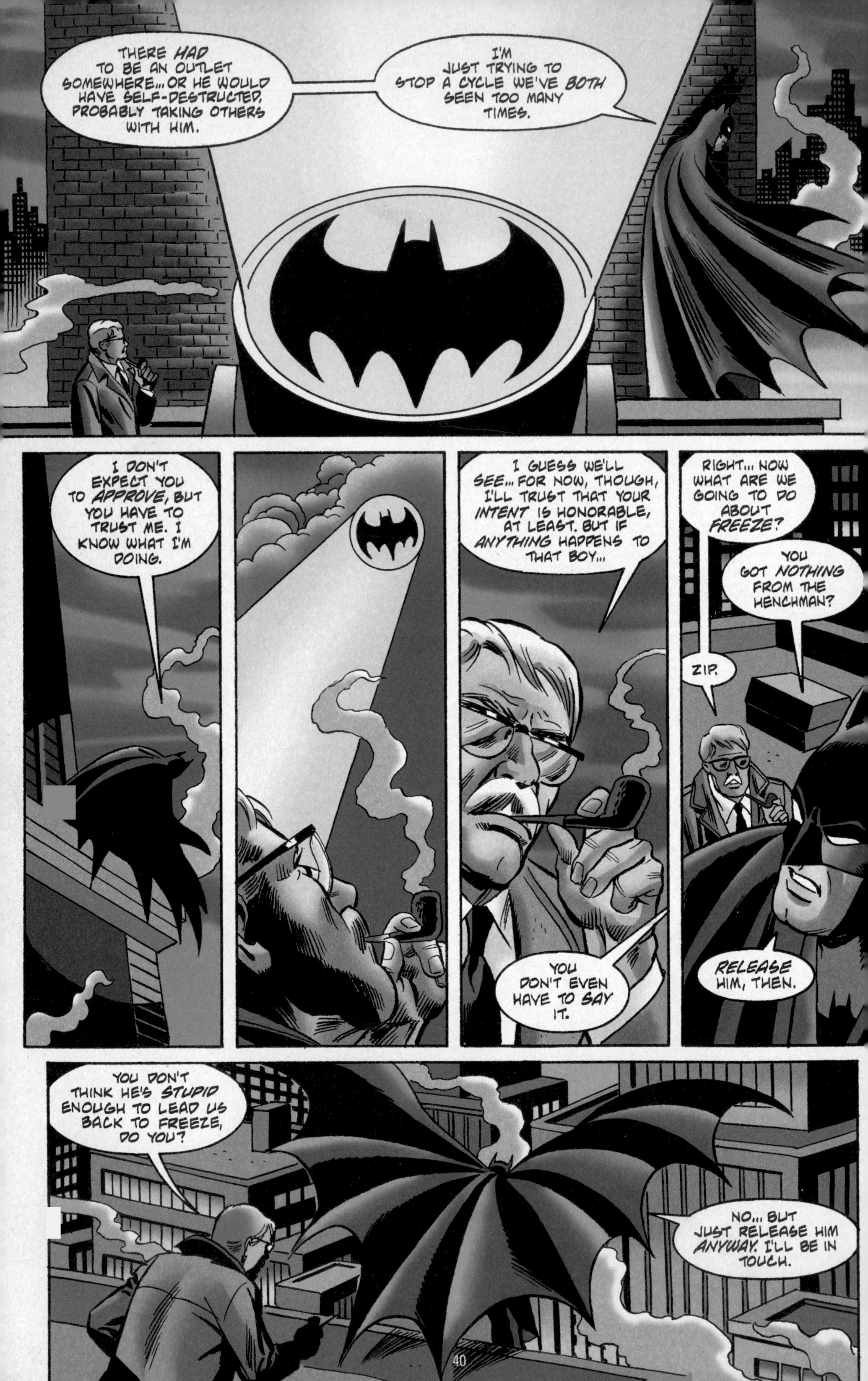
THERE HAD TO BE AN OUTLET SOMEWHERE... OR HE WOULD HAVE SELF-DESTRUCTED, PROBABLY TAKING OTHERS WITH HIM.
I'M JUST TRYING TO STOP A CYCLE WE'VE BOTH SEEN TOO MANY TIMES.
I DON'T EXPECT YOU TO APPROVE, BUT YOU HAVE TO TRUST ME. I KNOW WHAT I'M DOING.
I GUESS WE'LL SEE... FOR NOW, THOUGH, I'LL TRUST THAT YOUR INTENT IS HONORABLE, AT LEAST. BUT IF ANYTHING HAPPENS TO THAT BOY...
YOU DON'T EVEN HAVE TO SAY IT.
RIGHT... NOW WHAT ARE WE GOING TO DO ABOUT FREEZE?
YOU GOT NOTHING FROM THE HENCHMAN?
ZIP.
RELEASE HIM, THEN.
YOU DON'T THINK HE'S STUPID ENOUGH TO LEAD US BACK TO FREEZE, DO YOU?
NO... BUT JUST RELEASE HIM ANYWAY. I'LL BE IN TOUCH.

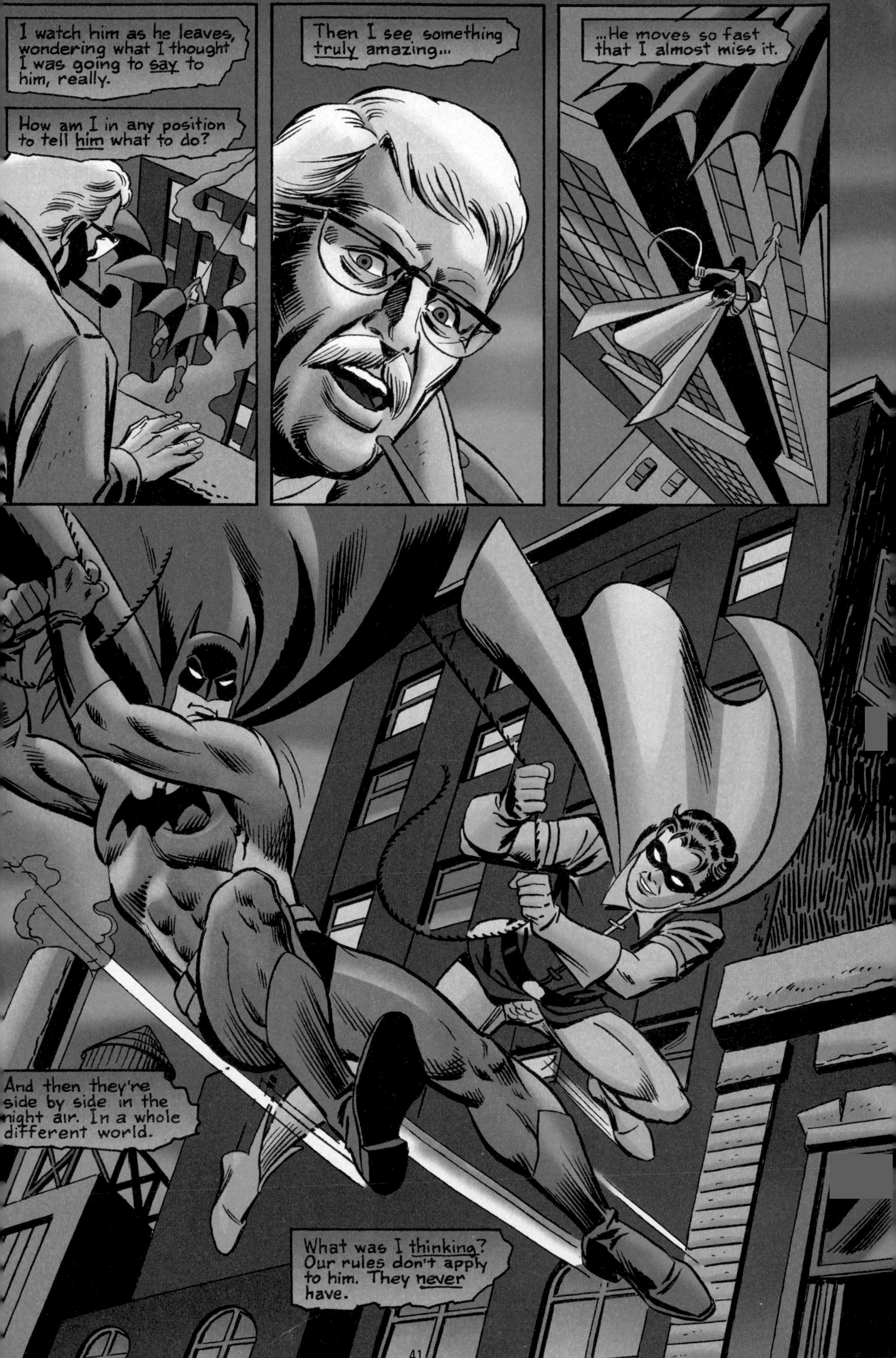
I watch him as he leaves, wondering what I thought I was going to say to him, really.
How am I in any position to tell him what to do?
Then I see something truly amazing...
...He moves so fast that I almost miss it.
And then they're side by side in the night air. In a whole different world.
What was I thinking? Our rules don't apply to him. They never have.

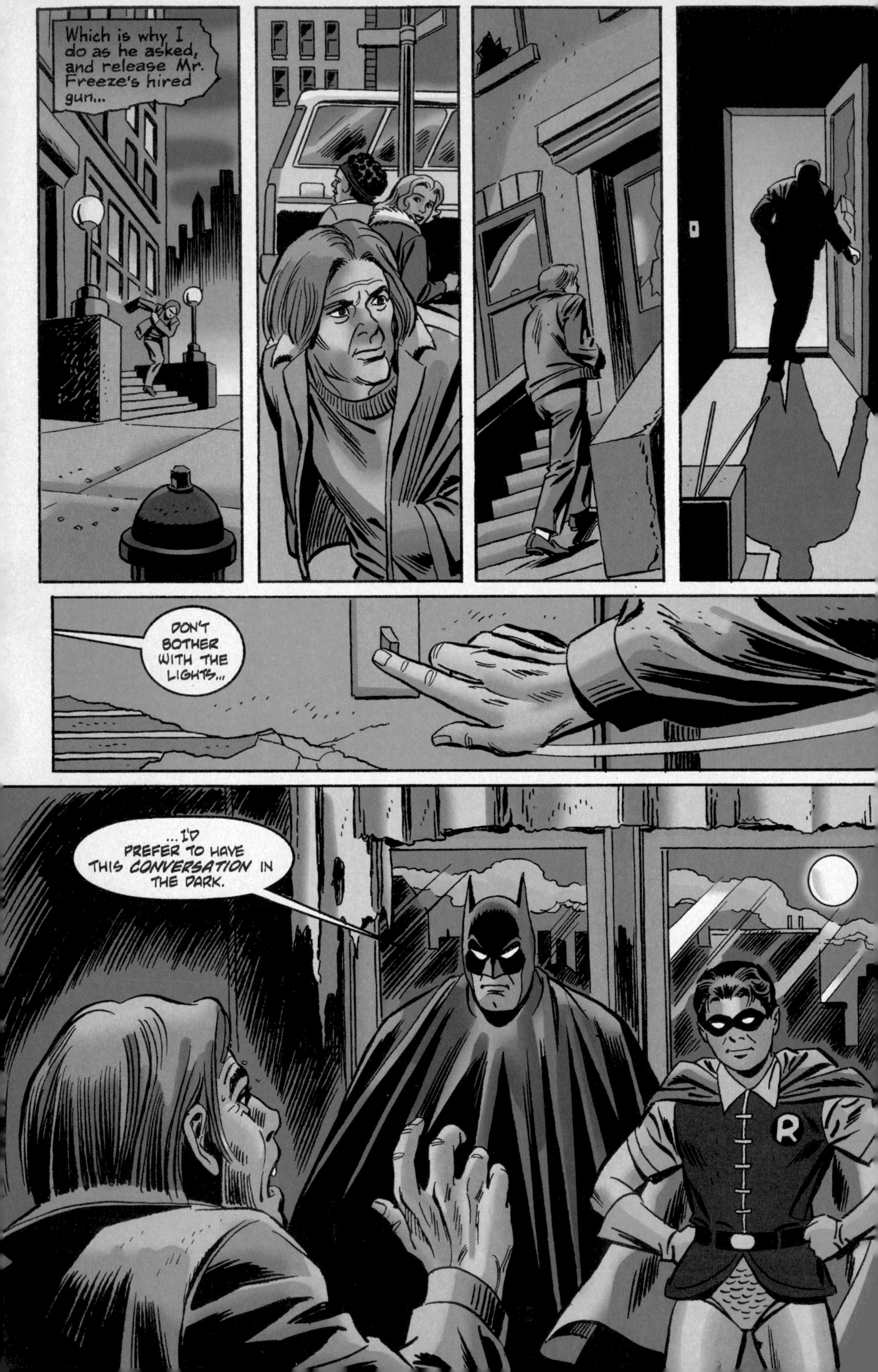
Which is why I do as he asked, and release Mr. Freeze's hired gun...
DON'T BOTHER WITH THE LIGHTS...
...I'D PREFER TO HAVE THIS CONVERSATION IN THE DARK.
R

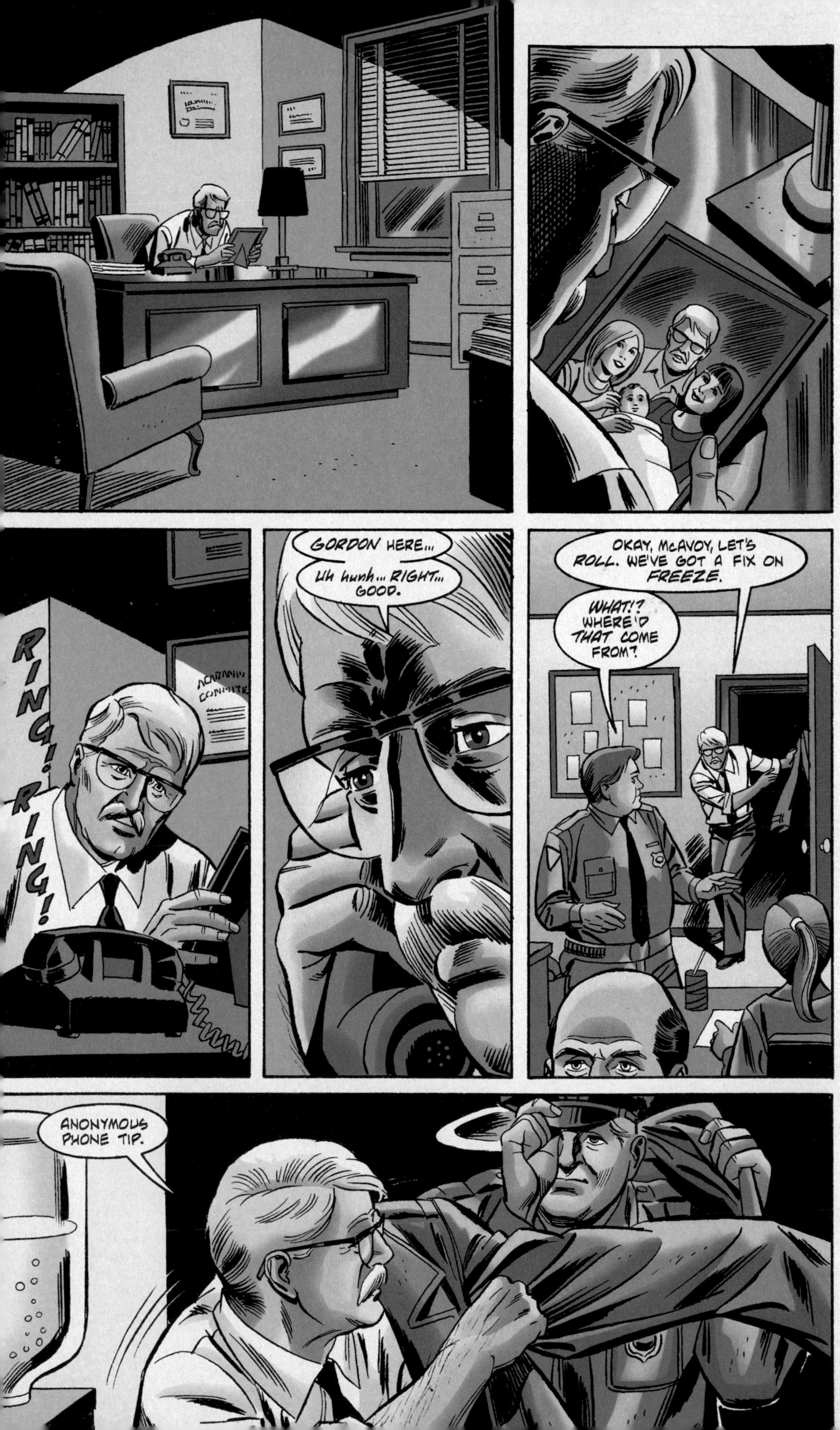
RING! RING!
GORDON HERE...
Uh hunh... RIGHT... GOOD.
OKAY, McAVOY, LET'S ROLL. WE'VE GOT A FIX ON FREEZE.
WHAT!? WHERE'D THAT COME FROM?
ANONYMOUS PHONE TIP.

WHAT THE HELL WAS THIS PLACE? WHERE'D ALL THIS STUFF *COME FROM?*

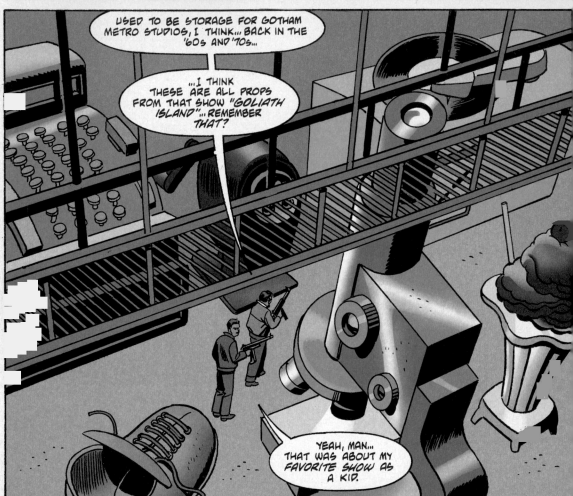

USED TO BE STORAGE FOR GOTHAM METRO STUDIOS, I THINK... BACK IN THE '60s AND '70s...

...I THINK THESE ARE ALL PROPS FROM THAT SHOW "GOLIATH ISLAND"... REMEMBER *THAT?*

YEAH, MAN... THAT WAS ABOUT MY *FAVORITE* SHOW AS A KID.

IT WAS OKAY... I LIKED "GORILLA WORLD" BETTER...

THE *MOVIE* OR THE *SHOW?* 'CAUSE THE MOVIE WAS GOOD, BUT THAT TV SHOW STUNK UP THE AIRWAVES...

YOU DON'T KNOW WHAT YOU'RE TALKIN' ABOUT.

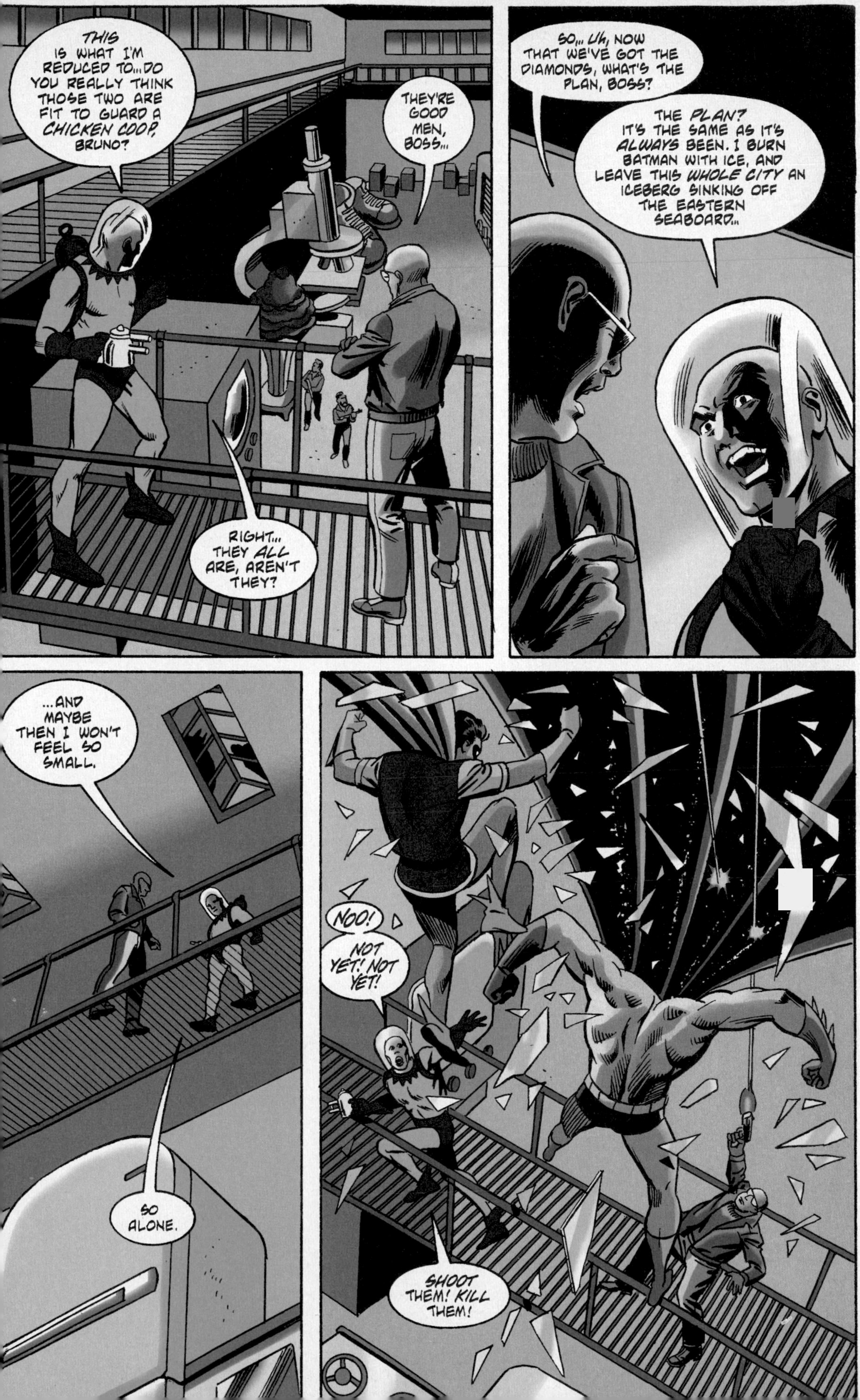
THIS IS WHAT I'M REDUCED TO... DO YOU REALLY THINK THOSE TWO ARE FIT TO GUARD A CHICKEN COOP, BRUNO?
THEY'RE GOOD MEN, BOSS...
RIGHT... THEY ALL ARE, AREN'T THEY?
SO... UH, NOW THAT WE'VE GOT THE DIAMONDS, WHAT'S THE PLAN, BOSS?
THE PLAN? IT'S THE SAME AS IT'S ALWAYS BEEN. I BURN BATMAN WITH ICE, AND LEAVE THIS WHOLE CITY AN ICEBERG SINKING OFF THE EASTERN SEABOARD...
...AND MAYBE THEN I WON'T FEEL SO SMALL.
SO ALONE.
NOO!
NOT YET! NOT YET!
SHOOT THEM! KILL THEM!

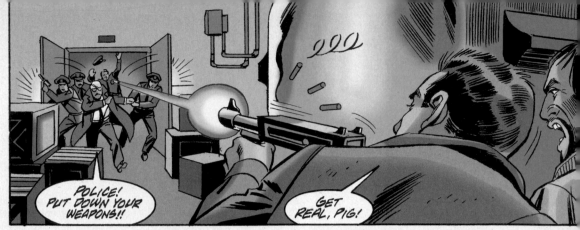

POLICE! PUT DOWN YOUR WEAPONS!!

GET REAL, PIG!

HELP THE *POLICE!* I'LL HANDLE FREEZE!

GOT IT!

NO SALE

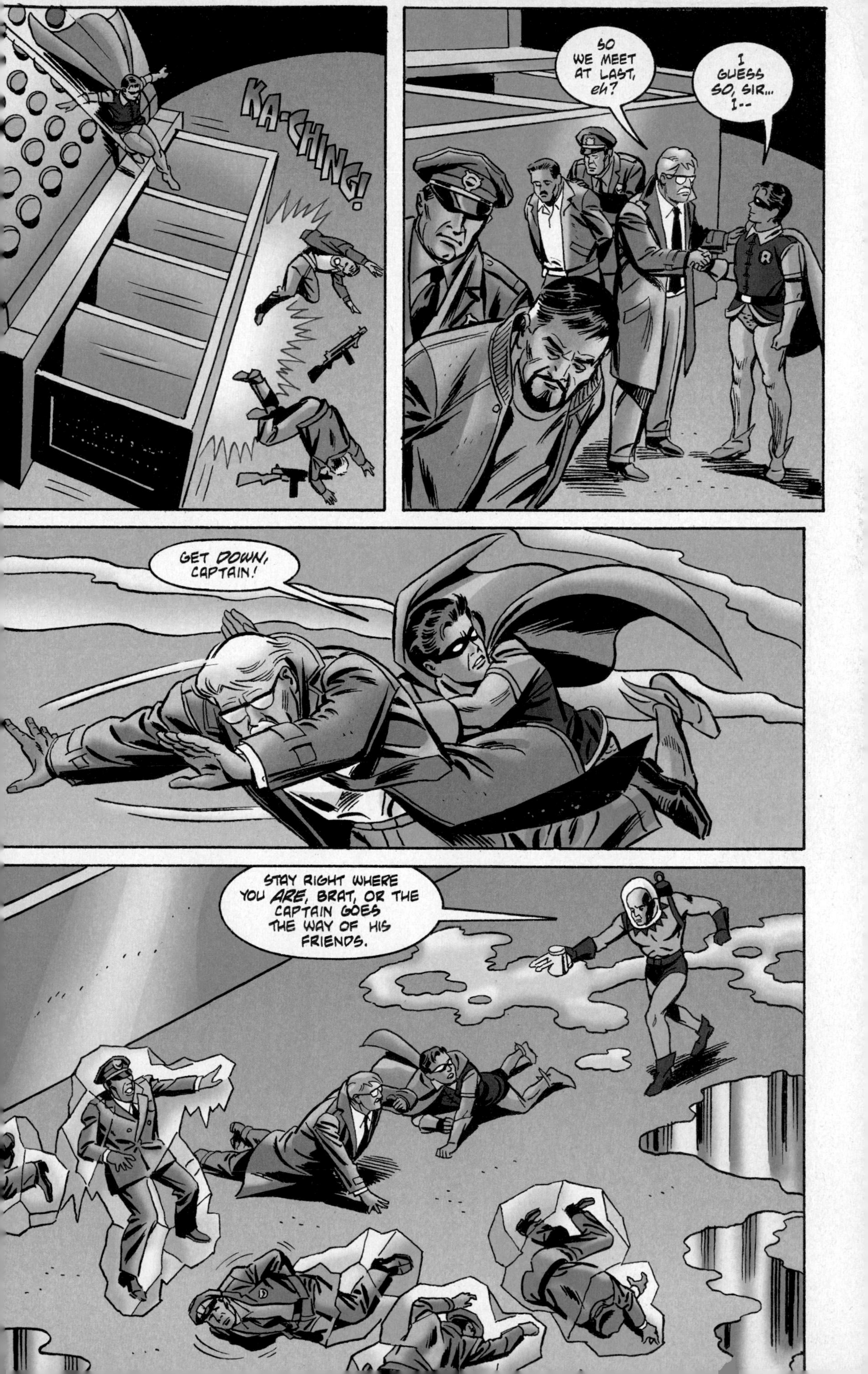
KA-CHING!
SO WE MEET AT LAST, eh?
I GUESS SO, SIR... I--
GET DOWN, CAPTAIN!
STAY RIGHT WHERE YOU ARE, BRAT, OR THE CAPTAIN GOES THE WAY OF HIS FRIENDS.

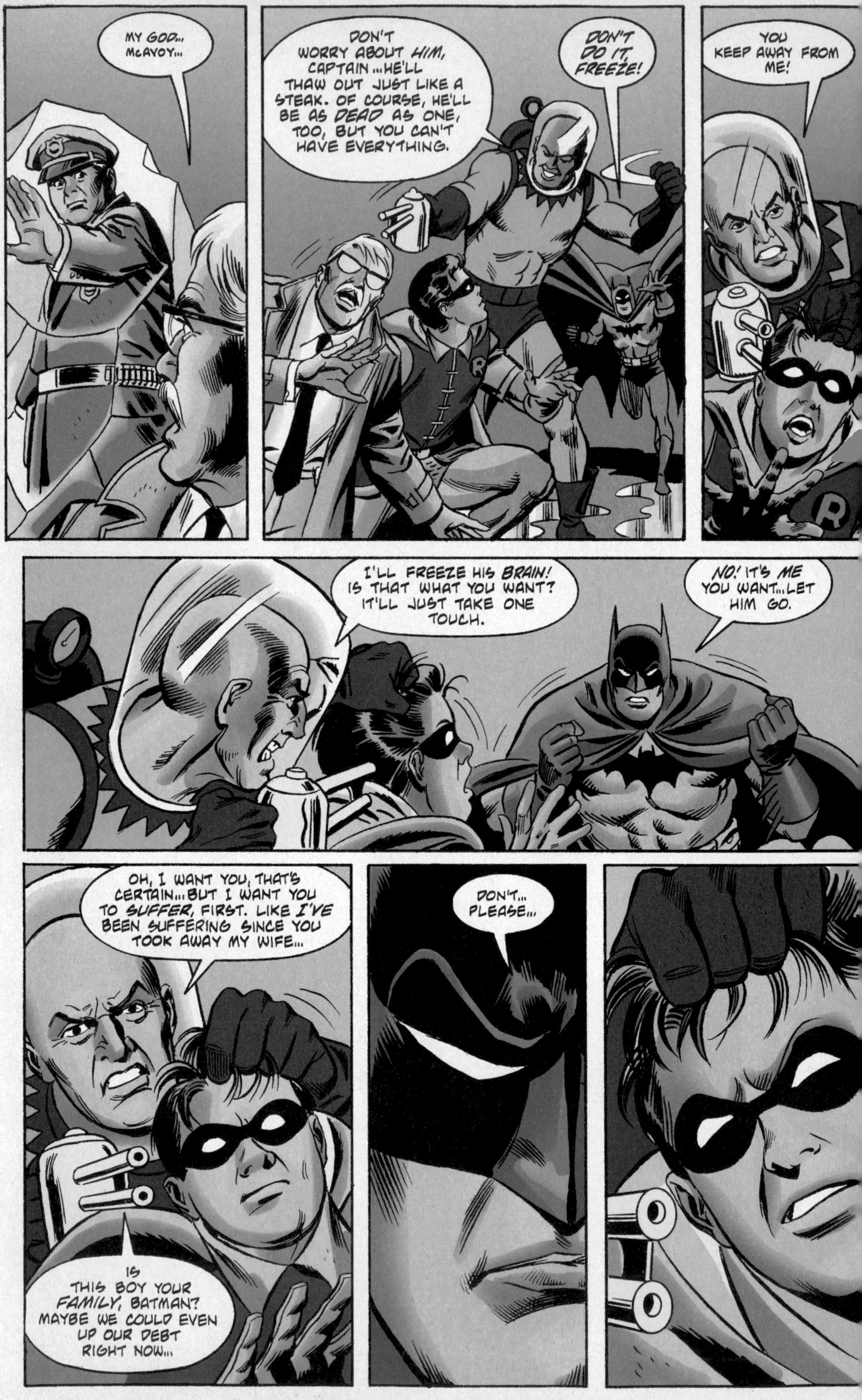

MY GOD... McAVOY...
DON'T WORRY ABOUT HIM, CAPTAIN ...HE'LL THAW OUT JUST LIKE A STEAK. OF COURSE, HE'LL BE AS DEAD AS ONE, TOO, BUT YOU CAN'T HAVE EVERYTHING.
DON'T DO IT, FREEZE!
YOU KEEP AWAY FROM ME!
I'LL FREEZE HIS BRAIN! IS THAT WHAT YOU WANT? IT'LL JUST TAKE ONE TOUCH.
NO! IT'S ME YOU WANT...LET HIM GO.
OH, I WANT YOU, THAT'S CERTAIN...BUT I WANT YOU TO SUFFER, FIRST. LIKE I'VE BEEN SUFFERING SINCE YOU TOOK AWAY MY WIFE...
IS THIS BOY YOUR FAMILY, BATMAN? MAYBE WE COULD EVEN UP OUR DEBT RIGHT NOW...
DON'T... PLEASE...

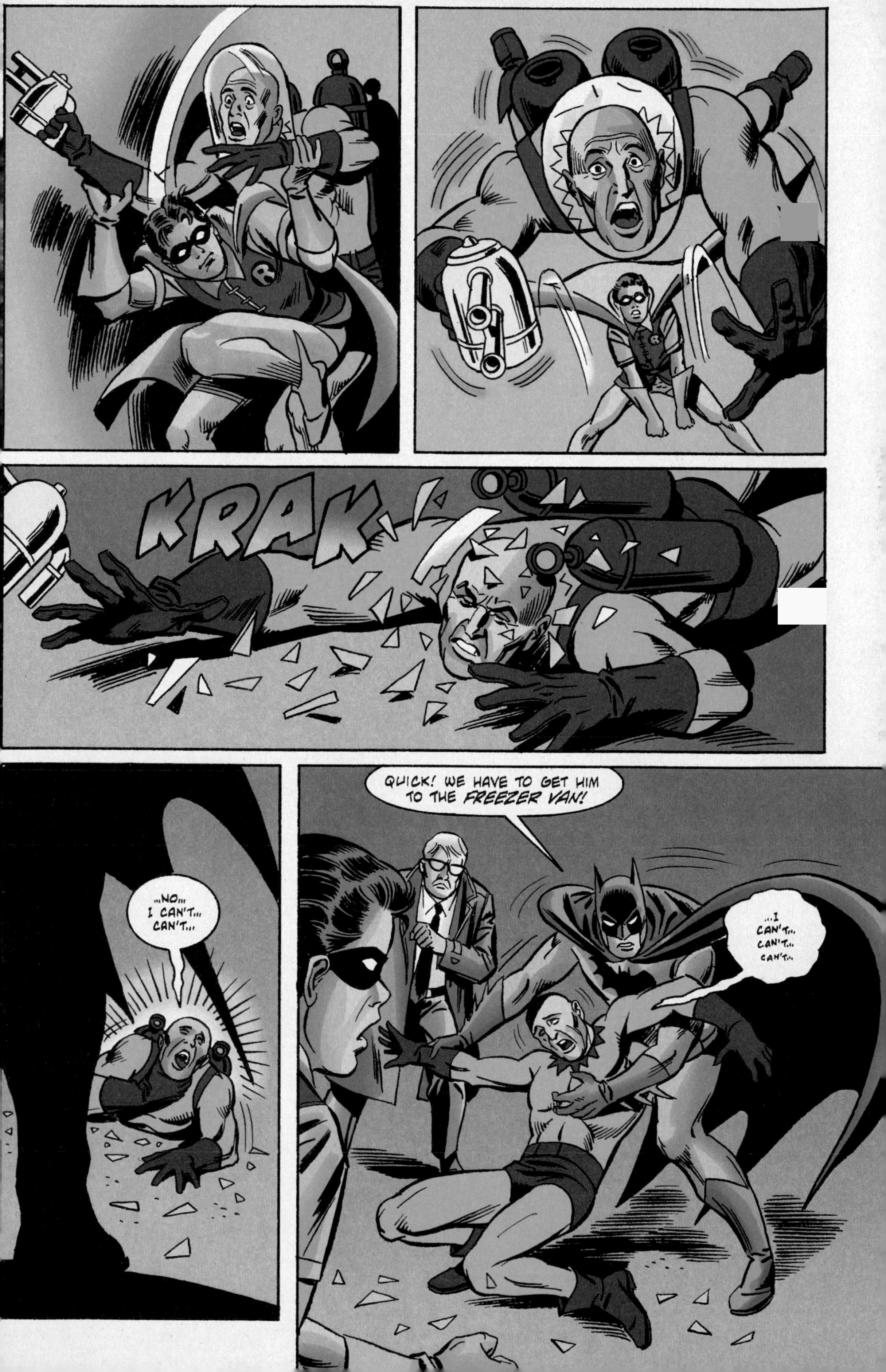
KRAK
...NO... I CAN'T... CAN'T...
QUICK! WE HAVE TO GET HIM TO THE FREEZER VAN!
...I CAN'T... CAN'T... CAN'T...

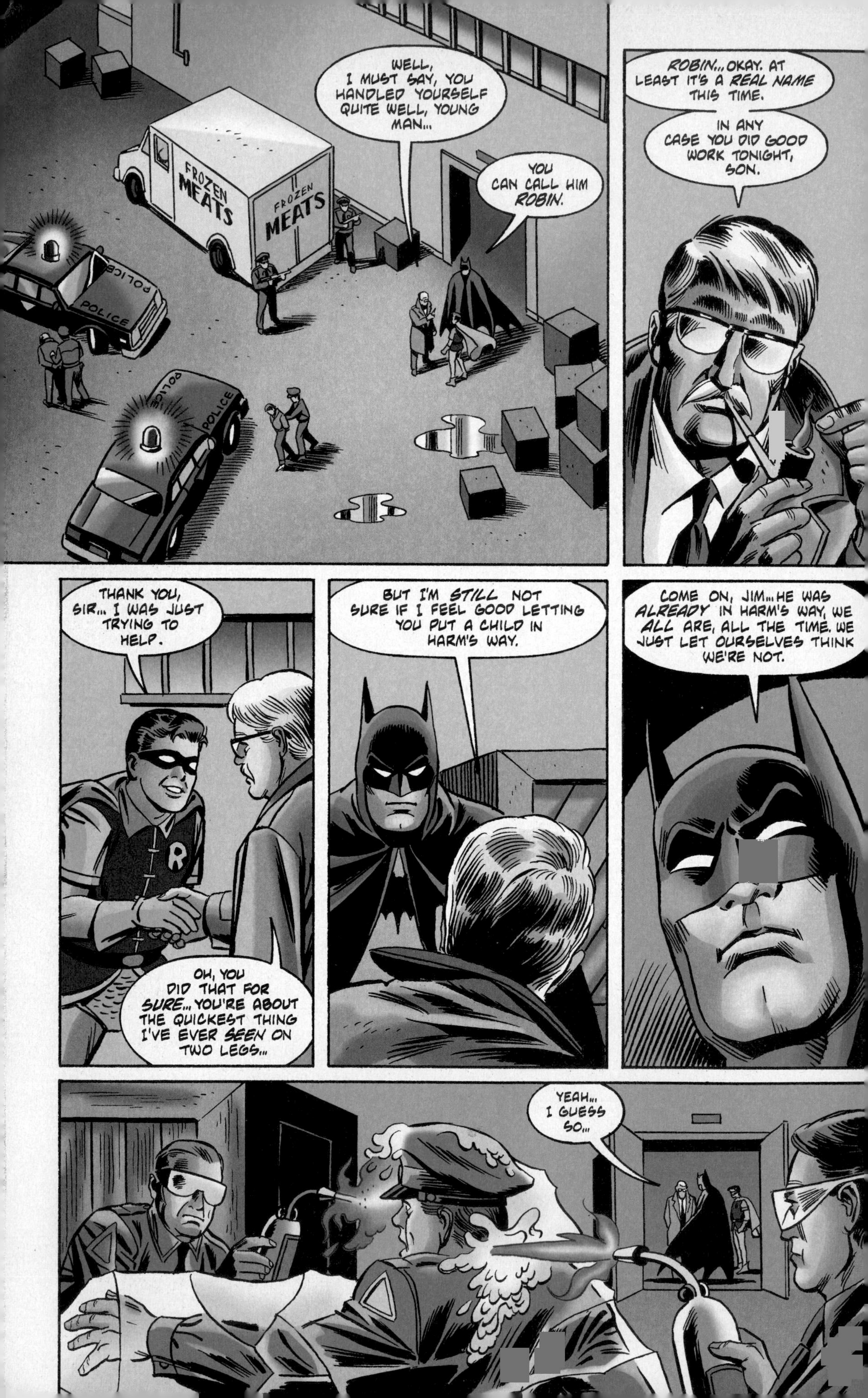
WELL, I MUST SAY, YOU HANDLED YOURSELF QUITE WELL, YOUNG MAN...
FROZEN MEATS
FROZEN MEATS
POLICE
POLICE
YOU CAN CALL HIM *ROBIN.*
ROBIN... OKAY. AT LEAST IT'S A *REAL NAME* THIS TIME.
IN ANY CASE YOU DID GOOD WORK TONIGHT, SON.
THANK YOU, SIR... I WAS JUST TRYING TO HELP.
OH, YOU DID THAT FOR *SURE...* YOU'RE ABOUT THE QUICKEST THING I'VE EVER *SEEN* ON TWO LEGS...
BUT I'M *STILL* NOT SURE IF I FEEL GOOD LETTING YOU PUT A CHILD IN HARM'S WAY.
COME ON, JIM... HE WAS *ALREADY* IN HARM'S WAY, WE *ALL* ARE, ALL THE TIME. WE JUST LET OURSELVES THINK WE'RE NOT.
YEAH... I GUESS SO...

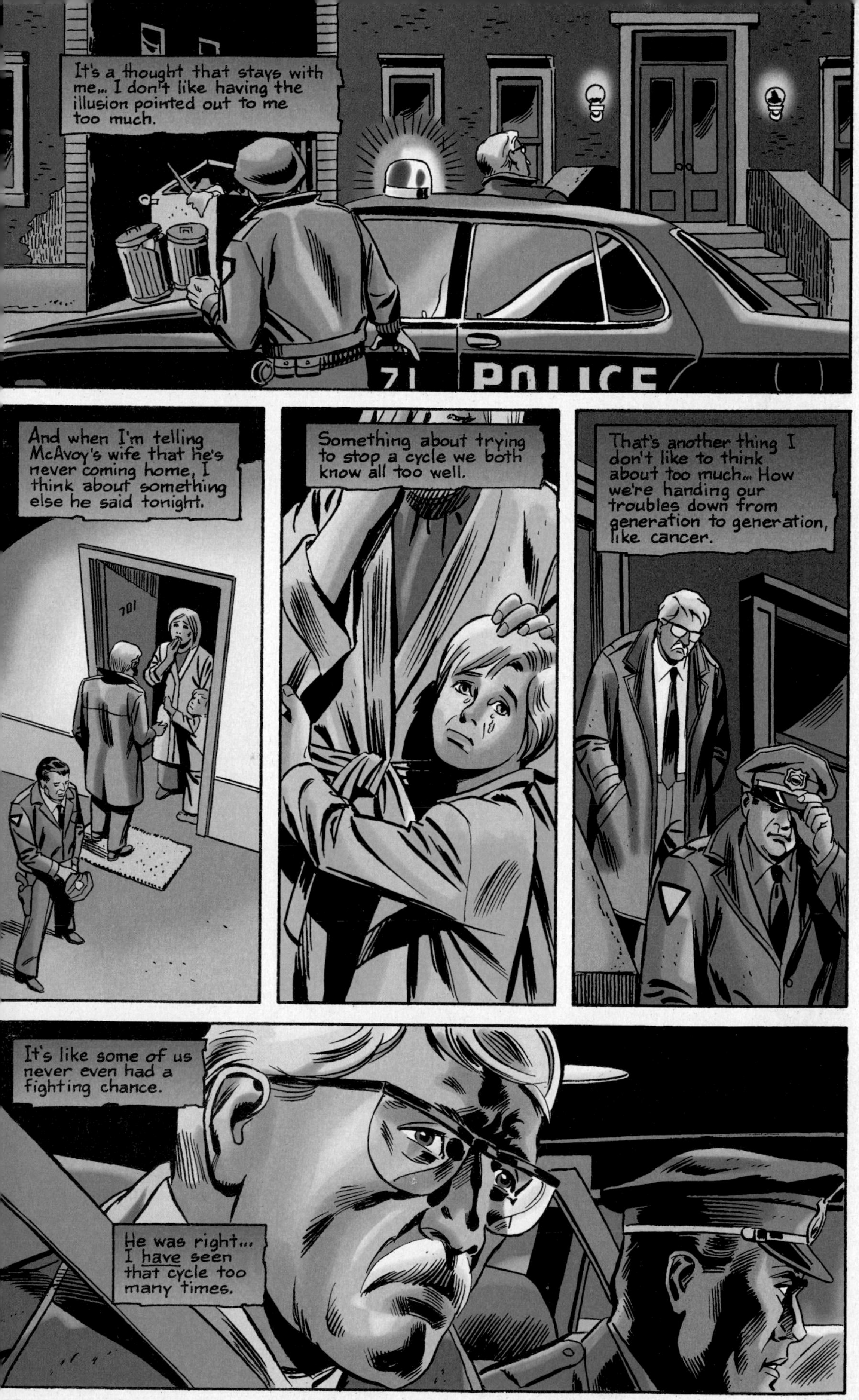
It's a thought that stays with me... I don't like having the illusion pointed out to me too much.
71 POLICE
And when I'm telling McAvoy's wife that he's never coming home, I think about something else he said tonight.
701
Something about trying to stop a cycle we both know all too well.
That's another thing I don't like to think about too much... How we're handing our troubles down from generation to generation, like cancer.
It's like some of us never even had a fighting chance.
He was right... I have seen that cycle too many times.

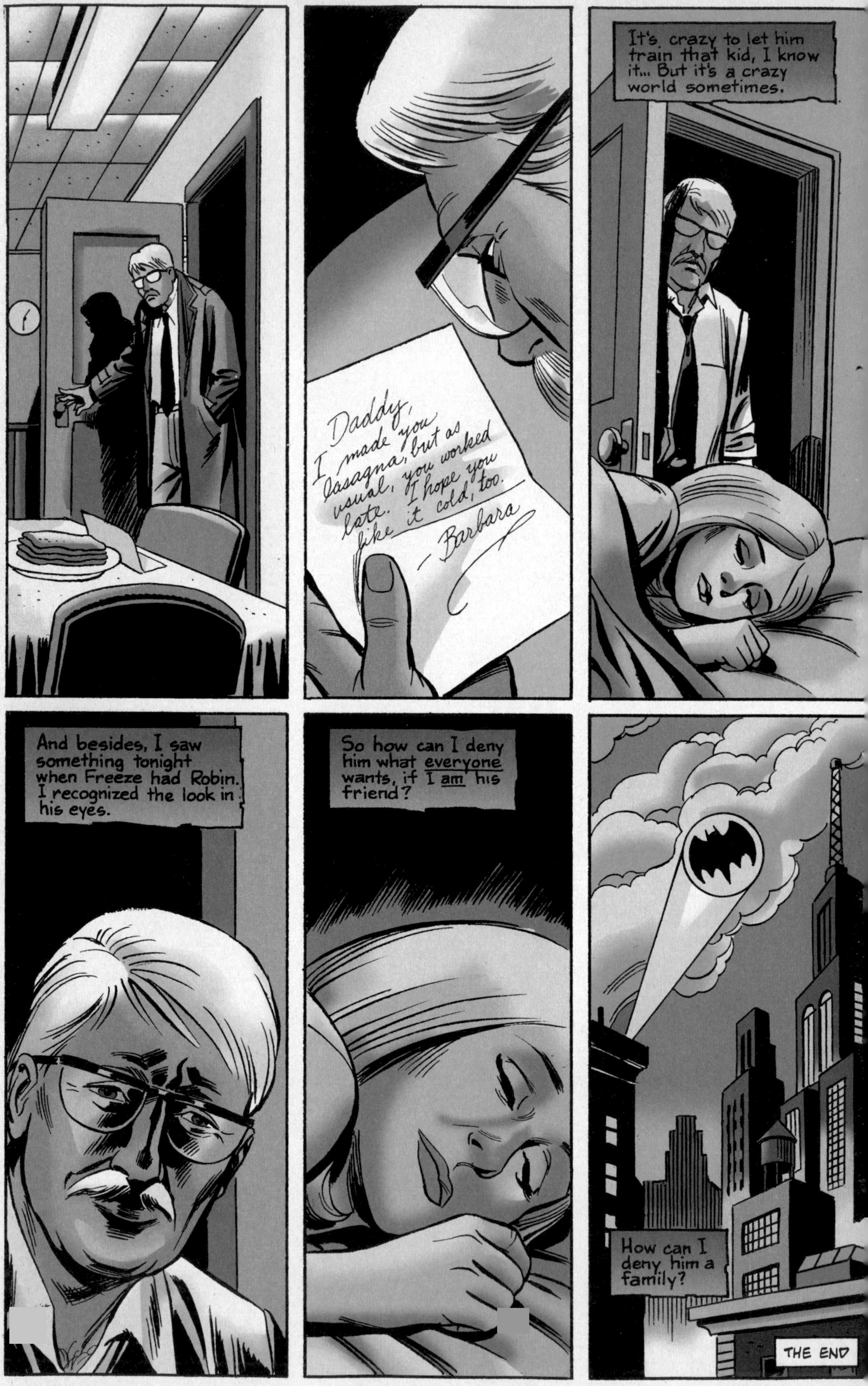
Daddy,
I made you lasagna, but as usual, you worked late. I hope you like it cold, too.
— Barbara
It's crazy to let him train that kid, I know it... But it's a crazy world sometimes.
And besides, I saw something tonight when Freeze had Robin. I recognized the look in his eyes.
So how can I deny him what everyone wants, if I am his friend?
How can I deny him a family?
THE END

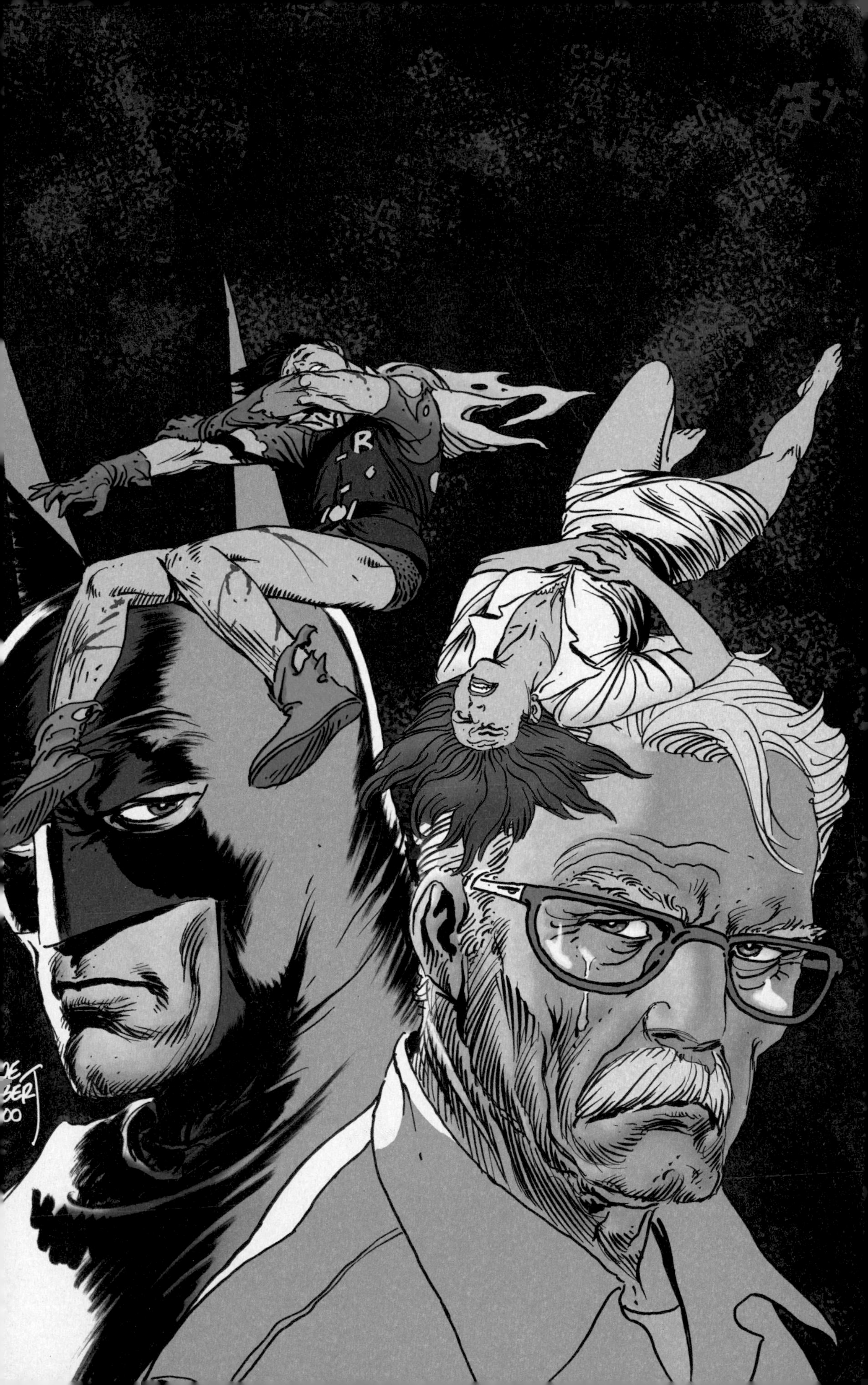

CHAPTER THREE

CASUALTIES OF WAR

Ed Brubaker
writer

Dick Giordano
penciller

Bob Smith
inker

Joe Kubert
cover artist

Glen Whitmore
colorist

Willie Schubert
letterer

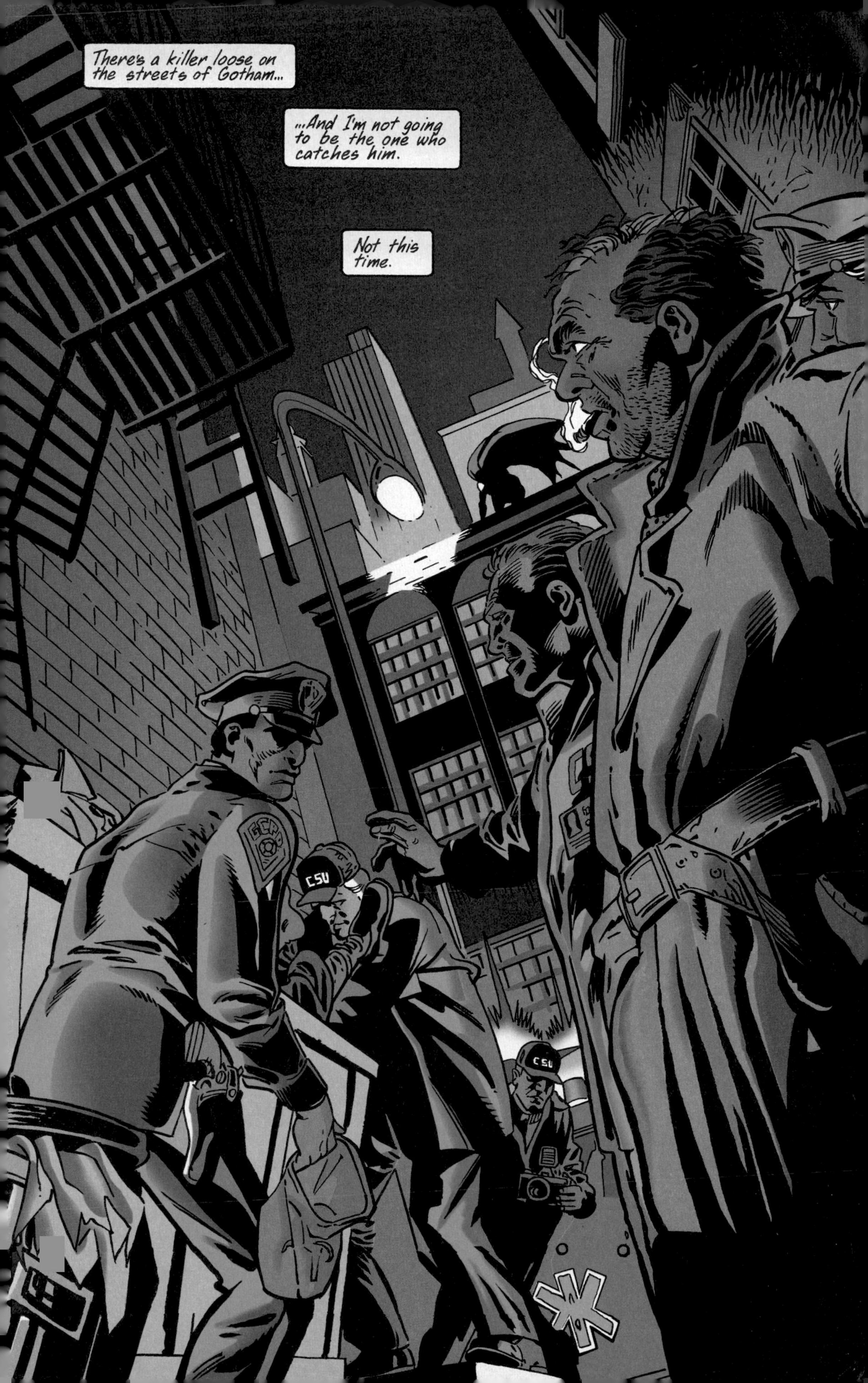

There's a killer loose on the streets of Gotham...
...And I'm not going to be the one who catches him.
Not this time.
CSU
CSU

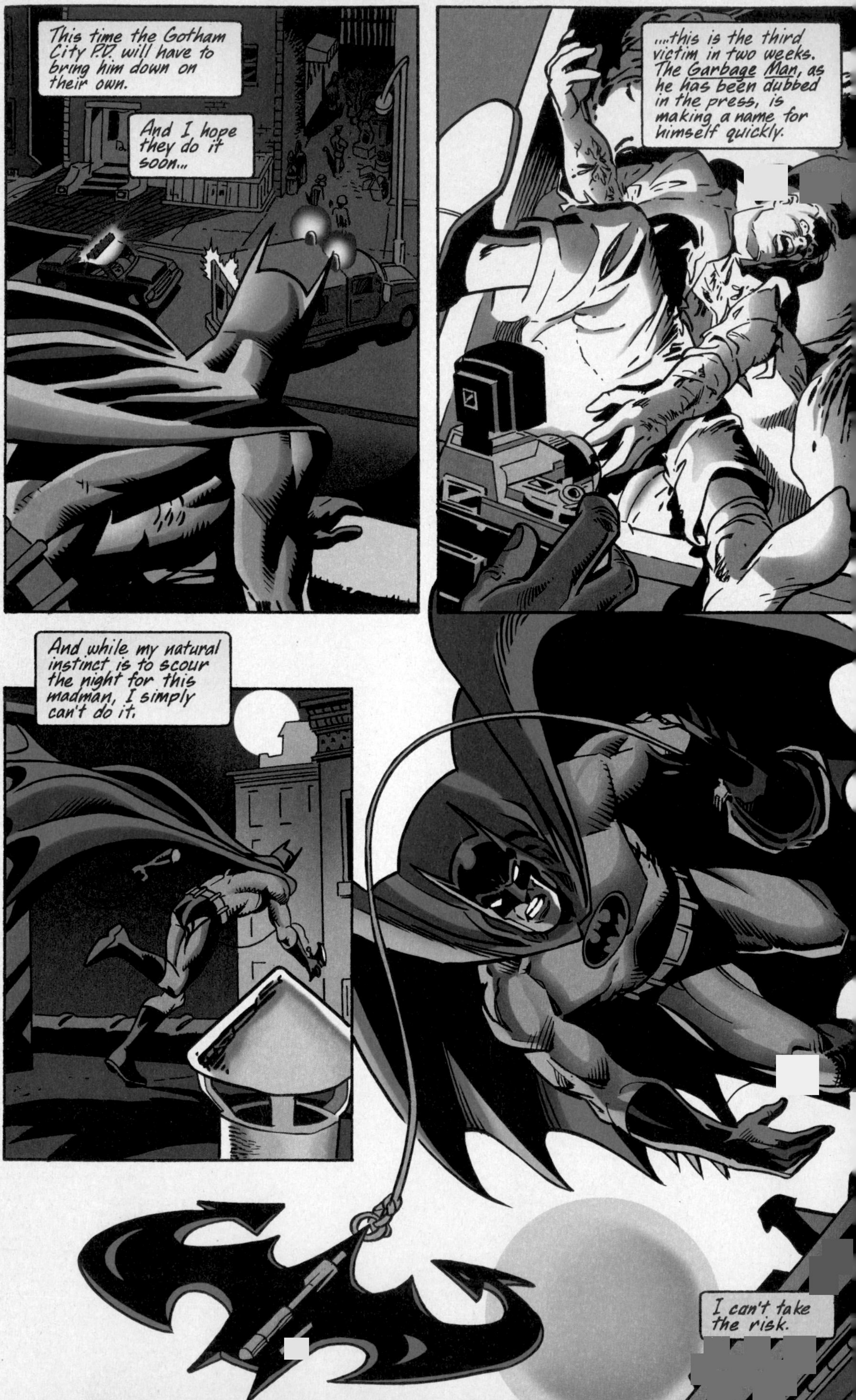
This time the Gotham City P.D. will have to bring him down on their own.
And I hope they do it soon...
...this is the third victim in two weeks. The Garbage Man, as he has been dubbed in the press, is making a name for himself quickly.
And while my natural instinct is to scour the night for this madman, I simply can't do it.
I can't take the risk.

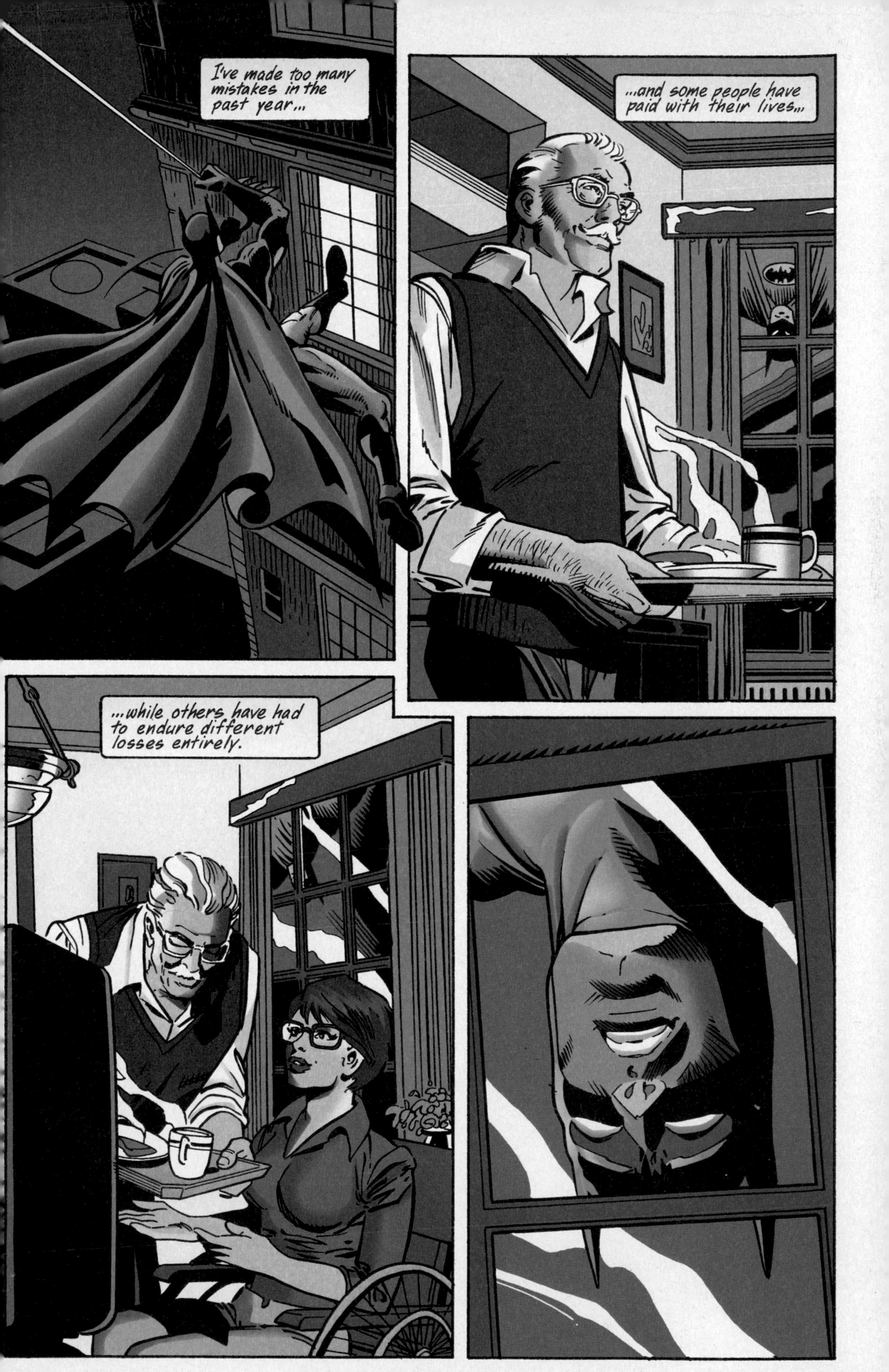
I've made too many mistakes in the past year...
...and some people have paid with their lives...
...while others have had to endure different losses entirely.

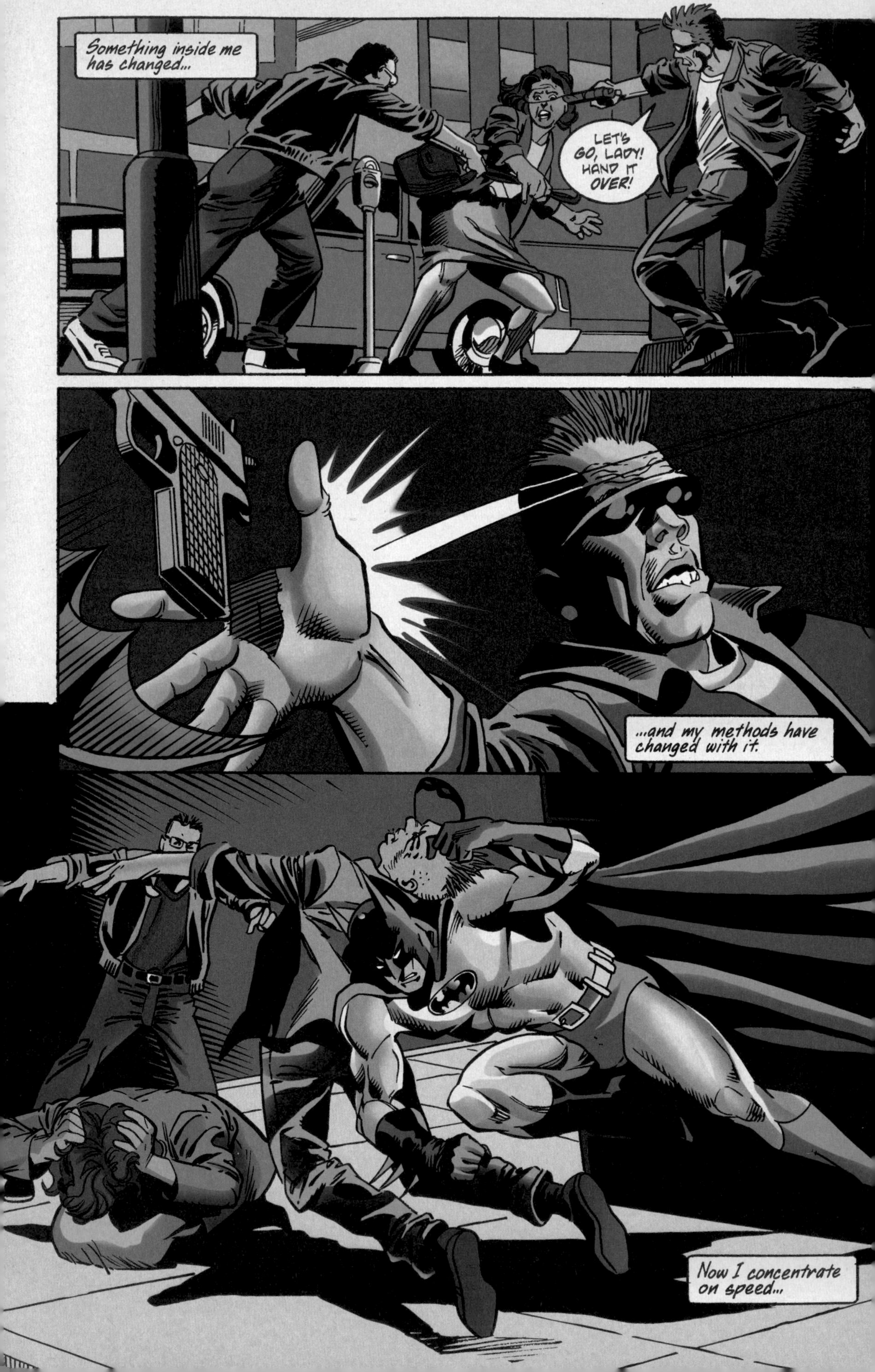
Something inside me has changed...
LET'S GO, LADY! HAND IT OVER!
...and my methods have changed with it.
Now I concentrate on speed...

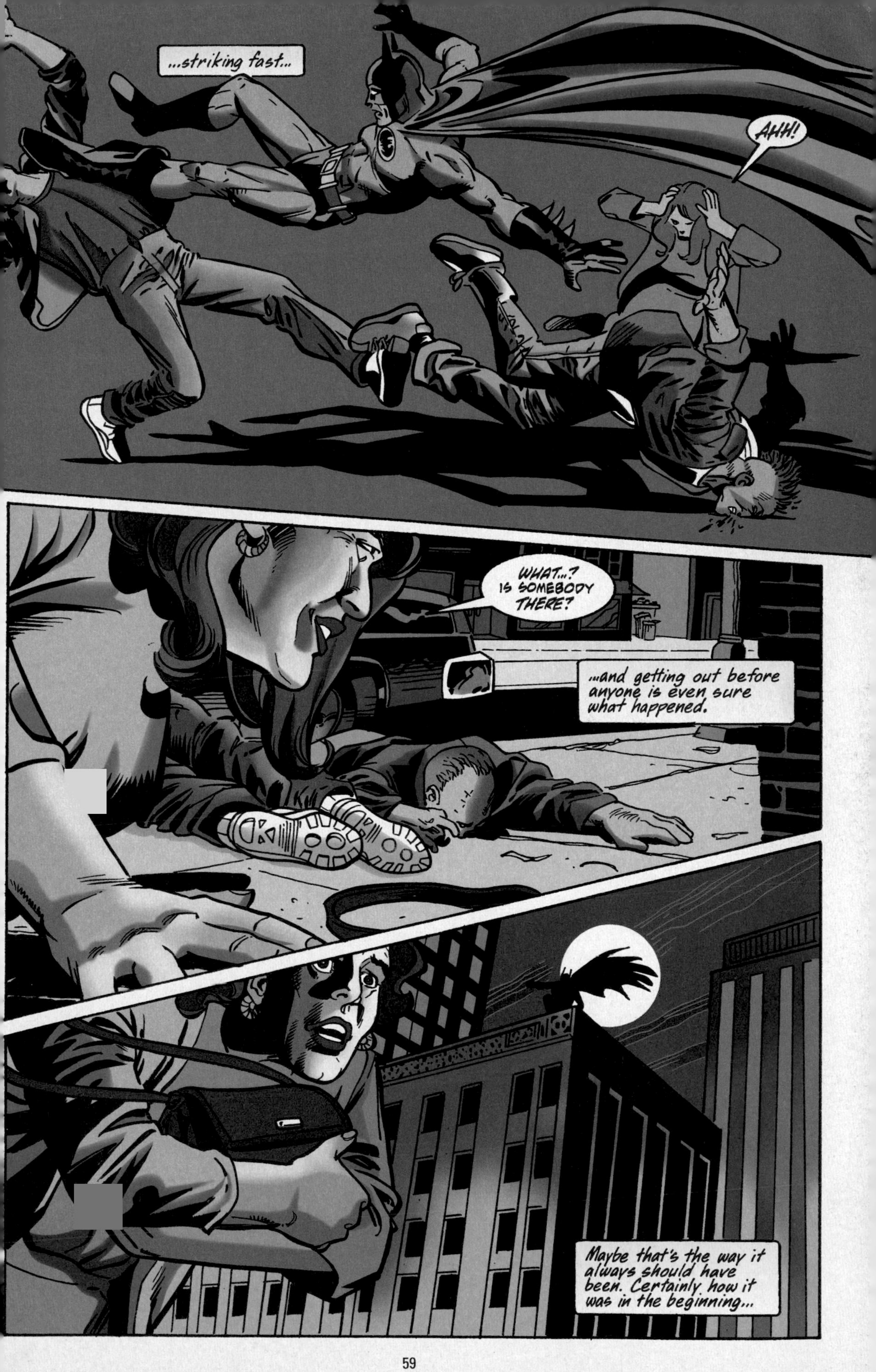
...striking fast...
AHH!
WHAT...? IS SOMEBODY THERE?
...and getting out before anyone is even sure what happened.
Maybe that's the way it always should have been. Certainly how it was in the beginning...

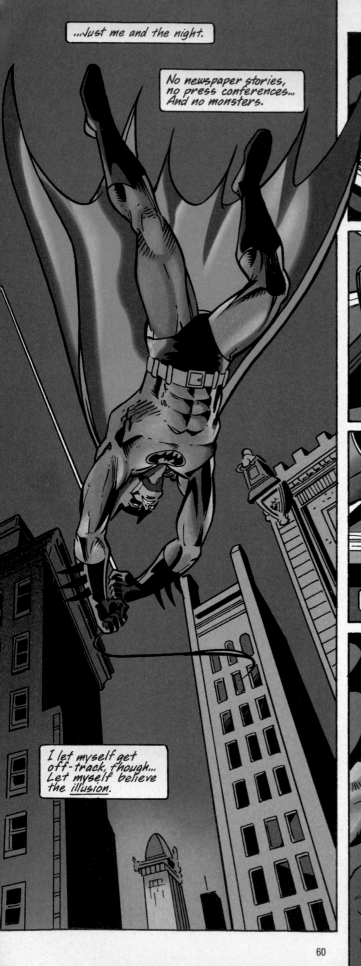

...Just me and the night.

No newspaper stories, no press conferences... And no monsters.

I let myself get off-track, though... Let myself believe the illusion.

Thought I could win.

So now it's back to my roots...

Owww!

...Swiftness...

...And solitude.

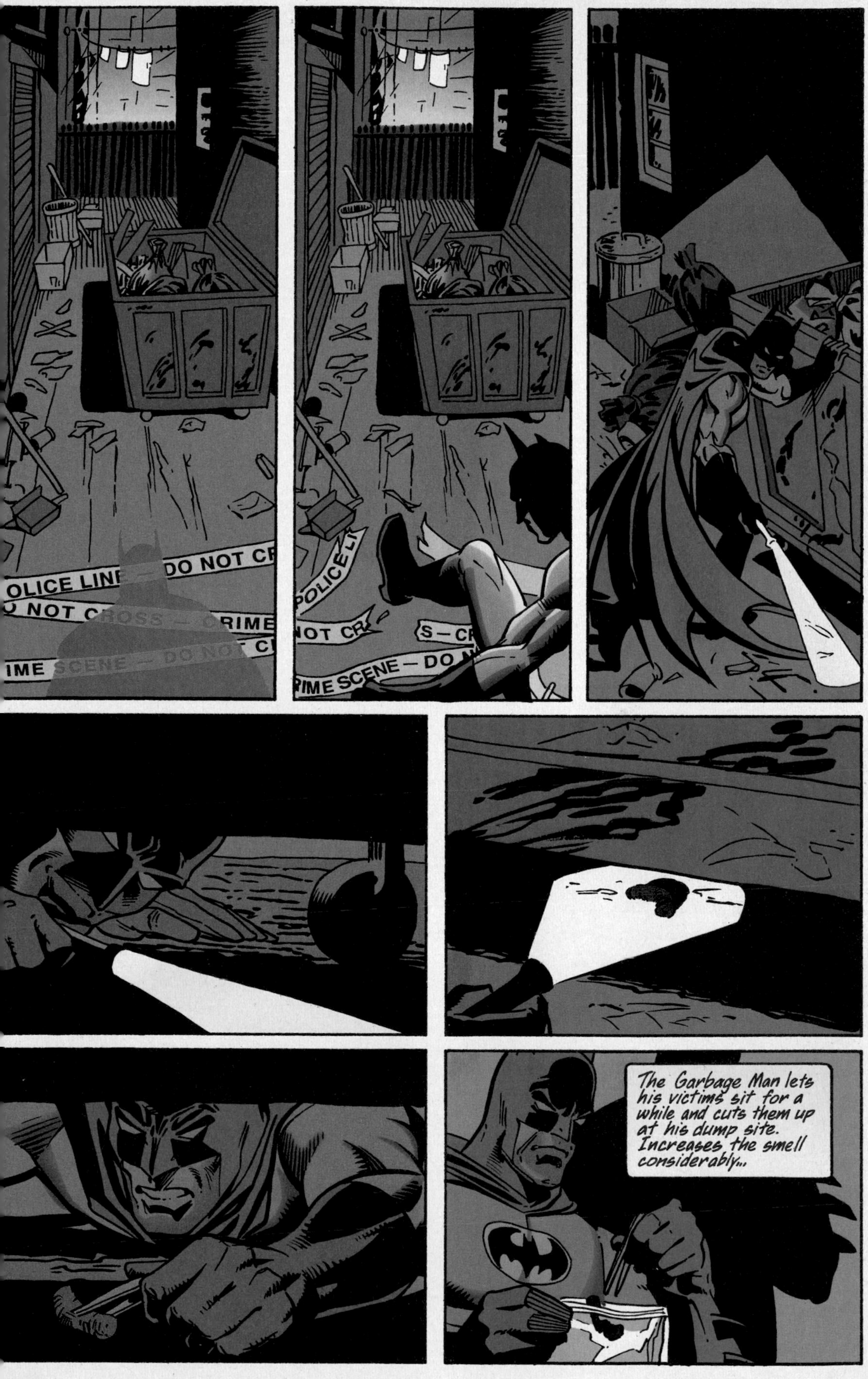
POLICE LINE — DO NOT CROSS — CRIME SCENE — DO NOT CROSS
The Garbage Man lets his victims sit for a while and cuts them up at his dump site. Increases the smell considerably...

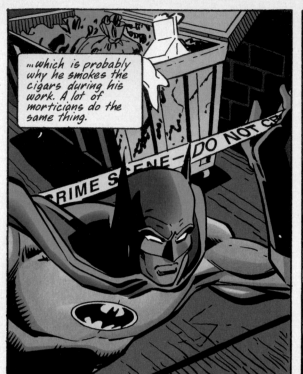

...which is probably why he smokes the cigars during his work. A lot of morticians do the same thing.

Under normal circumstances, the police would've noticed the cigar butts at these crime scenes... But here it's hard to know the difference between _trash_ and _evidence_.

It's getting like that all over the city.

HOMICIDE

THIS CITY IS REALLY GOING TO THE _DOGS_, BULLOCK... WHAT DO THEY PAY US FOR?

COMMISH? WHATTA _YOU_ DOIN' HERE AT THIS HOUR?

SHOULDN'T _YOU_ BE HOME WITH...?

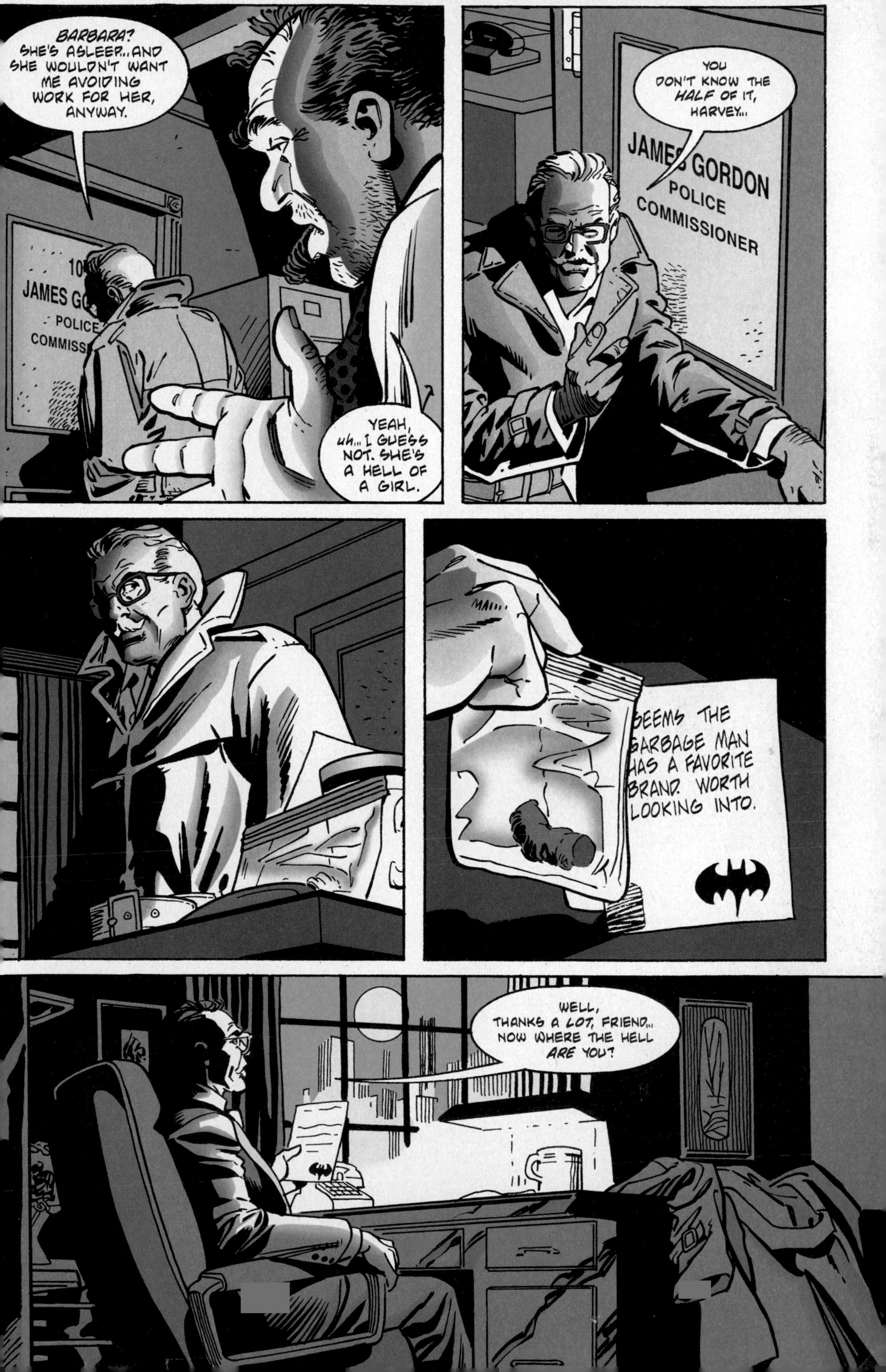
BARBARA? SHE'S ASLEEP... AND SHE WOULDN'T WANT ME AVOIDING WORK FOR HER, ANYWAY.
JAMES GORDON POLICE COMMISSIONER
YEAH, uh... I GUESS NOT. SHE'S A HELL OF A GIRL.
YOU DON'T KNOW THE HALF OF IT, HARVEY...
JAMES GORDON POLICE COMMISSIONER
SEEMS THE GARBAGE MAN HAS A FAVORITE BRAND. WORTH LOOKING INTO.
WELL, THANKS A LOT, FRIEND... NOW WHERE THE HELL ARE YOU?

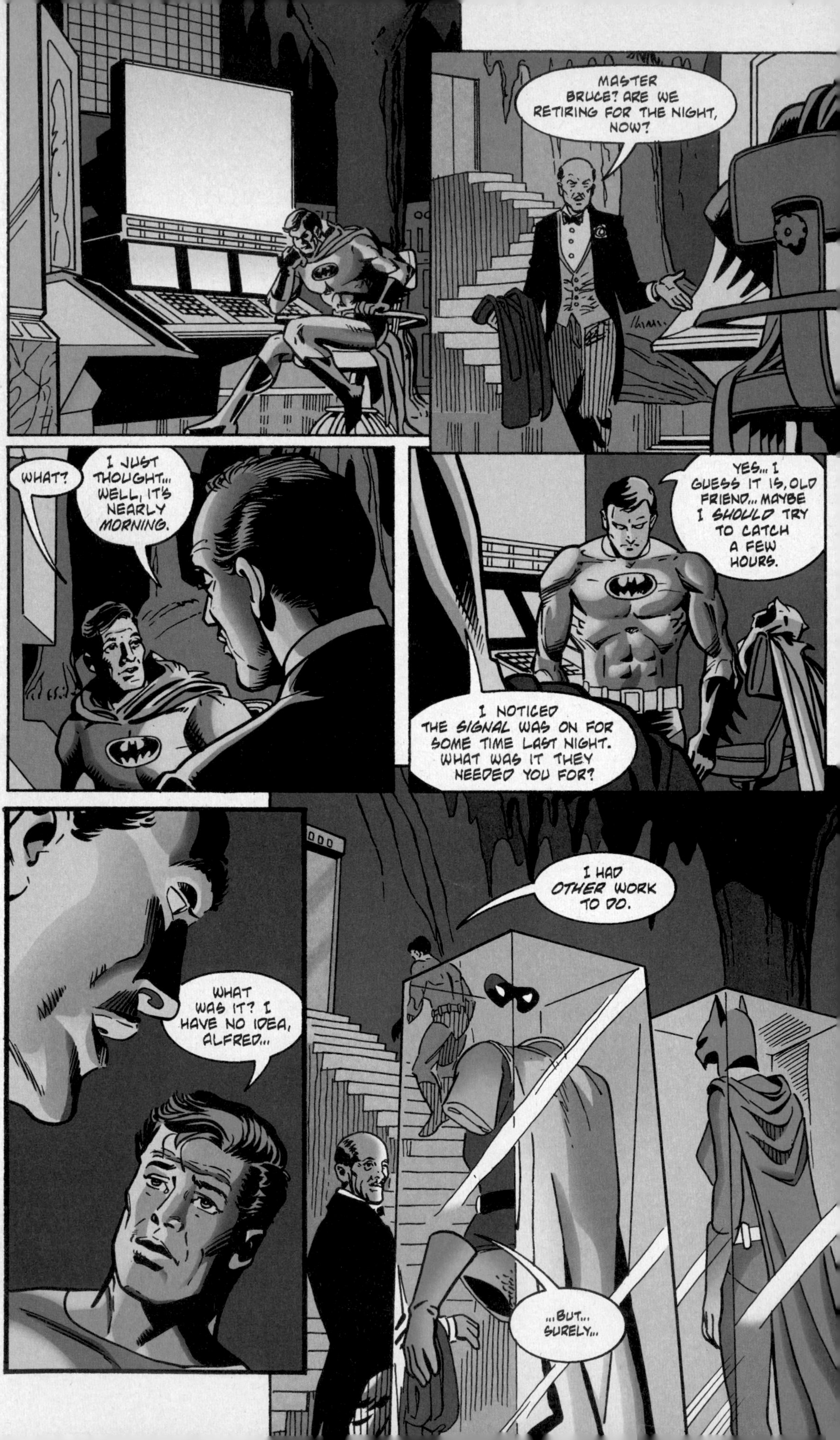
MASTER BRUCE? ARE WE RETIRING FOR THE NIGHT, NOW?
WHAT?
I JUST THOUGHT... WELL, IT'S NEARLY MORNING.
YES... I GUESS IT IS, OLD FRIEND... MAYBE I SHOULD TRY TO CATCH A FEW HOURS.
I NOTICED THE SIGNAL WAS ON FOR SOME TIME LAST NIGHT. WHAT WAS IT THEY NEEDED YOU FOR?
WHAT WAS IT? I HAVE NO IDEA, ALFRED...
I HAD OTHER WORK TO DO.
...BUT... SURELY...

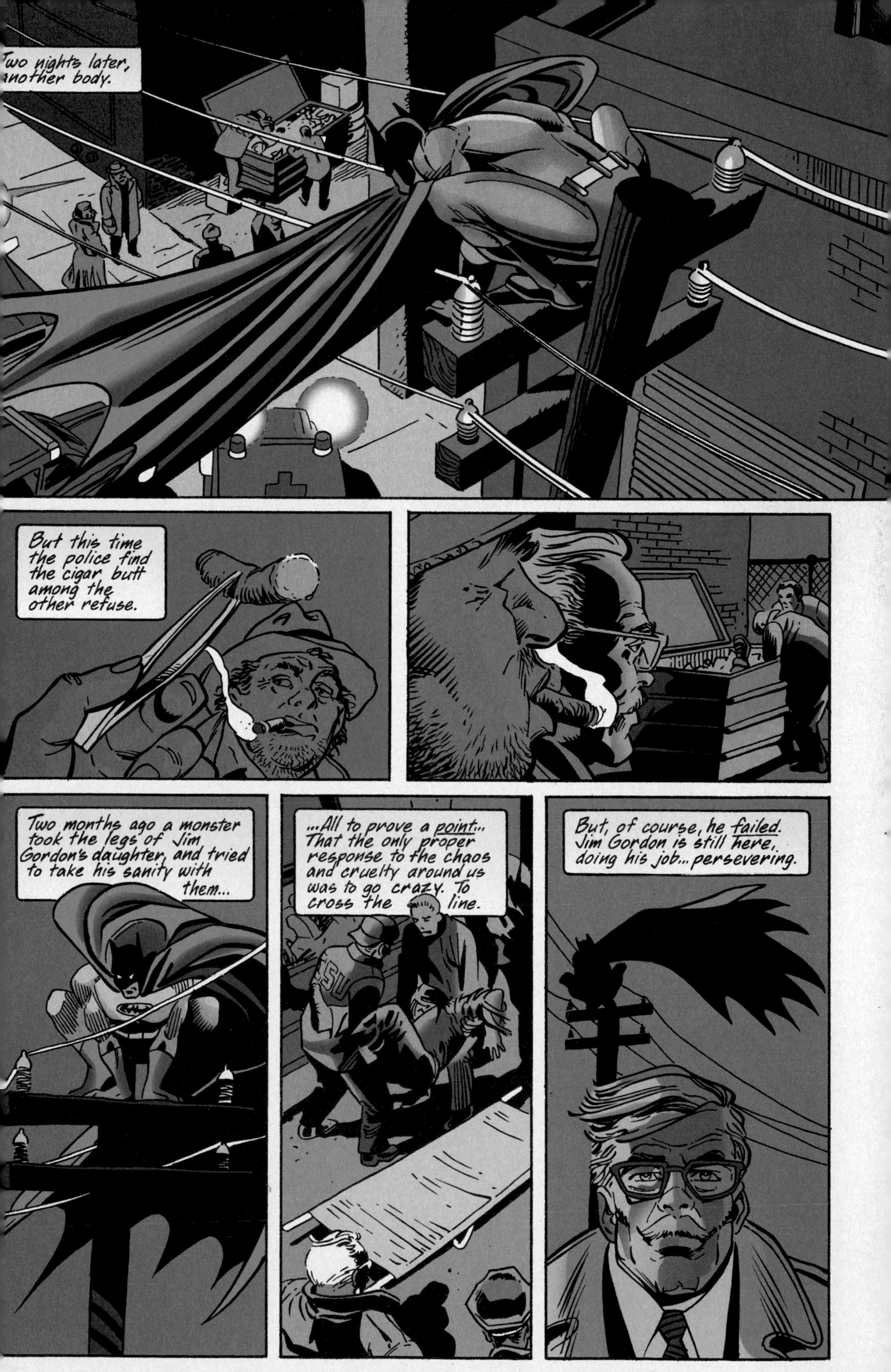
Two nights later, another body.
But this time the police find the cigar butt among the other refuse.
Two months ago a monster took the legs of Jim Gordon's daughter, and tried to take his sanity with them...
...All to prove a point... That the only proper response to the chaos and cruelty around us was to go crazy. To cross the line.
ESU
But, of course, he failed. Jim Gordon is still here, doing his job... persevering.

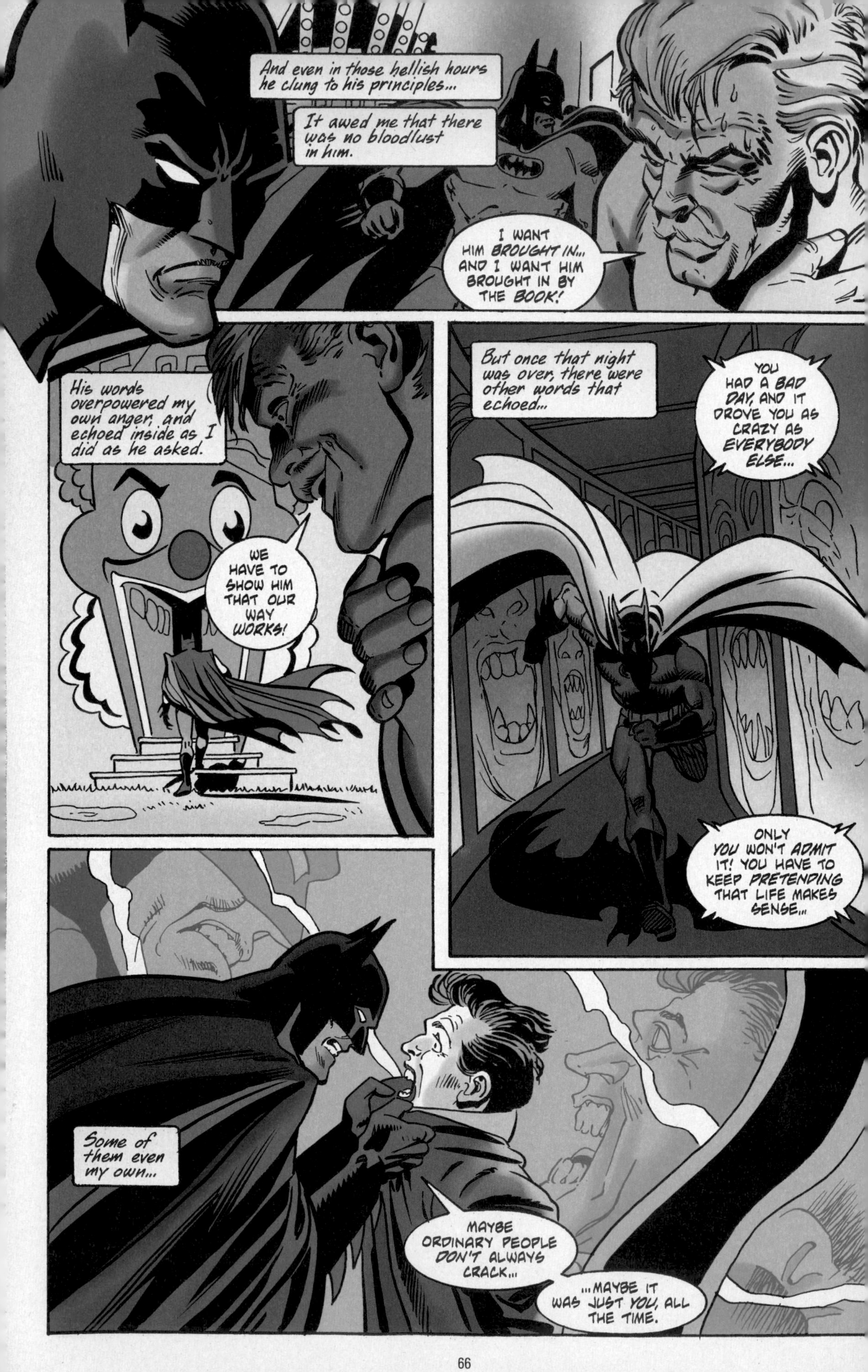

And even in those hellish hours he clung to his principles...
It awed me that there was no bloodlust in him.
I WANT HIM BROUGHT IN... AND I WANT HIM BROUGHT IN BY THE BOOK!
His words overpowered my own anger, and echoed inside as I did as he asked.
WE HAVE TO SHOW HIM THAT OUR WAY WORKS!
But once that night was over, there were other words that echoed...
YOU HAD A BAD DAY, AND IT DROVE YOU AS CRAZY AS EVERYBODY ELSE...
ONLY YOU WON'T ADMIT IT! YOU HAVE TO KEEP PRETENDING THAT LIFE MAKES SENSE...
Some of them even my own...
MAYBE ORDINARY PEOPLE DON'T ALWAYS CRACK...
...MAYBE IT WAS JUST YOU, ALL THE TIME.

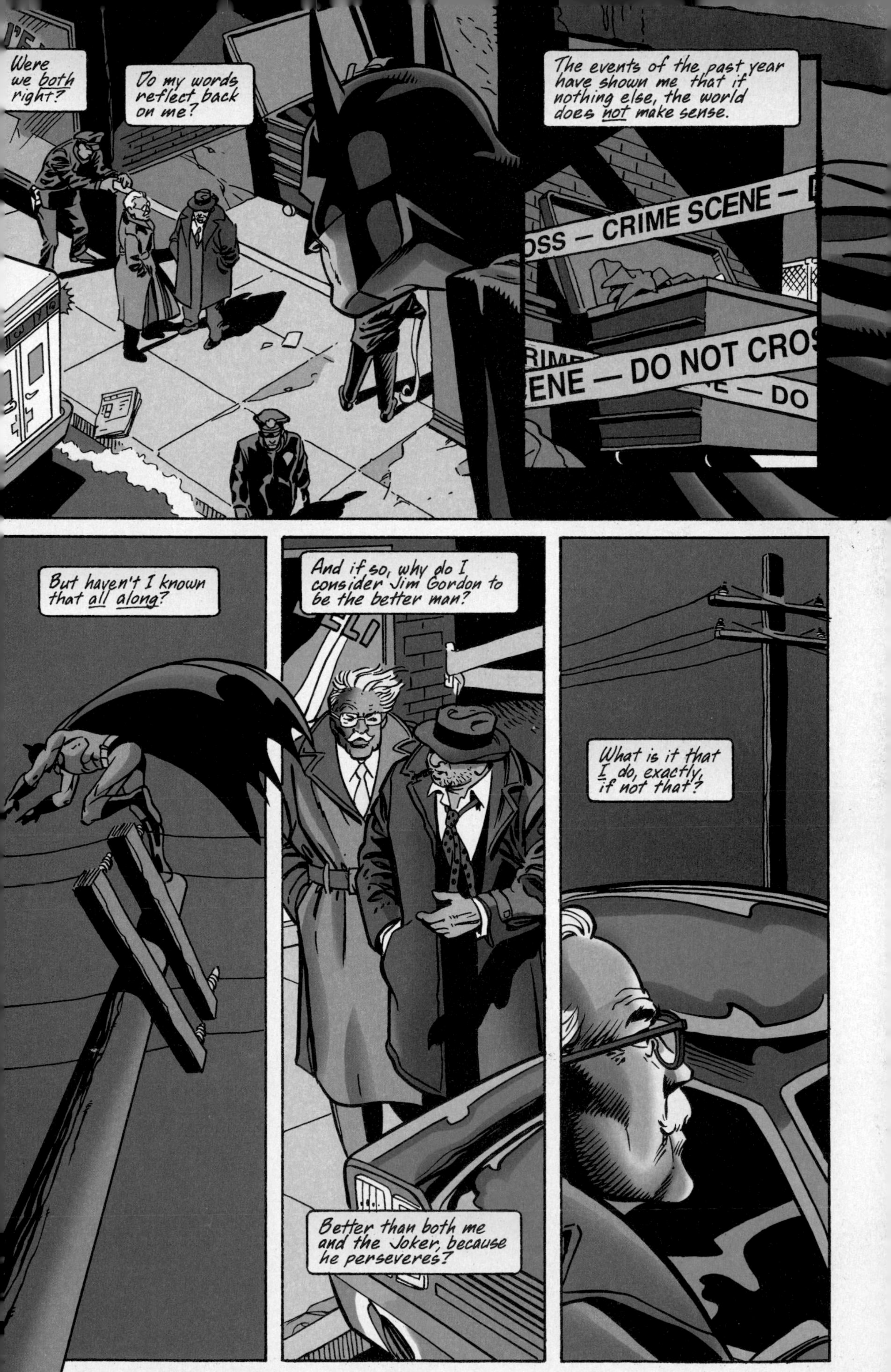
Were we both right?
Do my words reflect back on me?
The events of the past year have shown me that if nothing else, the world does not make sense.
CROSS — CRIME SCENE — D
CRIME SCENE — DO NOT CROSS
But haven't I known that all along?
And if so, why do I consider Jim Gordon to be the better man?
Better than both me and the Joker, because he perseveres?
What is it that I do, exactly, if not that?

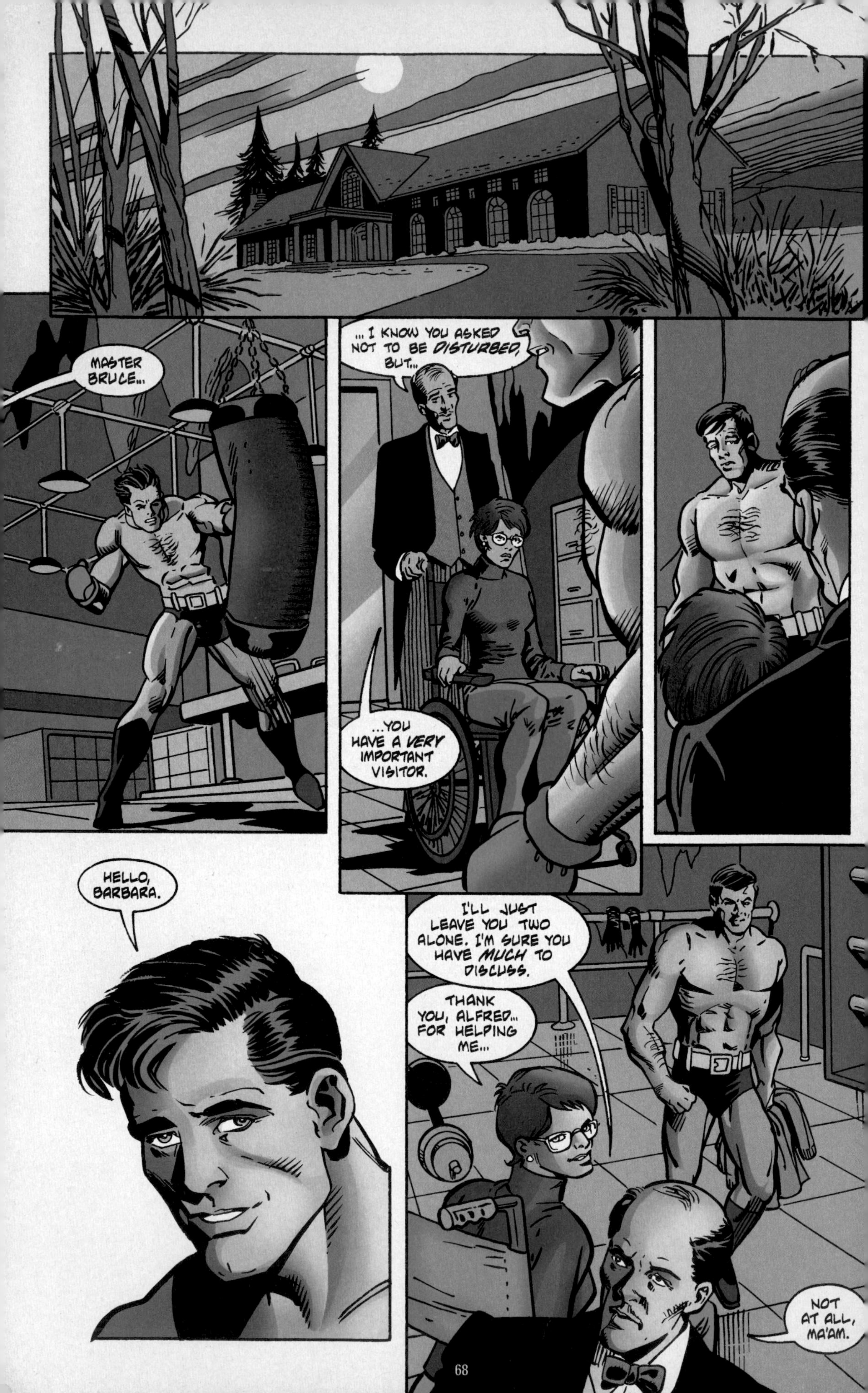
MASTER BRUCE...
... I KNOW YOU ASKED NOT TO BE DISTURBED, BUT...
...YOU HAVE A VERY IMPORTANT VISITOR.
HELLO, BARBARA.
I'LL JUST LEAVE YOU TWO ALONE. I'M SURE YOU HAVE MUCH TO DISCUSS.
THANK YOU, ALFRED... FOR HELPING ME...
NOT AT ALL, MA'AM.

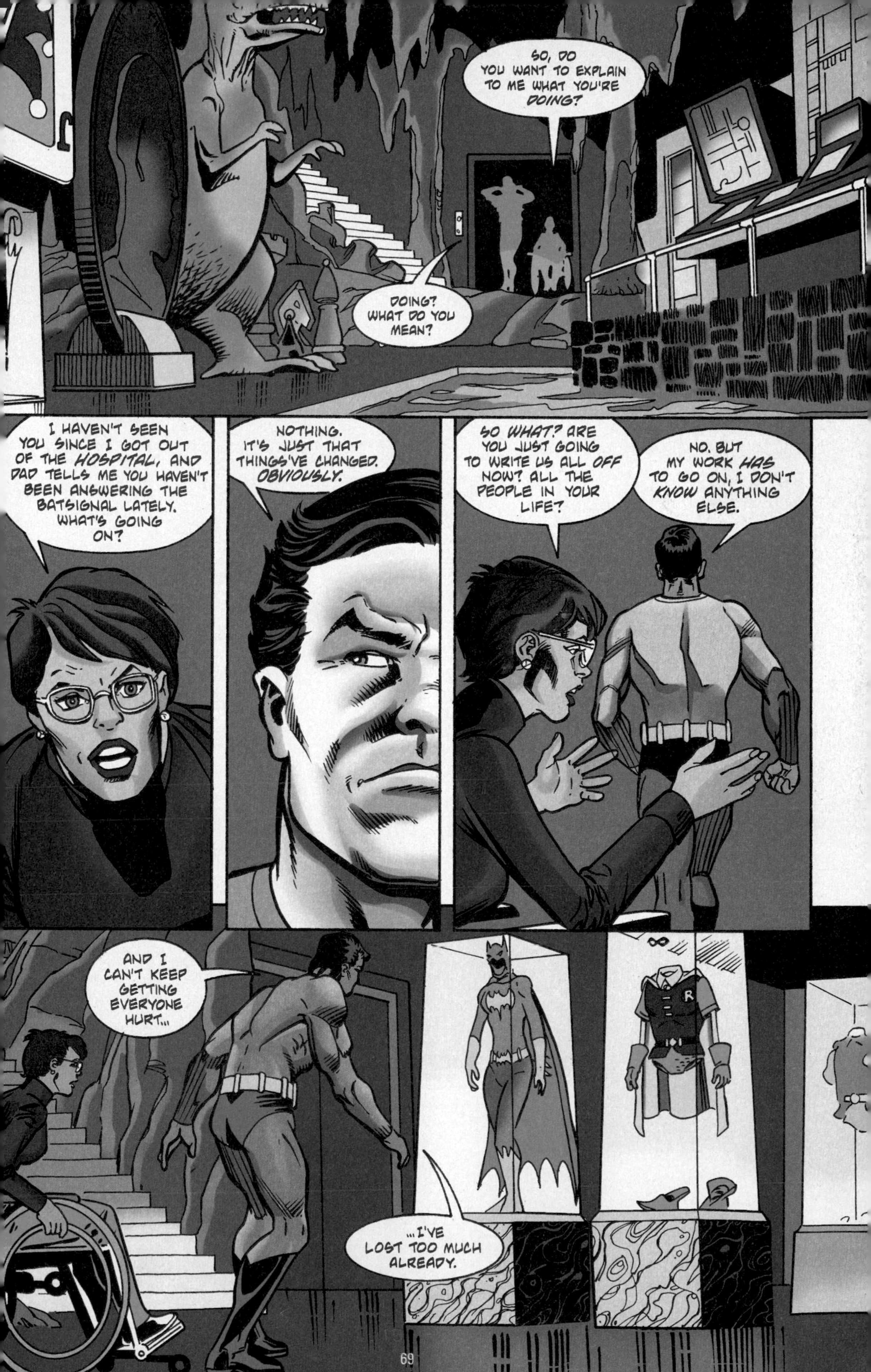

SO, DO YOU WANT TO EXPLAIN TO ME WHAT YOU'RE *DOING?*
DOING? WHAT DO YOU MEAN?
I HAVEN'T SEEN YOU SINCE I GOT OUT OF THE *HOSPITAL*, AND DAD TELLS ME YOU HAVEN'T BEEN ANSWERING THE BATSIGNAL LATELY. WHAT'S GOING ON?
NOTHING. IT'S JUST THAT THINGS'VE CHANGED. *OBVIOUSLY.*
SO *WHAT?* ARE YOU JUST GOING TO WRITE US ALL *OFF* NOW? ALL THE PEOPLE IN YOUR LIFE?
NO. BUT MY WORK *HAS* TO GO ON, I DON'T *KNOW* ANYTHING ELSE.
AND I CAN'T KEEP GETTING EVERYONE HURT...
...I'VE LOST TOO MUCH ALREADY.

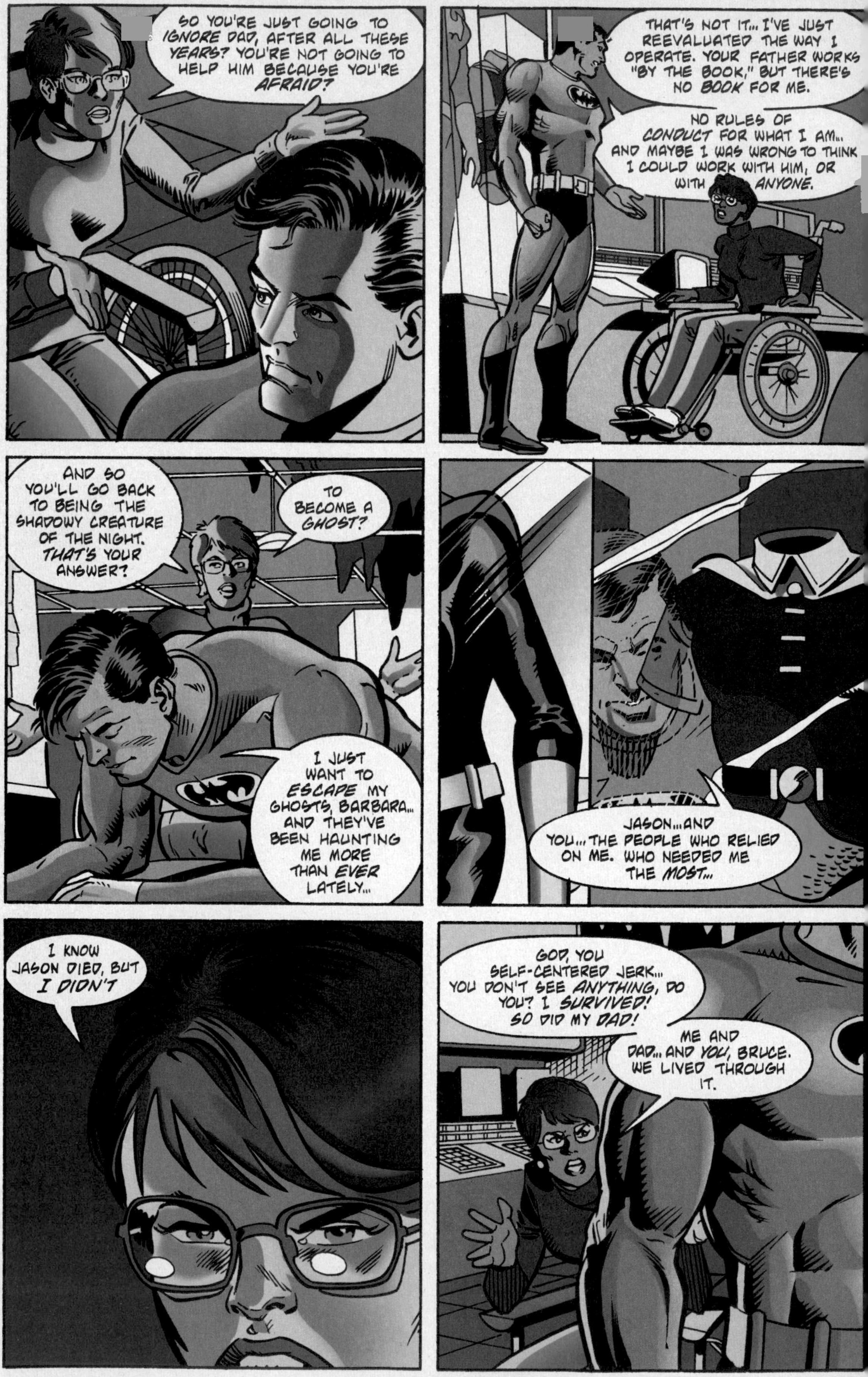
SO YOU'RE JUST GOING TO IGNORE DAD, AFTER ALL THESE YEARS? YOU'RE NOT GOING TO HELP HIM BECAUSE YOU'RE AFRAID?
THAT'S NOT IT... I'VE JUST REEVALUATED THE WAY I OPERATE. YOUR FATHER WORKS "BY THE BOOK," BUT THERE'S NO BOOK FOR ME.
NO RULES OF CONDUCT FOR WHAT I AM... AND MAYBE I WAS WRONG TO THINK I COULD WORK WITH HIM, OR WITH ANYONE.
AND SO YOU'LL GO BACK TO BEING THE SHADOWY CREATURE OF THE NIGHT. THAT'S YOUR ANSWER?
TO BECOME A GHOST?
I JUST WANT TO ESCAPE MY GHOSTS, BARBARA... AND THEY'VE BEEN HAUNTING ME MORE THAN EVER LATELY...
JASON...AND YOU... THE PEOPLE WHO RELIED ON ME. WHO NEEDED ME THE MOST...
I KNOW JASON DIED, BUT I DIDN'T
GOD, YOU SELF-CENTERED JERK... YOU DON'T SEE ANYTHING, DO YOU? I SURVIVED! SO DID MY DAD!
ME AND DAD... AND YOU, BRUCE. WE LIVED THROUGH IT.

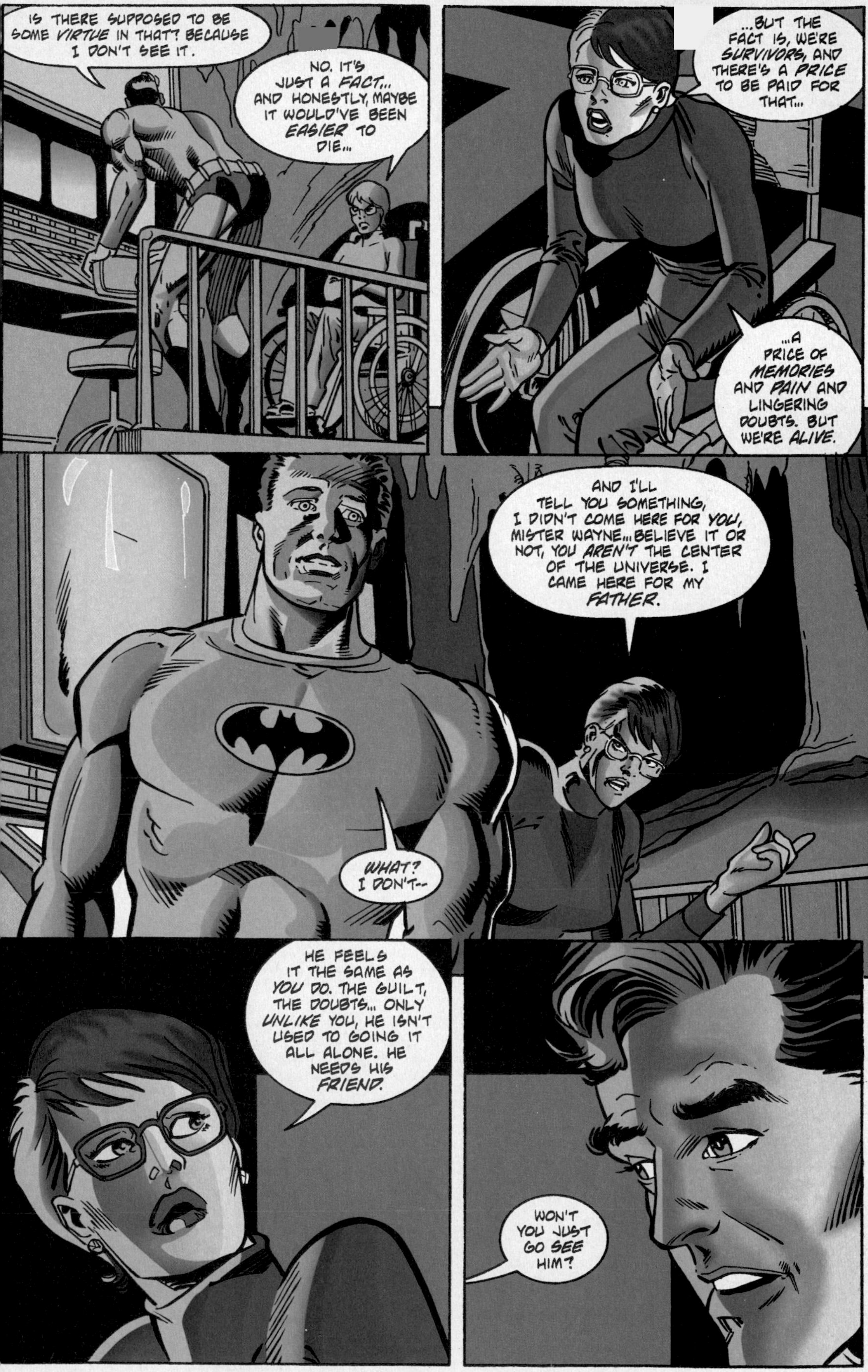

IS THERE SUPPOSED TO BE SOME VIRTUE IN THAT? BECAUSE I DON'T SEE IT.
NO. IT'S JUST A FACT... AND HONESTLY, MAYBE IT WOULD'VE BEEN EASIER TO DIE...
...BUT THE FACT IS, WE'RE SURVIVORS, AND THERE'S A PRICE TO BE PAID FOR THAT...
...A PRICE OF MEMORIES AND PAIN AND LINGERING DOUBTS. BUT WE'RE ALIVE.
AND I'LL TELL YOU SOMETHING, I DIDN'T COME HERE FOR YOU, MISTER WAYNE... BELIEVE IT OR NOT, YOU AREN'T THE CENTER OF THE UNIVERSE. I CAME HERE FOR MY FATHER.
WHAT? I DON'T--
HE FEELS IT THE SAME AS YOU DO. THE GUILT, THE DOUBTS... ONLY UNLIKE YOU, HE ISN'T USED TO GOING IT ALL ALONE. HE NEEDS HIS FRIEND.
WON'T YOU JUST GO SEE HIM?

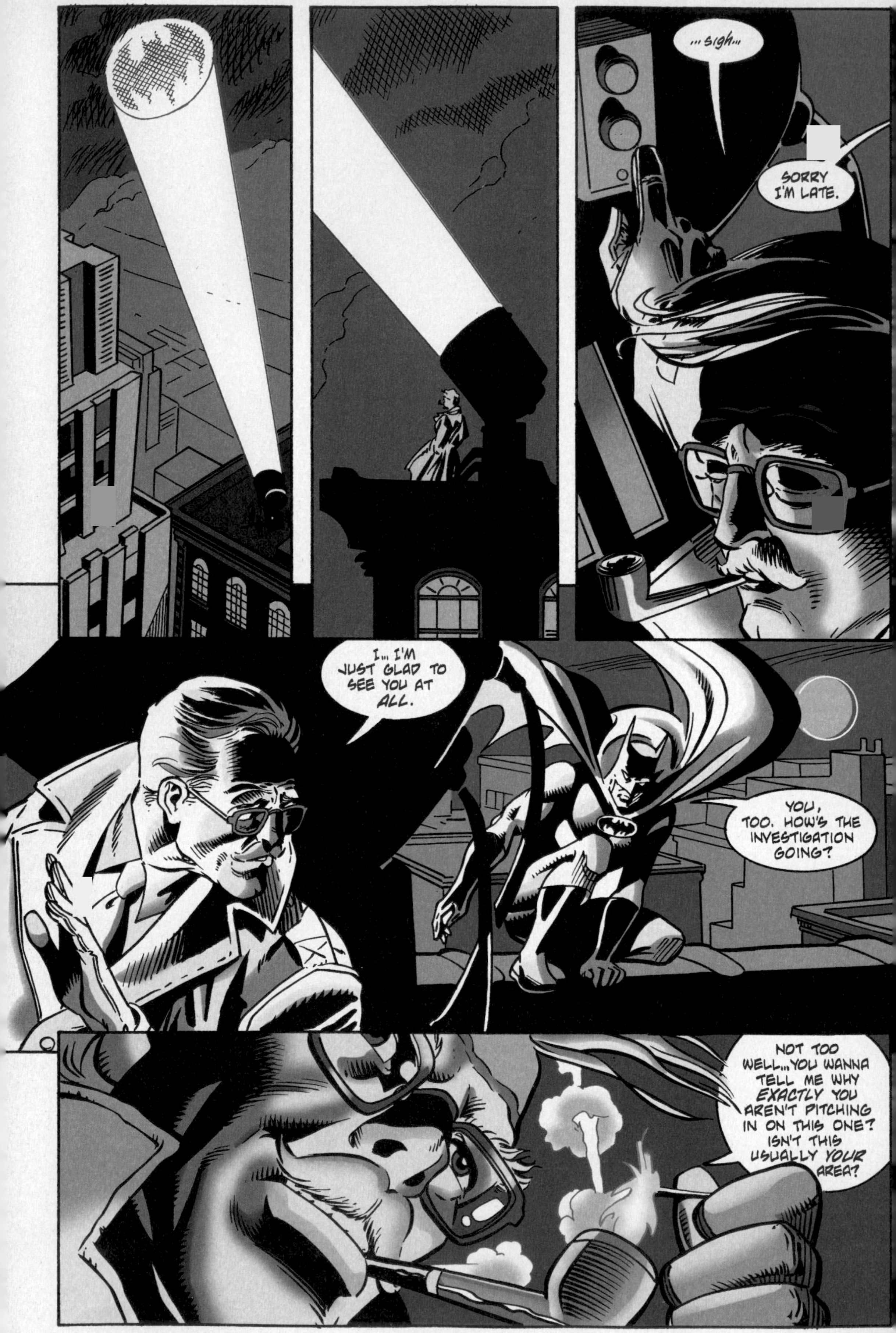
...sigh...
SORRY I'M LATE.
I... I'M JUST GLAD TO SEE YOU AT ALL.
YOU, TOO. HOW'S THE INVESTIGATION GOING?
NOT TOO WELL... YOU WANNA TELL ME WHY EXACTLY YOU AREN'T PITCHING IN ON THIS ONE? ISN'T THIS USUALLY YOUR AREA?

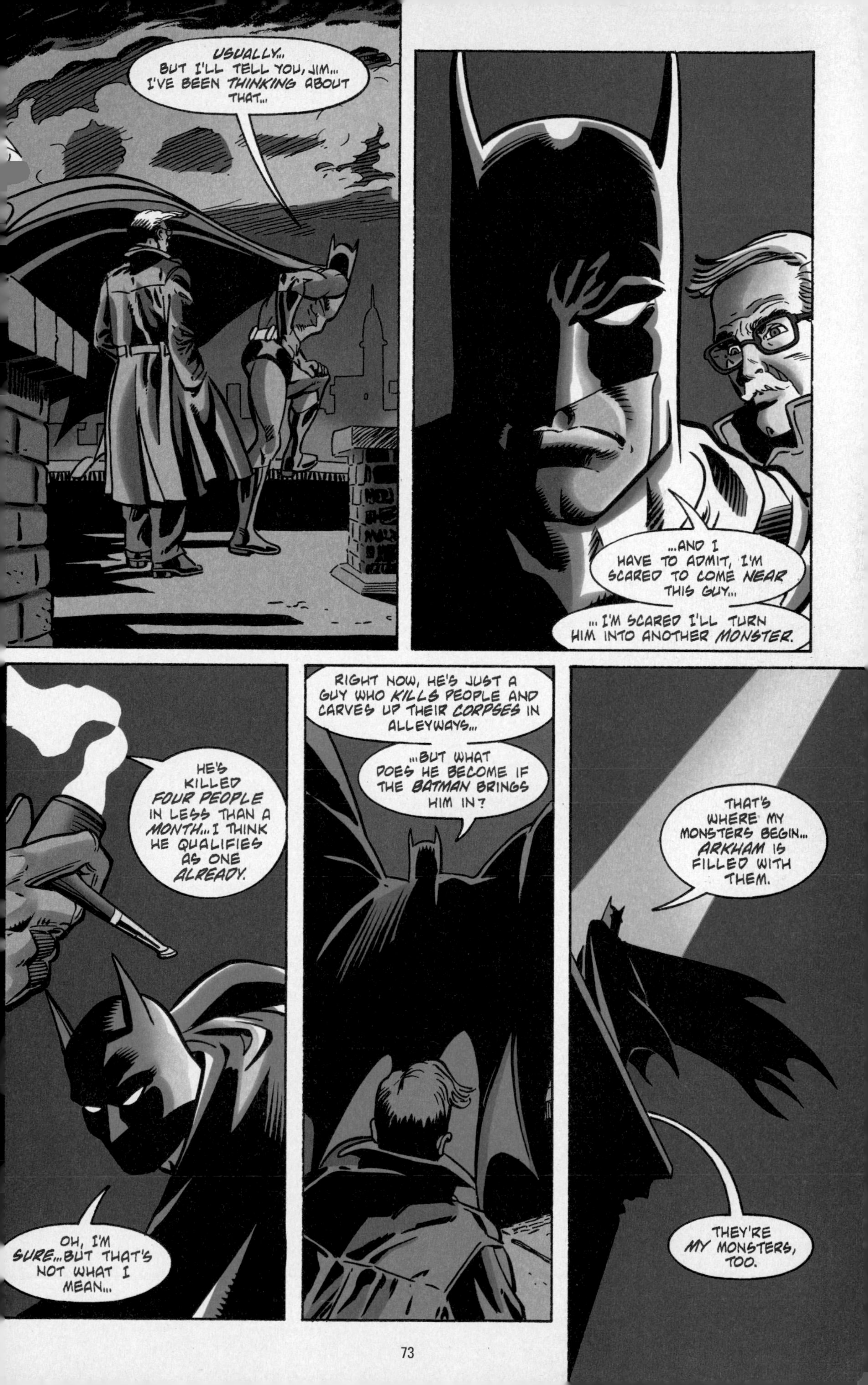
USUALLY... BUT I'LL TELL YOU, JIM... I'VE BEEN THINKING ABOUT THAT...
...AND I HAVE TO ADMIT, I'M SCARED TO COME NEAR THIS GUY...
...I'M SCARED I'LL TURN HIM INTO ANOTHER MONSTER.
HE'S KILLED FOUR PEOPLE IN LESS THAN A MONTH... I THINK HE QUALIFIES AS ONE ALREADY.
OH, I'M SURE... BUT THAT'S NOT WHAT I MEAN...
RIGHT NOW, HE'S JUST A GUY WHO KILLS PEOPLE AND CARVES UP THEIR CORPSES IN ALLEYWAYS...
...BUT WHAT DOES HE BECOME IF THE BATMAN BRINGS HIM IN?
THAT'S WHERE MY MONSTERS BEGIN... ARKHAM IS FILLED WITH THEM.
THEY'RE MY MONSTERS, TOO.

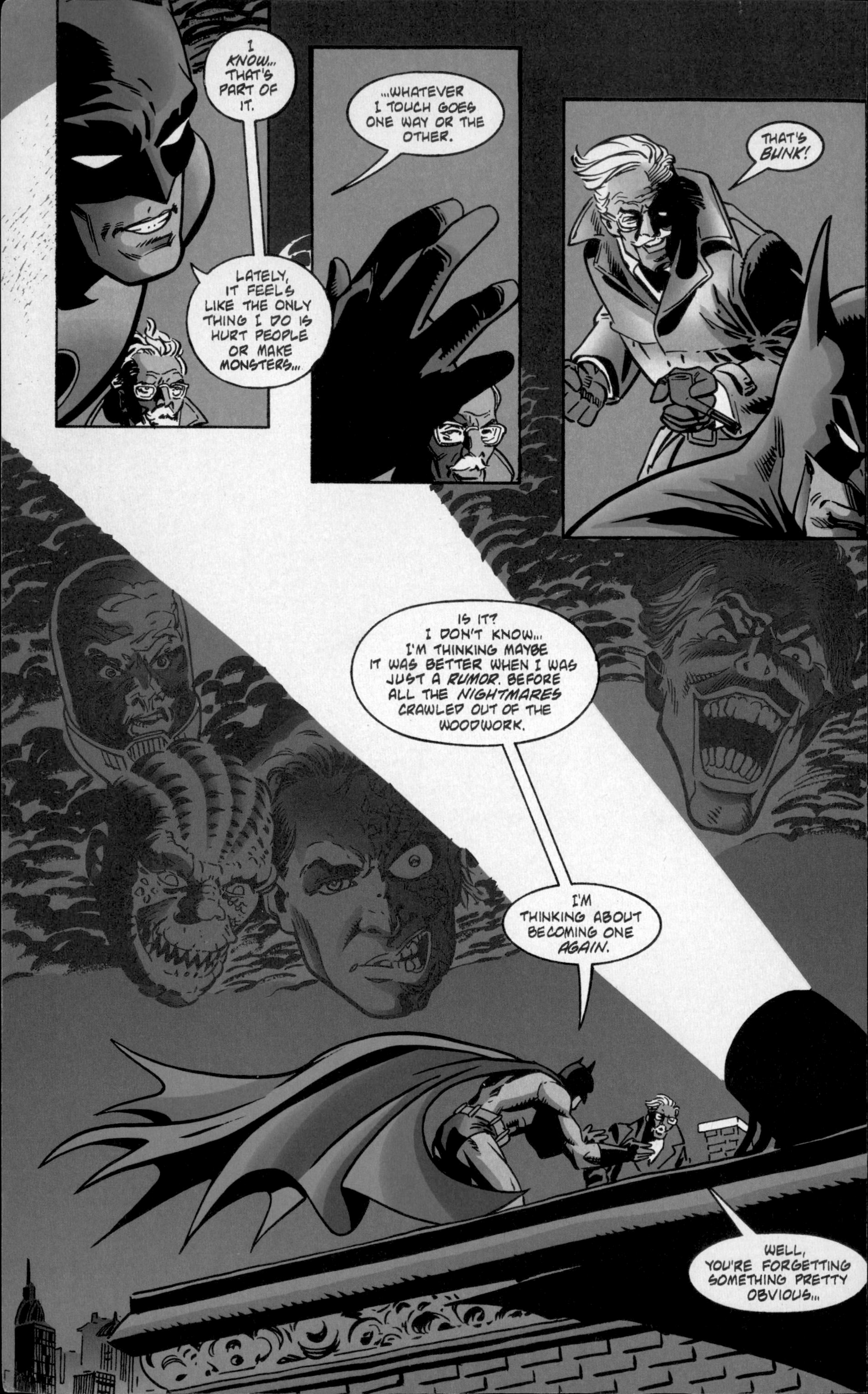
I KNOW... THAT'S PART OF IT.
LATELY, IT FEELS LIKE THE ONLY THING I DO IS HURT PEOPLE OR MAKE MONSTERS...
...WHATEVER I TOUCH GOES ONE WAY OR THE OTHER.
THAT'S BUNK!
IS IT? I DON'T KNOW... I'M THINKING MAYBE IT WAS BETTER WHEN I WAS JUST A RUMOR. BEFORE ALL THE NIGHTMARES CRAWLED OUT OF THE WOODWORK.
I'M THINKING ABOUT BECOMING ONE AGAIN.
WELL, YOU'RE FORGETTING SOMETHING PRETTY OBVIOUS...

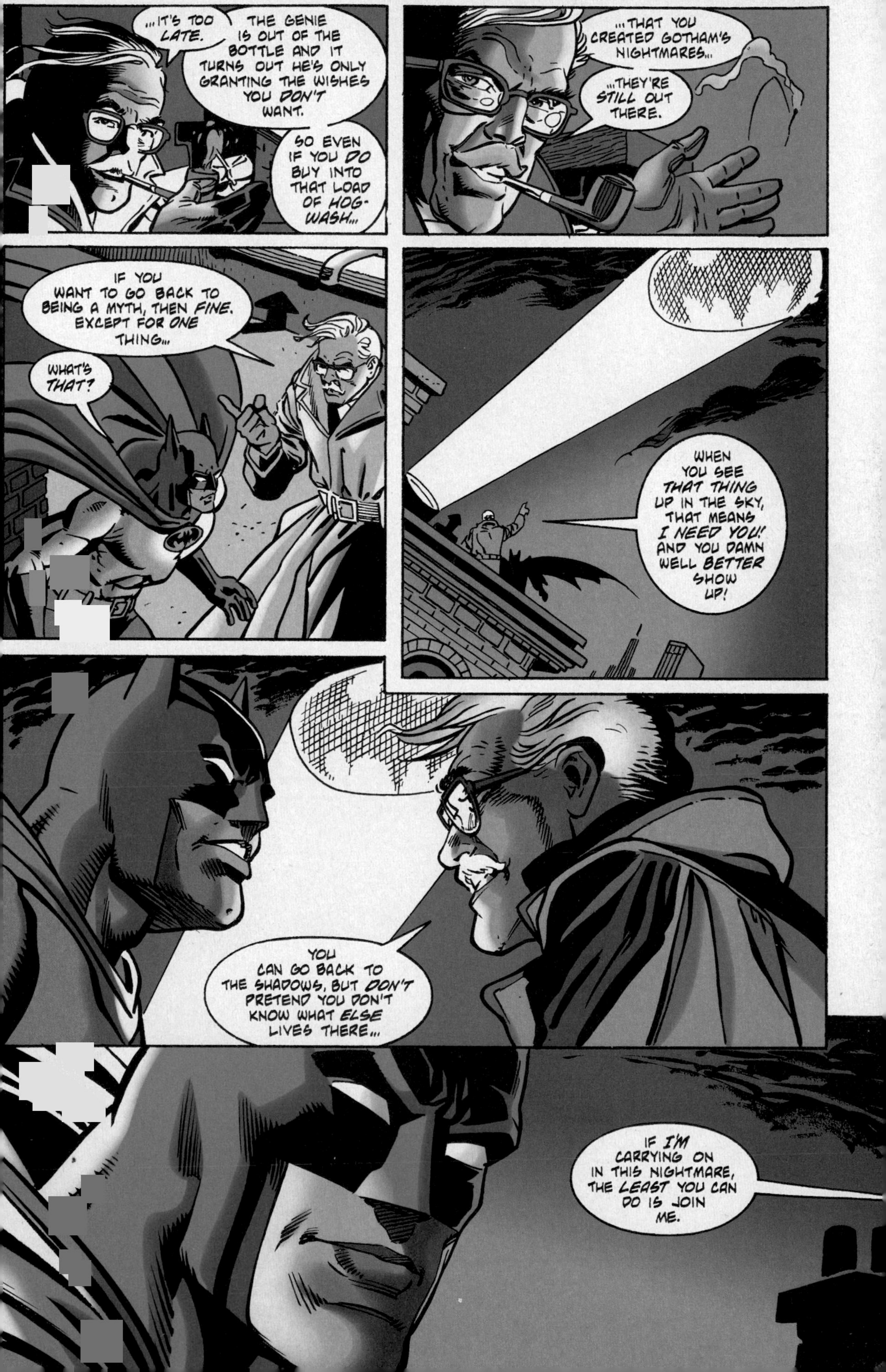
...IT'S TOO LATE.
THE GENIE IS OUT OF THE BOTTLE AND IT TURNS OUT HE'S ONLY GRANTING THE WISHES YOU DON'T WANT.
SO EVEN IF YOU DO BUY INTO THAT LOAD OF HOG-WASH...
...THAT YOU CREATED GOTHAM'S NIGHTMARES...
...THEY'RE STILL OUT THERE.
IF YOU WANT TO GO BACK TO BEING A MYTH, THEN FINE. EXCEPT FOR ONE THING...
WHAT'S THAT?
WHEN YOU SEE THAT THING UP IN THE SKY, THAT MEANS I NEED YOU! AND YOU DAMN WELL BETTER SHOW UP!
YOU CAN GO BACK TO THE SHADOWS, BUT DON'T PRETEND YOU DON'T KNOW WHAT ELSE LIVES THERE...
IF I'M CARRYING ON IN THIS NIGHTMARE, THE LEAST YOU CAN DO IS JOIN ME.

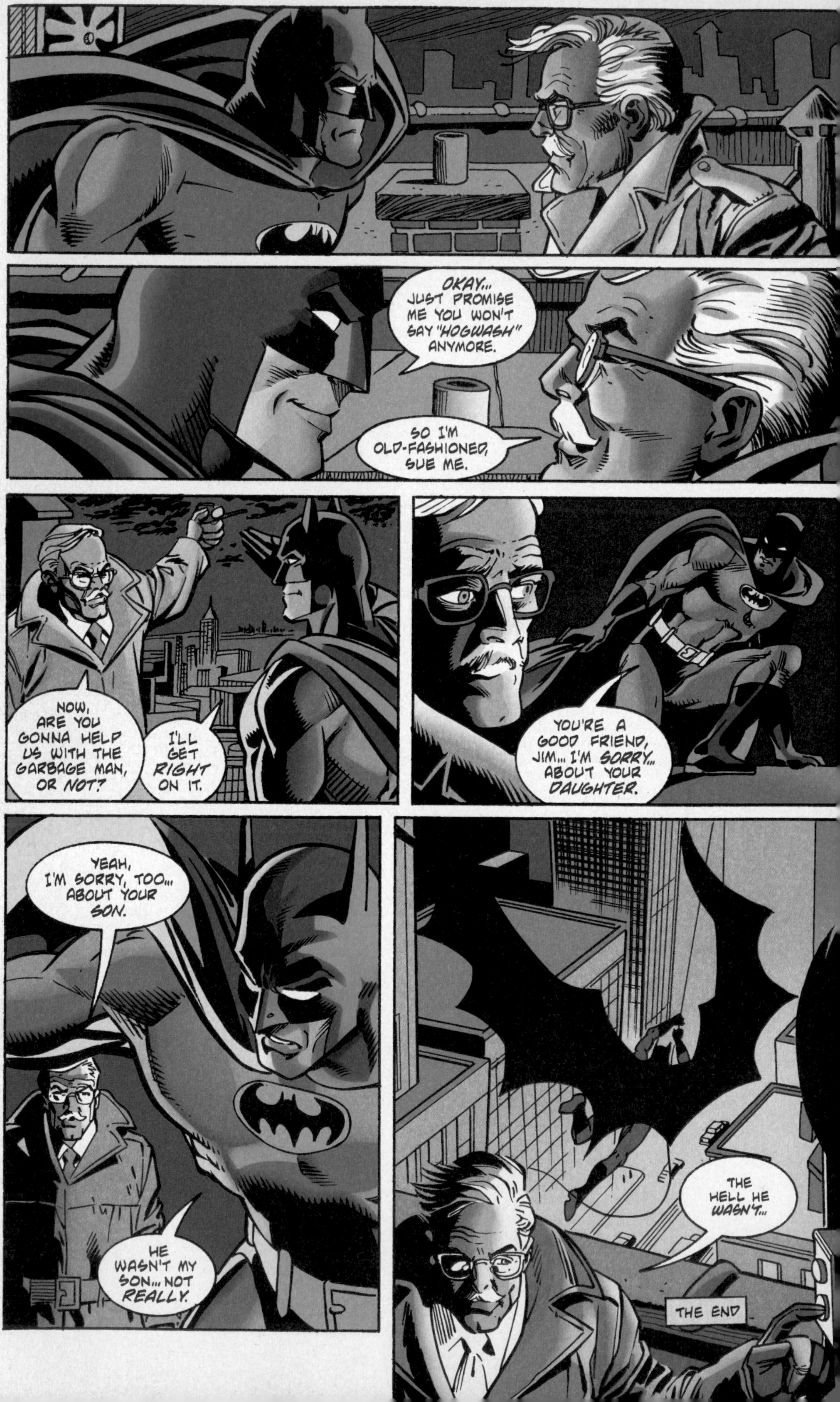
OKAY... JUST PROMISE ME YOU WON'T SAY "HOGWASH" ANYMORE.
SO I'M OLD-FASHIONED, SUE ME.
NOW, ARE YOU GONNA HELP US WITH THE GARBAGE MAN, OR NOT?
I'LL GET RIGHT ON IT.
YOU'RE A GOOD FRIEND, JIM... I'M SORRY... ABOUT YOUR DAUGHTER.
YEAH, I'M SORRY, TOO... ABOUT YOUR SON.
HE WASN'T MY SON... NOT REALLY.
THE HELL HE WASN'T...
THE END

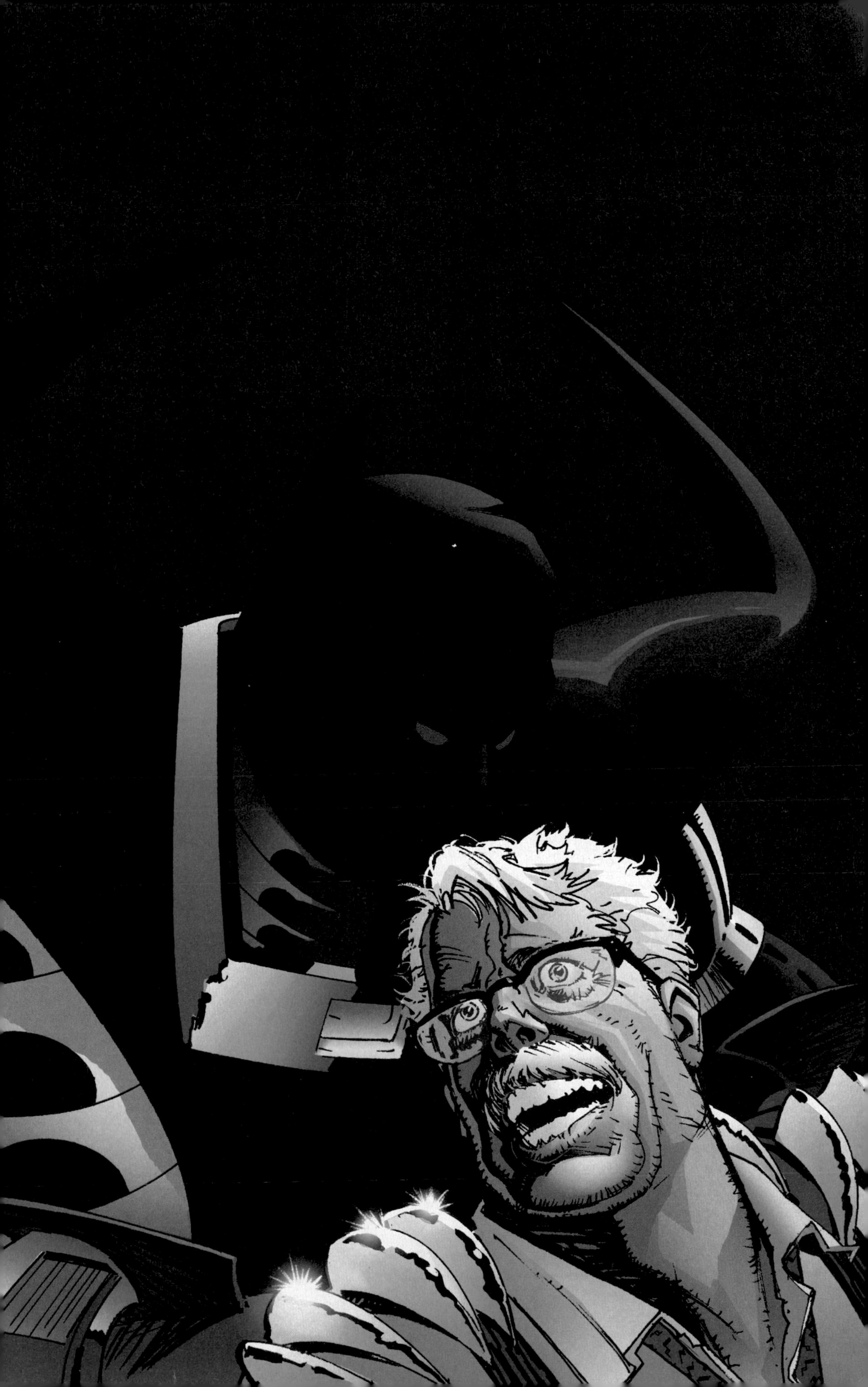

CHAPTER FOUR

THE ULTIMATE BETRAYAL

Chuck Dixon
writer

Brent Anderson
artist

Howard Chaykin
cover artist

John Kalisz
colorist

Willie Schubert
letterer

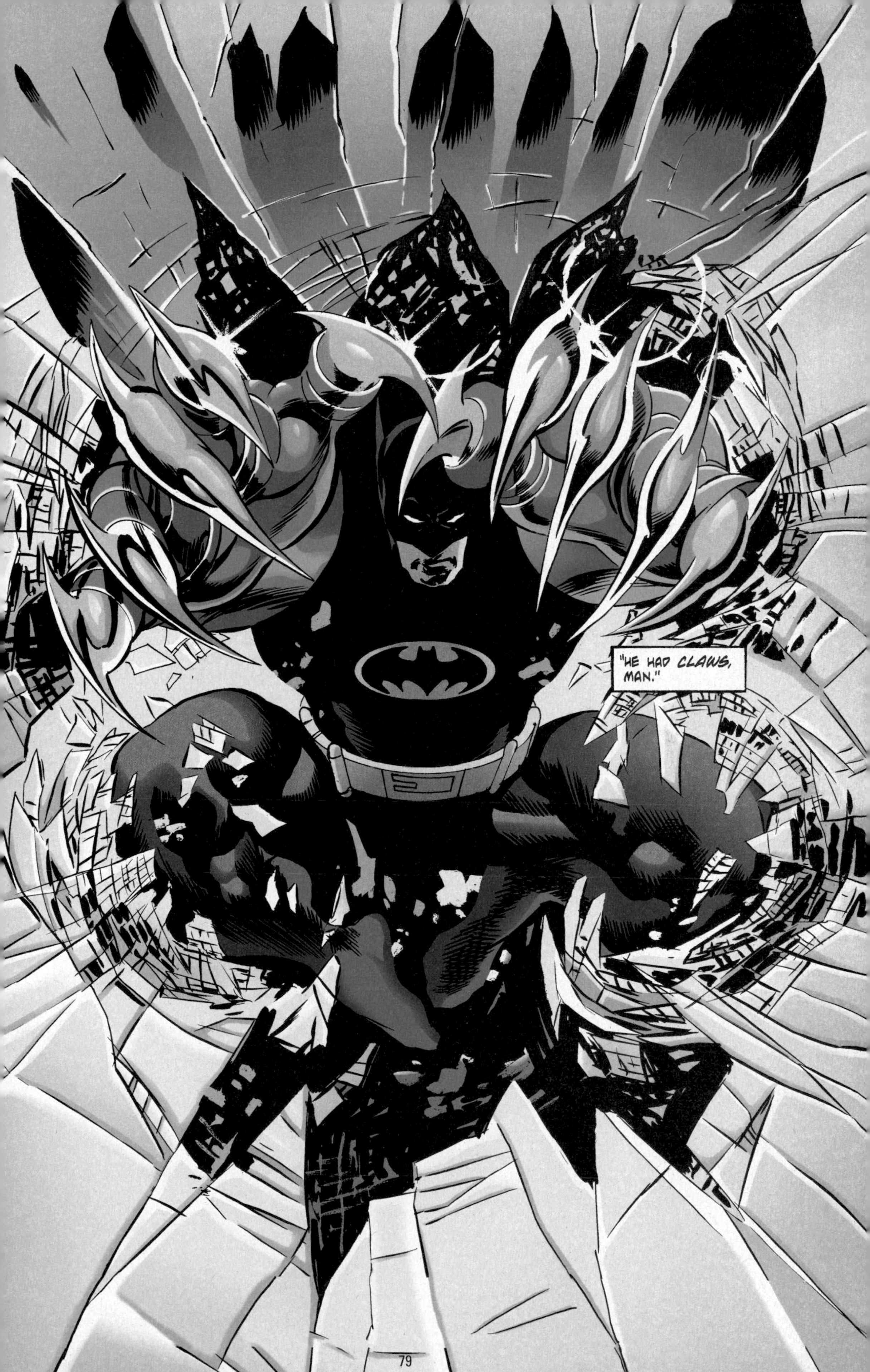
"HE HAD CLAWS, MAN."

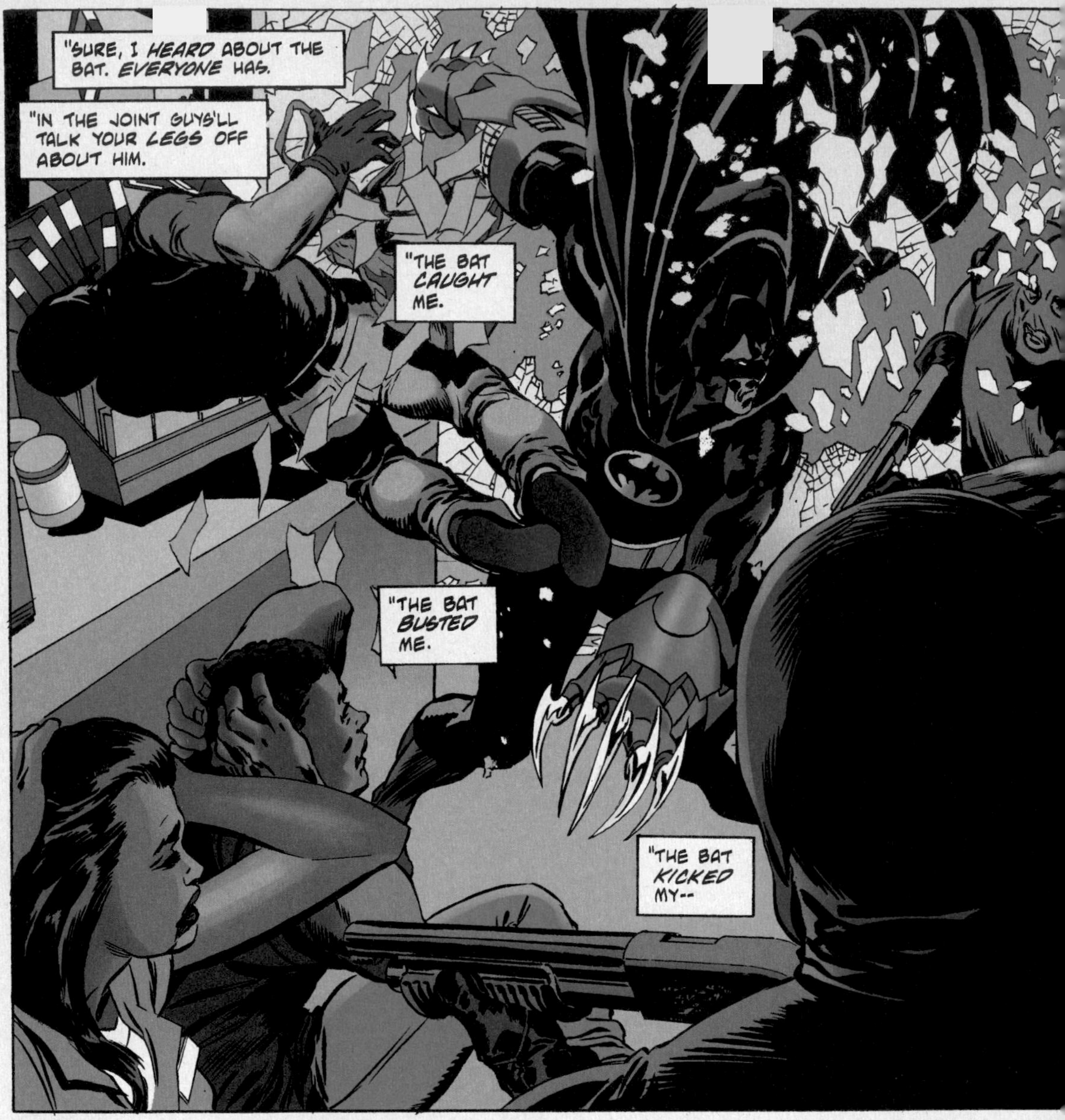
"SURE, I HEARD ABOUT THE BAT. EVERYONE HAS.
"IN THE JOINT GUYS'LL TALK YOUR LEGS OFF ABOUT HIM.
"THE BAT CAUGHT ME.
"THE BAT BUSTED ME.
"THE BAT KICKED MY--

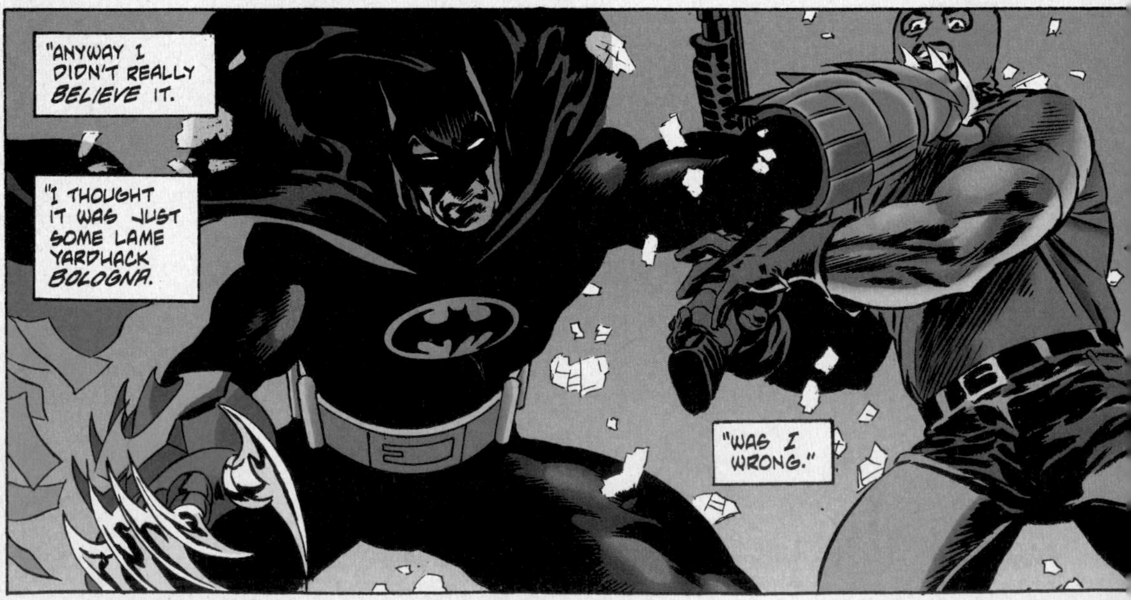
"ANYWAY I DIDN'T REALLY BELIEVE IT.
"I THOUGHT IT WAS JUST SOME LAME YARDHACK BOLOGNA.
"WAS I WRONG."

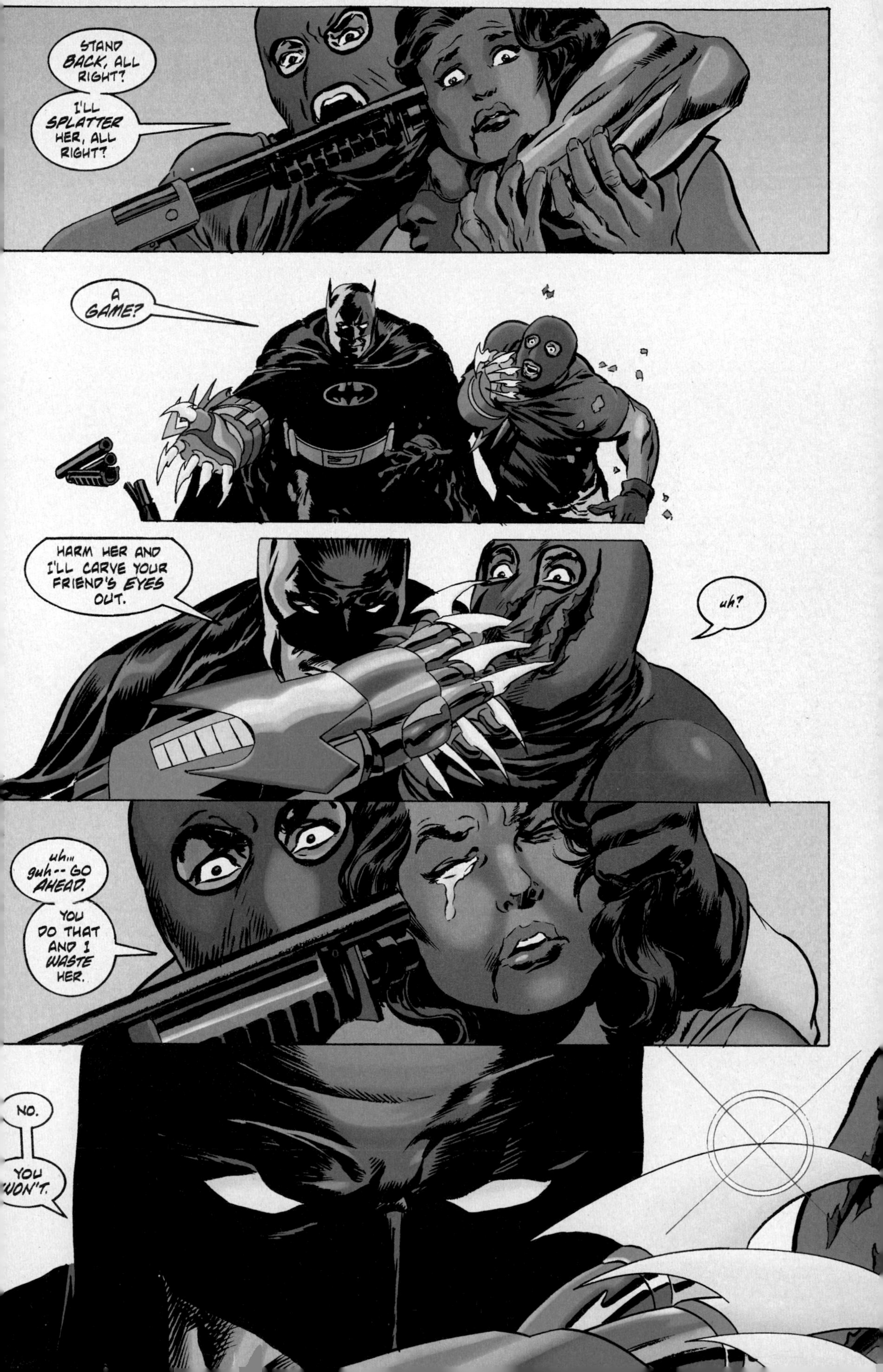
STAND BACK, ALL RIGHT?
I'LL SPLATTER HER, ALL RIGHT?
A GAME?
HARM HER AND I'LL CARVE YOUR FRIEND'S EYES OUT.
uh?
uh... guh-- GO AHEAD.
YOU DO THAT AND I WASTE HER.
NO.
YOU WON'T.

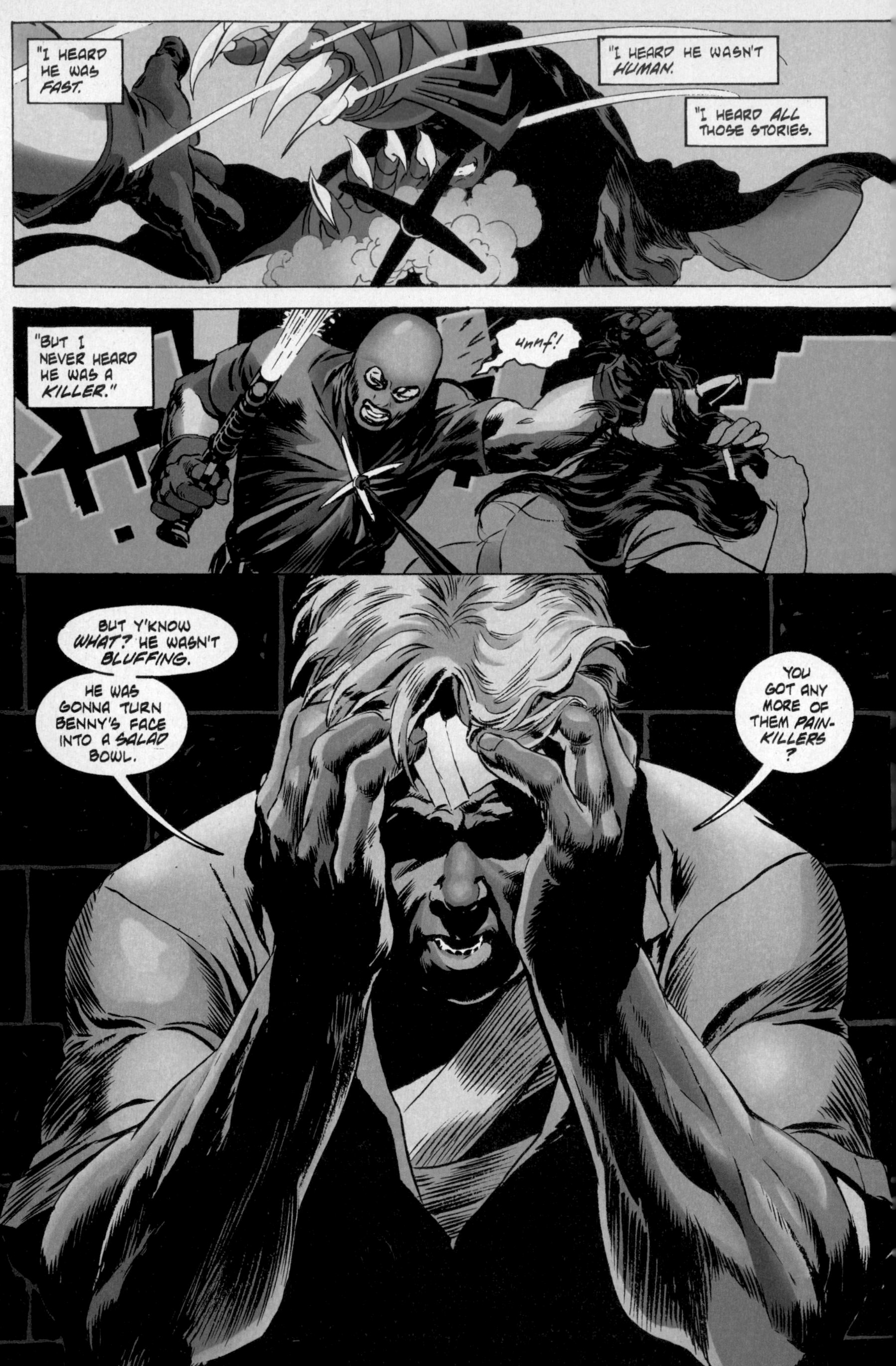
"I HEARD HE WAS FAST.
"I HEARD HE WASN'T HUMAN.
"I HEARD ALL THOSE STORIES.
"BUT I NEVER HEARD HE WAS A KILLER."
unnf!
BUT Y'KNOW WHAT? HE WASN'T BLUFFING.
HE WAS GONNA TURN BENNY'S FACE INTO A SALAD BOWL.
YOU GOT ANY MORE OF THEM PAIN-KILLERS?

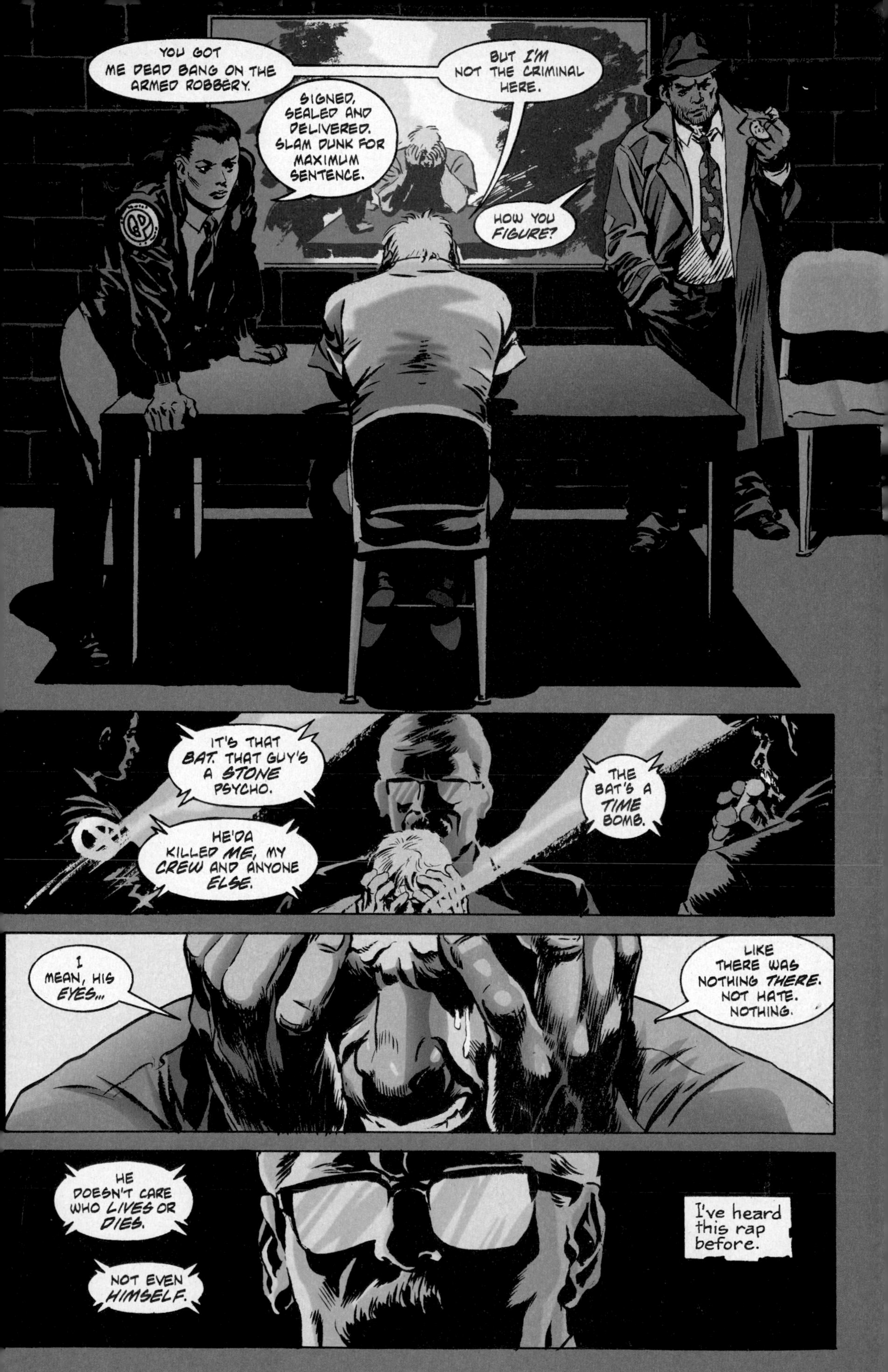
YOU GOT ME DEAD BANG ON THE ARMED ROBBERY.
BUT I'M NOT THE CRIMINAL HERE.
SIGNED, SEALED AND DELIVERED. SLAM DUNK FOR MAXIMUM SENTENCE.
HOW YOU FIGURE?
IT'S THAT BAT. THAT GUY'S A STONE PSYCHO.
HE'DA KILLED ME, MY CREW AND ANYONE ELSE.
THE BAT'S A TIME BOMB.
I MEAN, HIS EYES...
LIKE THERE WAS NOTHING THERE. NOT HATE. NOTHING.
HE DOESN'T CARE WHO LIVES OR DIES.
NOT EVEN HIMSELF.
I've heard this rap before.

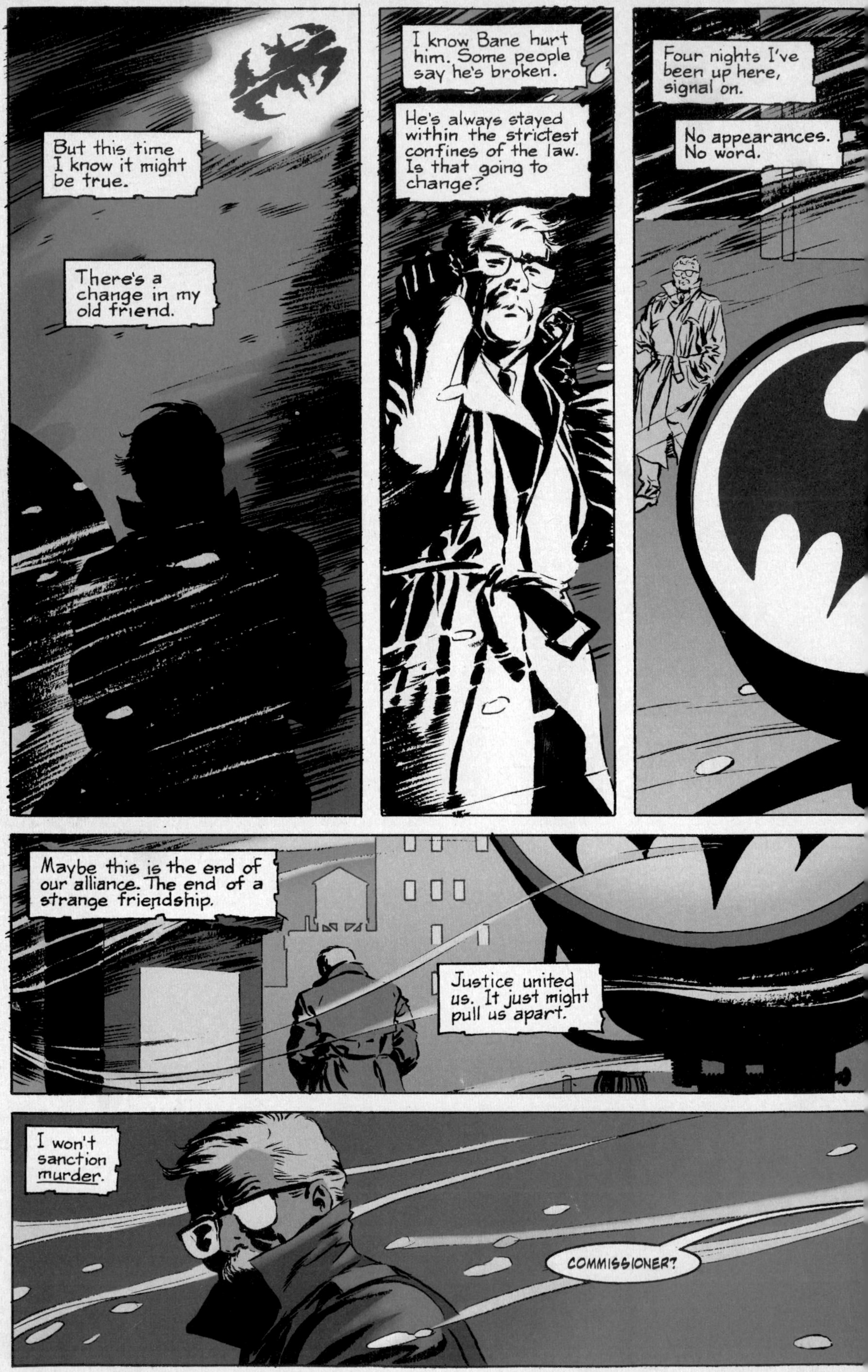
But this time I know it might be true.
There's a change in my old friend.
I know Bane hurt him. Some people say he's broken.
He's always stayed within the strictest confines of the law. Is that going to change?
Four nights I've been up here, signal on.
No appearances. No word.
Maybe this is the end of our alliance. The end of a strange friendship.
Justice united us. It just might pull us apart.
I won't sanction murder.
COMMISSIONER?

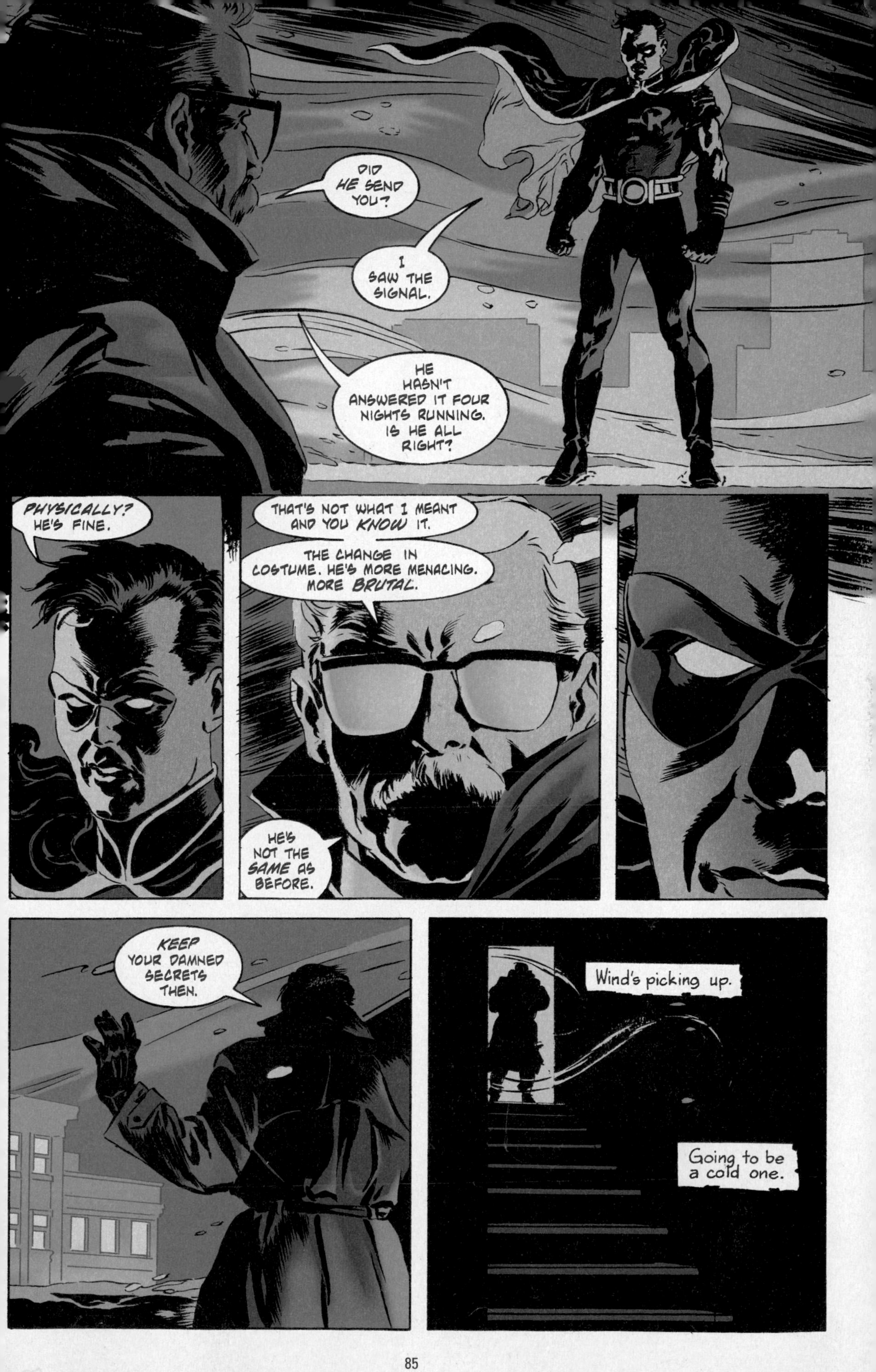
DID HE SEND YOU?
I SAW THE SIGNAL.
HE HASN'T ANSWERED IT FOUR NIGHTS RUNNING. IS HE ALL RIGHT?
PHYSICALLY? HE'S FINE.
THAT'S NOT WHAT I MEANT AND YOU KNOW IT.
THE CHANGE IN COSTUME. HE'S MORE MENACING. MORE BRUTAL.
HE'S NOT THE SAME AS BEFORE.
KEEP YOUR DAMNED SECRETS THEN.
Wind's picking up.
Going to be a cold one.

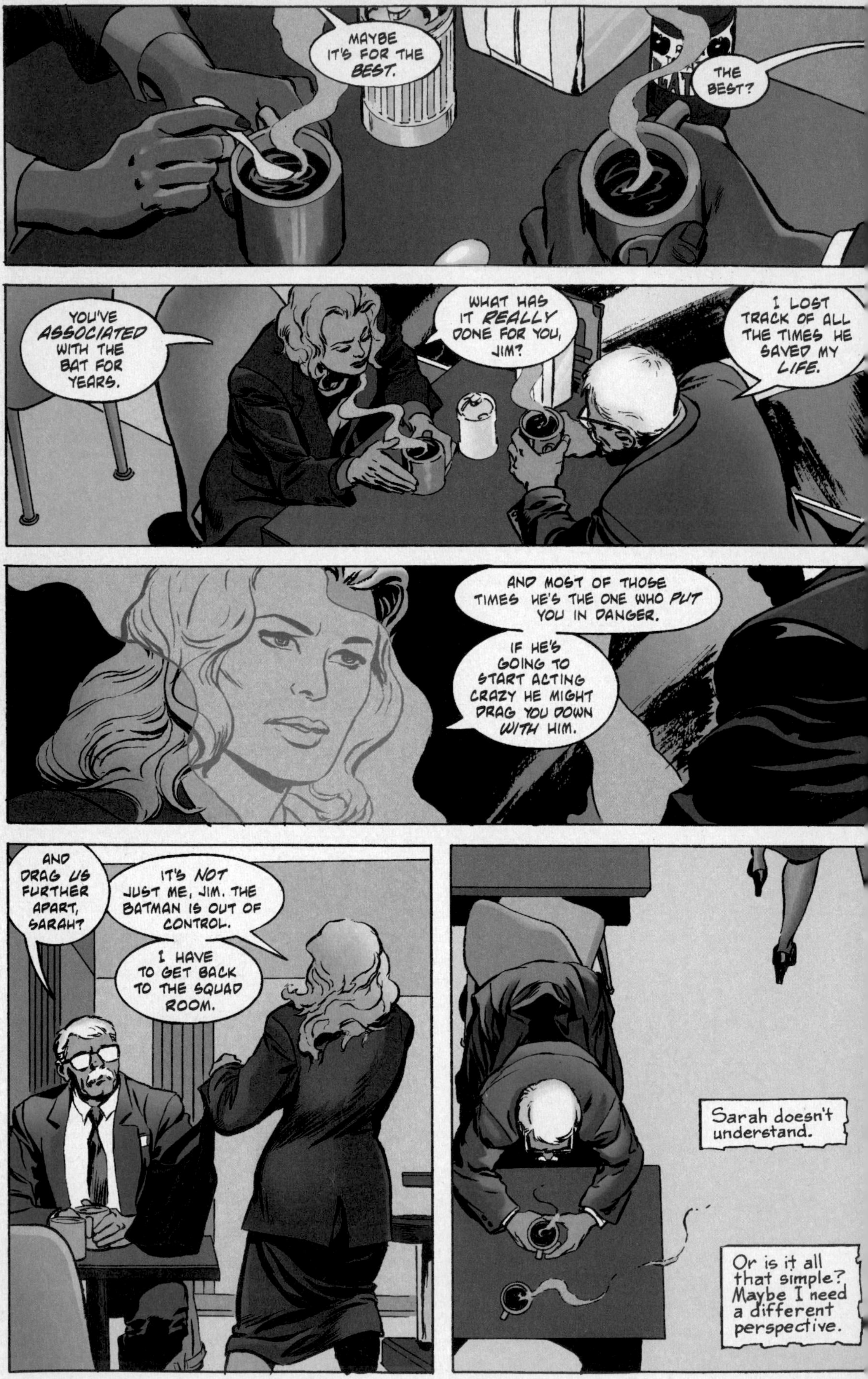

MAYBE IT'S FOR THE BEST.
THE BEST?
YOU'VE ASSOCIATED WITH THE BAT FOR YEARS.
WHAT HAS IT REALLY DONE FOR YOU, JIM?
I LOST TRACK OF ALL THE TIMES HE SAVED MY LIFE.
AND MOST OF THOSE TIMES HE'S THE ONE WHO PUT YOU IN DANGER.
IF HE'S GOING TO START ACTING CRAZY HE MIGHT DRAG YOU DOWN WITH HIM.
AND DRAG US FURTHER APART, SARAH?
IT'S NOT JUST ME, JIM. THE BATMAN IS OUT OF CONTROL.
I HAVE TO GET BACK TO THE SQUAD ROOM.
Sarah doesn't understand.
Or is it all that simple? Maybe I need a different perspective.

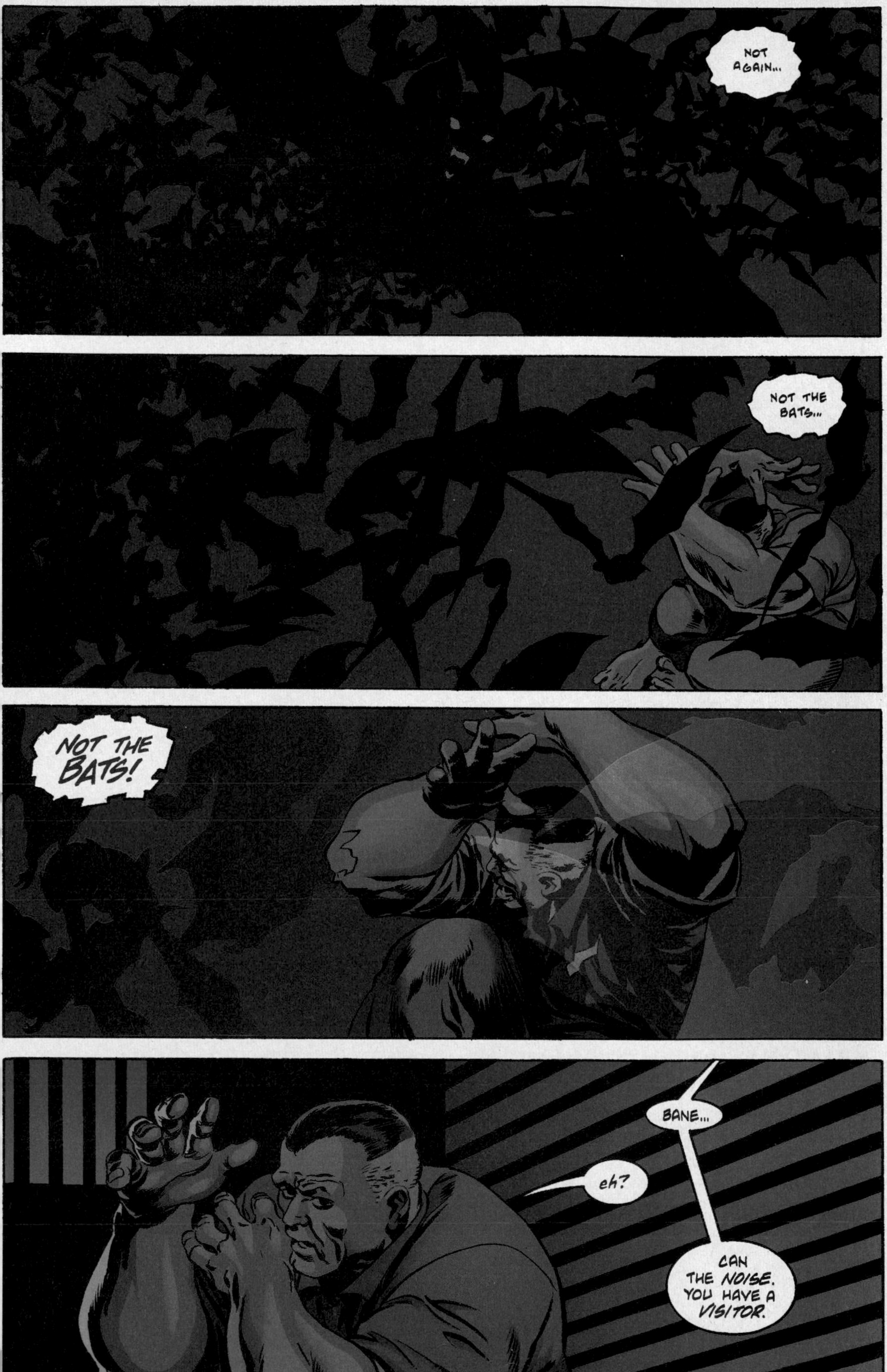
NOT AGAIN...
NOT THE BATS...
NOT THE BATS!
BANE...
eh?
CAN THE NOISE. YOU HAVE A VISITOR.

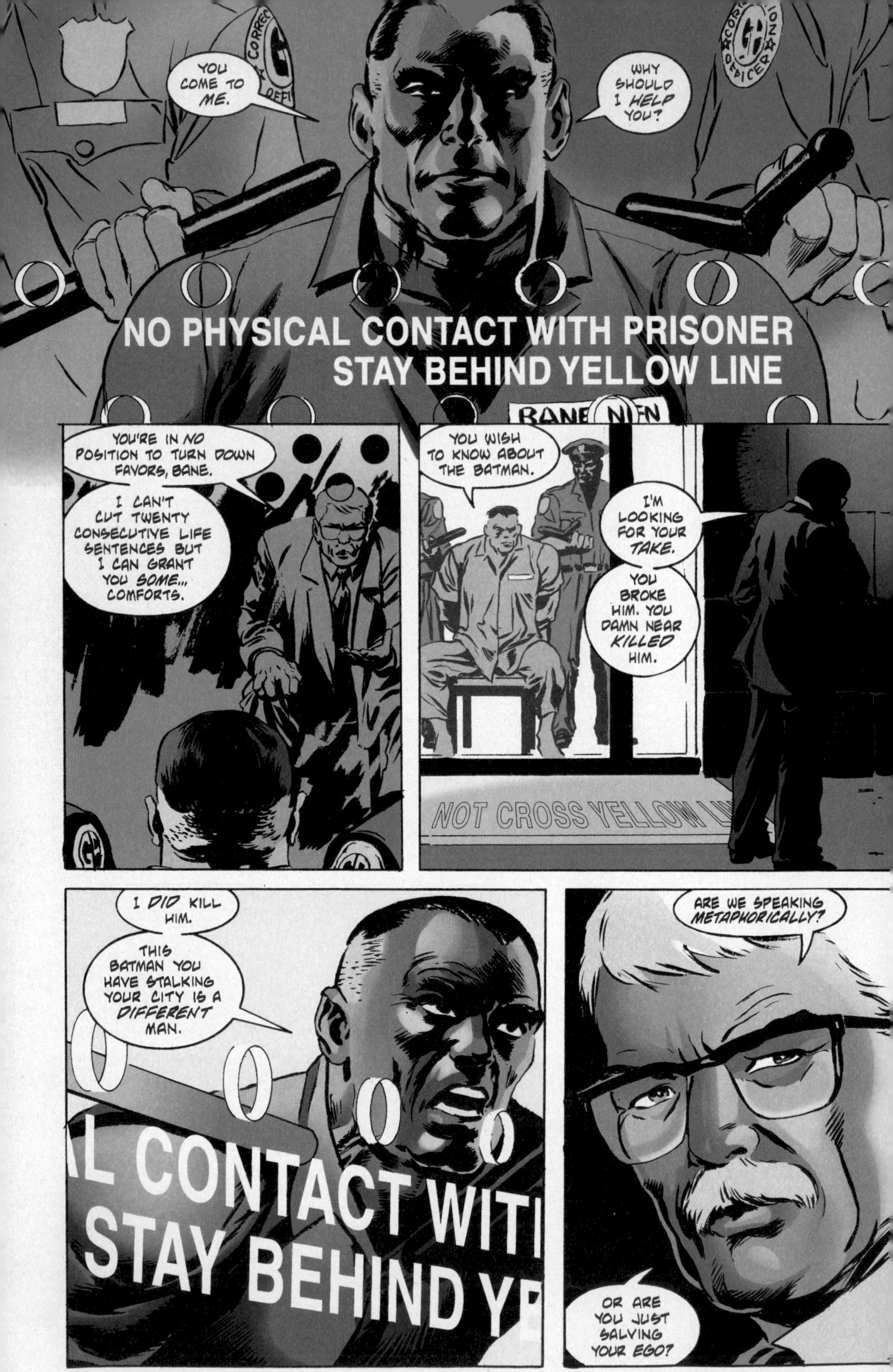

YOU COME TO ME.
WHY SHOULD I HELP YOU?
NO PHYSICAL CONTACT WITH PRISONER
STAY BEHIND YELLOW LINE
BANE
YOU'RE IN NO POSITION TO TURN DOWN FAVORS, BANE.
I CAN'T CUT TWENTY CONSECUTIVE LIFE SENTENCES BUT I CAN GRANT YOU SOME... COMFORTS.
YOU WISH TO KNOW ABOUT THE BATMAN.
I'M LOOKING FOR YOUR TAKE.
YOU BROKE HIM. YOU DAMN NEAR KILLED HIM.
NOT CROSS YELLOW L
I DID KILL HIM.
THIS BATMAN YOU HAVE STALKING YOUR CITY IS A DIFFERENT MAN.
L CONTACT WIT
STAY BEHIND Y
ARE WE SPEAKING METAPHORICALLY?
OR ARE YOU JUST SALVING YOUR EGO?

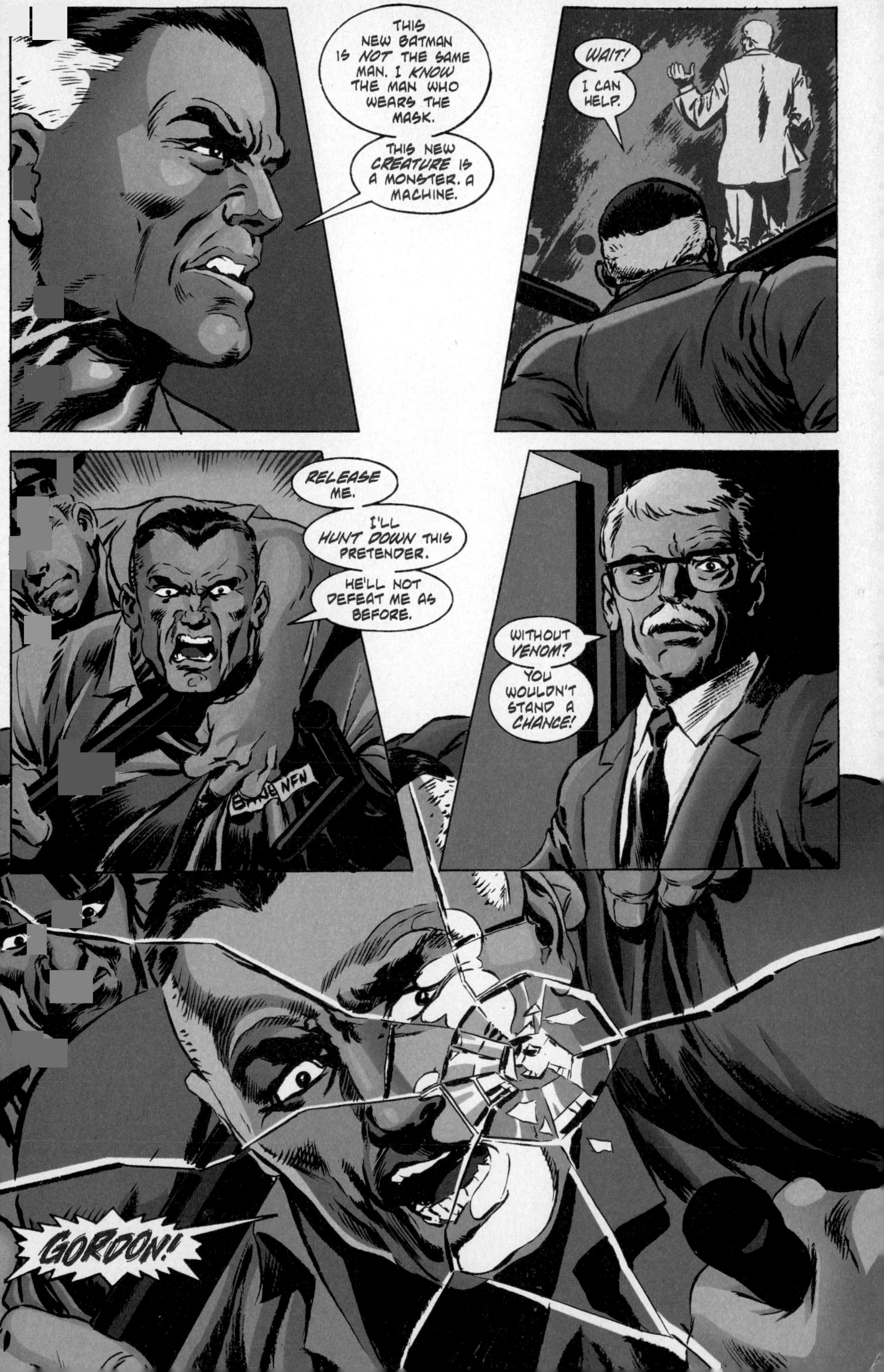
THIS NEW BATMAN IS *NOT* THE SAME MAN. I *KNOW* THE MAN WHO WEARS THE MASK.
THIS NEW *CREATURE* IS A MONSTER. A MACHINE.
WAIT!
I CAN HELP.
RELEASE ME.
I'LL *HUNT DOWN* THIS PRETENDER.
HE'LL NOT DEFEAT ME AS BEFORE.
WITHOUT *VENOM?*
YOU WOULDN'T STAND A *CHANCE!*
GORDON!

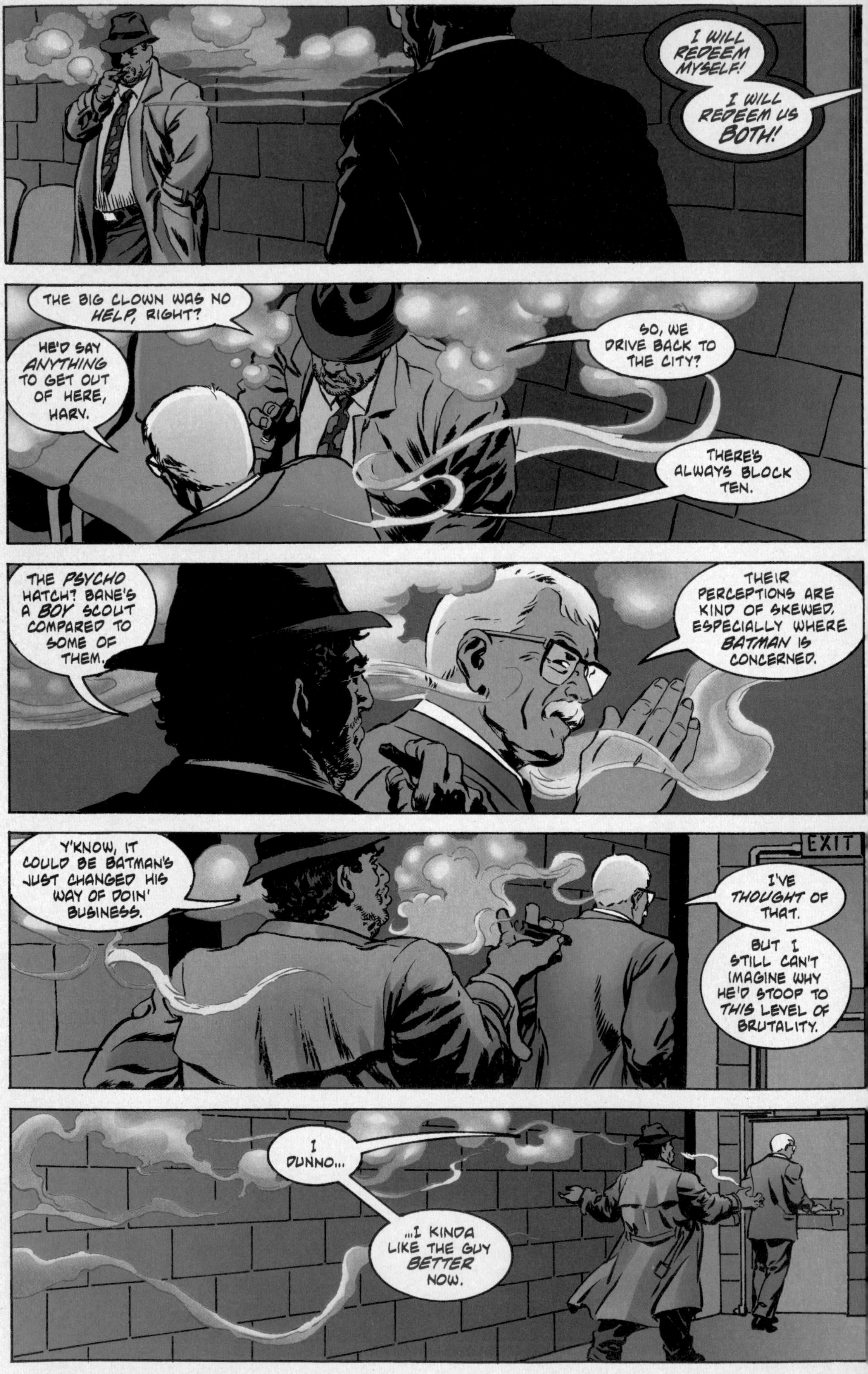
I WILL REDEEM MYSELF!
I WILL REDEEM US BOTH!
THE BIG CLOWN WAS NO HELP, RIGHT?
HE'D SAY ANYTHING TO GET OUT OF HERE, HARV.
SO, WE DRIVE BACK TO THE CITY?
THERE'S ALWAYS BLOCK TEN.
THE PSYCHO HATCH? BANE'S A BOY SCOUT COMPARED TO SOME OF THEM.
THEIR PERCEPTIONS ARE KIND OF SKEWED, ESPECIALLY WHERE BATMAN IS CONCERNED.
EXIT
Y'KNOW, IT COULD BE BATMAN'S JUST CHANGED HIS WAY OF DOIN' BUSINESS.
I'VE THOUGHT OF THAT.
BUT I STILL CAN'T IMAGINE WHY HE'D STOOP TO THIS LEVEL OF BRUTALITY.
I DUNNO...
...I KINDA LIKE THE GUY BETTER NOW.

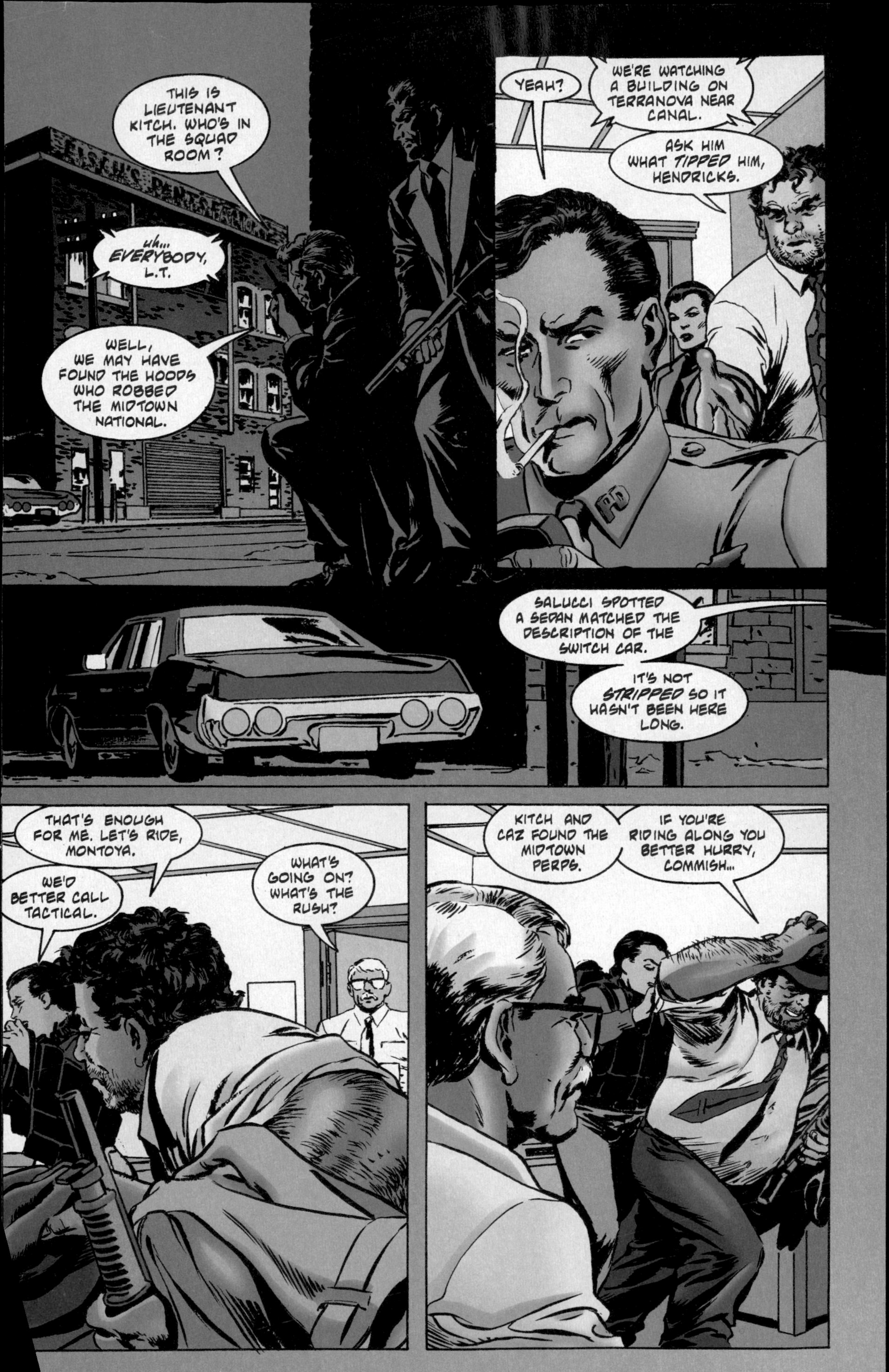
THIS IS LIEUTENANT KITCH. WHO'S IN THE SQUAD ROOM?
uh... EVERYBODY, L.T.
WELL, WE MAY HAVE FOUND THE HOODS WHO ROBBED THE MIDTOWN NATIONAL.
YEAH?
WE'RE WATCHING A BUILDING ON TERRANOVA NEAR CANAL.
ASK HIM WHAT TIPPED HIM, HENDRICKS.
SALUCCI SPOTTED A SEDAN MATCHED THE DESCRIPTION OF THE SWITCH CAR.
IT'S NOT STRIPPED SO IT HASN'T BEEN HERE LONG.
THAT'S ENOUGH FOR ME. LET'S RIDE, MONTOYA.
WE'D BETTER CALL TACTICAL.
WHAT'S GOING ON? WHAT'S THE RUSH?
KITCH AND CAZ FOUND THE MIDTOWN PERPS.
IF YOU'RE RIDING ALONG YOU BETTER HURRY, COMMISH...

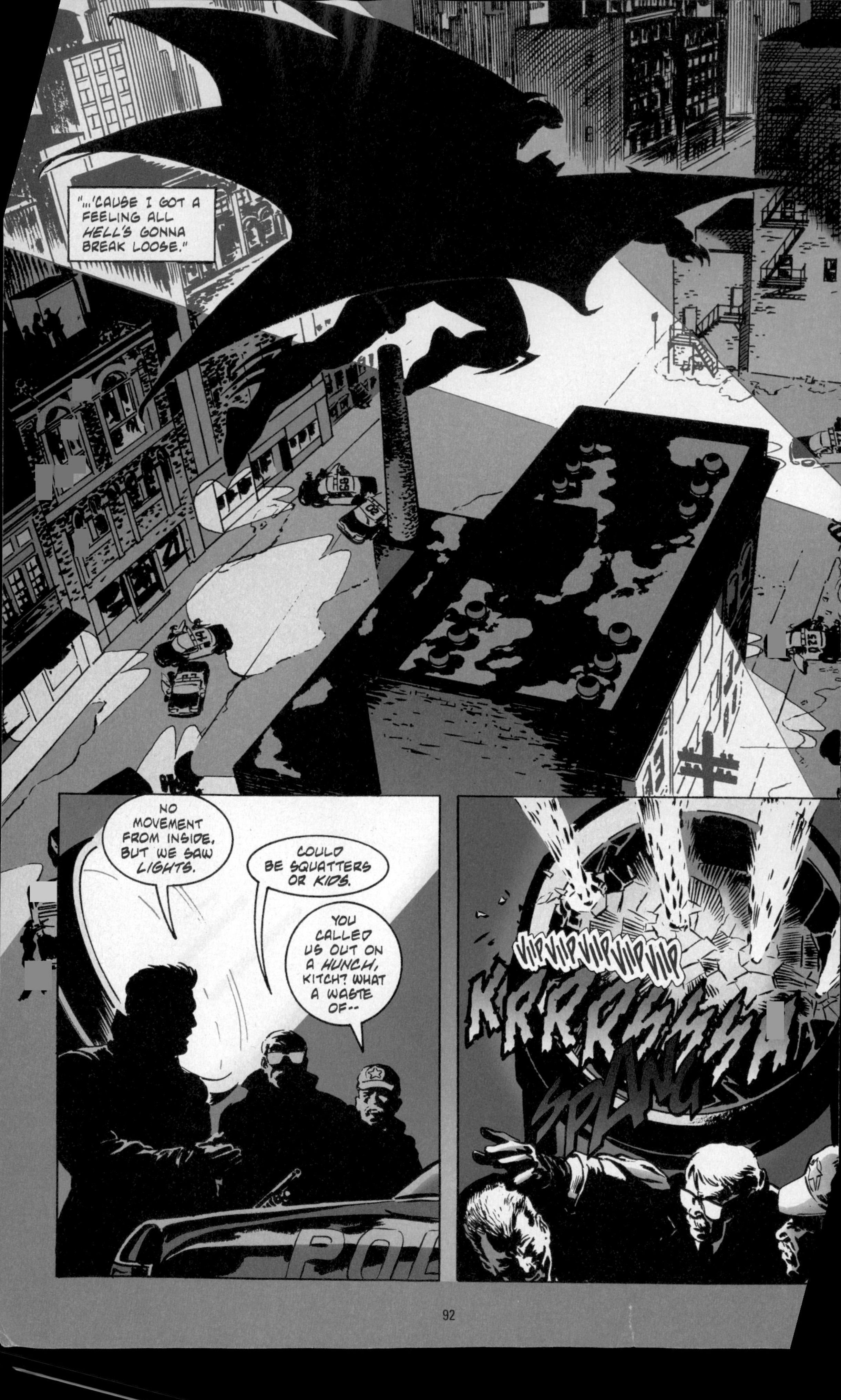
"...'CAUSE I GOT A FEELING ALL HELL'S GONNA BREAK LOOSE."
NO MOVEMENT FROM INSIDE, BUT WE SAW LIGHTS.
COULD BE SQUATTERS OR KIDS.
YOU CALLED US OUT ON A HUNCH, KITCH? WHAT A WASTE OF--
POL
VIIP VIIP VIIP VIIP VIIP
SPLANG

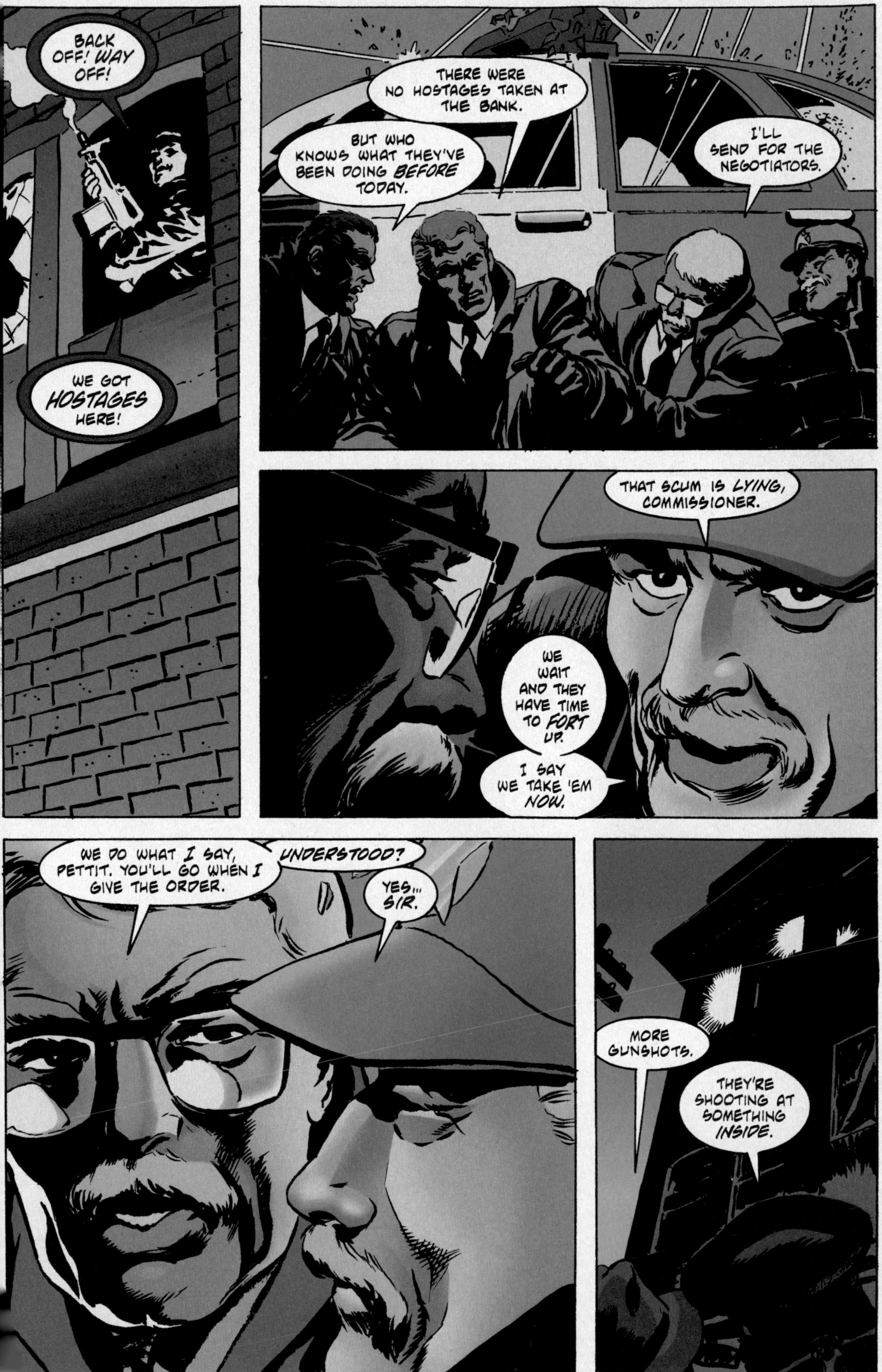
BACK OFF! WAY OFF!
WE GOT HOSTAGES HERE!
THERE WERE NO HOSTAGES TAKEN AT THE BANK.
BUT WHO KNOWS WHAT THEY'VE BEEN DOING BEFORE TODAY.
I'LL SEND FOR THE NEGOTIATORS.
THAT SCUM IS LYING, COMMISSIONER.
WE WAIT AND THEY HAVE TIME TO FORT UP.
I SAY WE TAKE 'EM NOW.
WE DO WHAT I SAY, PETTIT. YOU'LL GO WHEN I GIVE THE ORDER.
UNDERSTOOD?
YES... SIR.
MORE GUNSHOTS.
THEY'RE SHOOTING AT SOMETHING INSIDE.

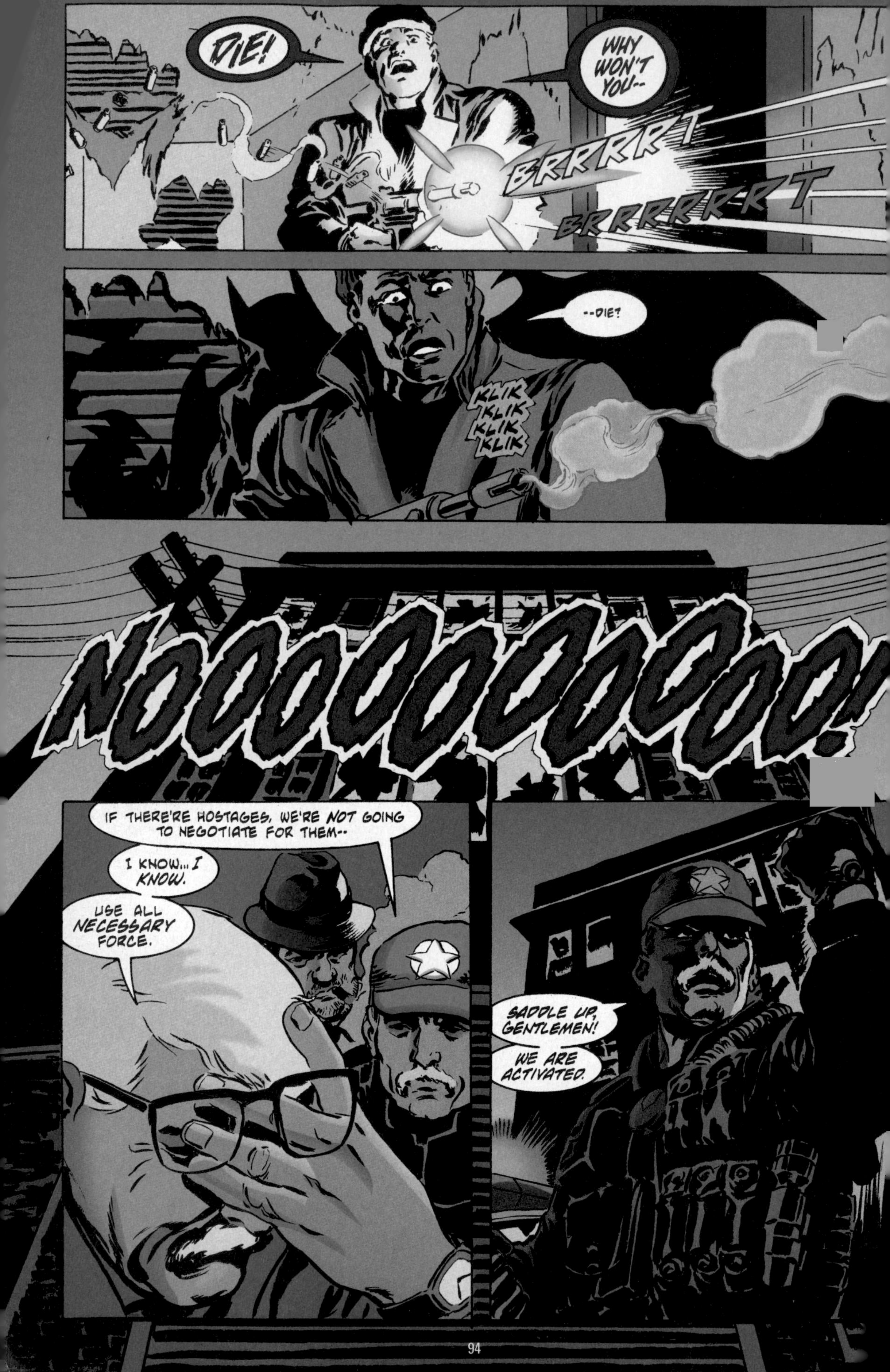
DIE!
WHY WON'T YOU--
BRRRRRT
BRRRRRRRT
--DIE?
KLIK KLIK KLIK KLIK
NOOOOOOOOOO!
IF THERE'RE HOSTAGES, WE'RE NOT GOING TO NEGOTIATE FOR THEM--
I KNOW... I KNOW.
USE ALL NECESSARY FORCE.
SADDLE UP, GENTLEMEN!
WE ARE ACTIVATED.

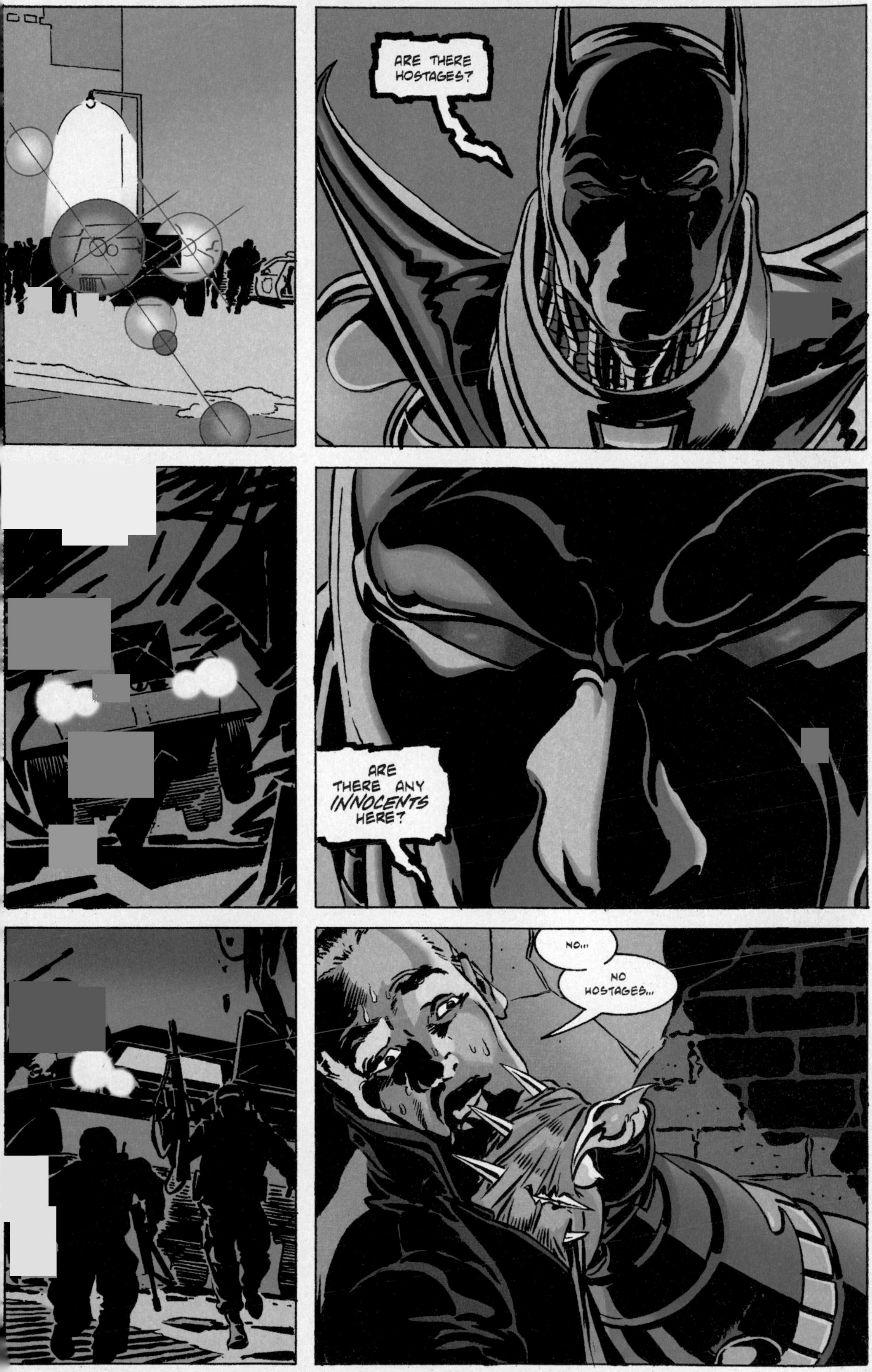
ARE THERE HOSTAGES?
ARE THERE ANY INNOCENTS HERE?
NO...
NO HOSTAGES...

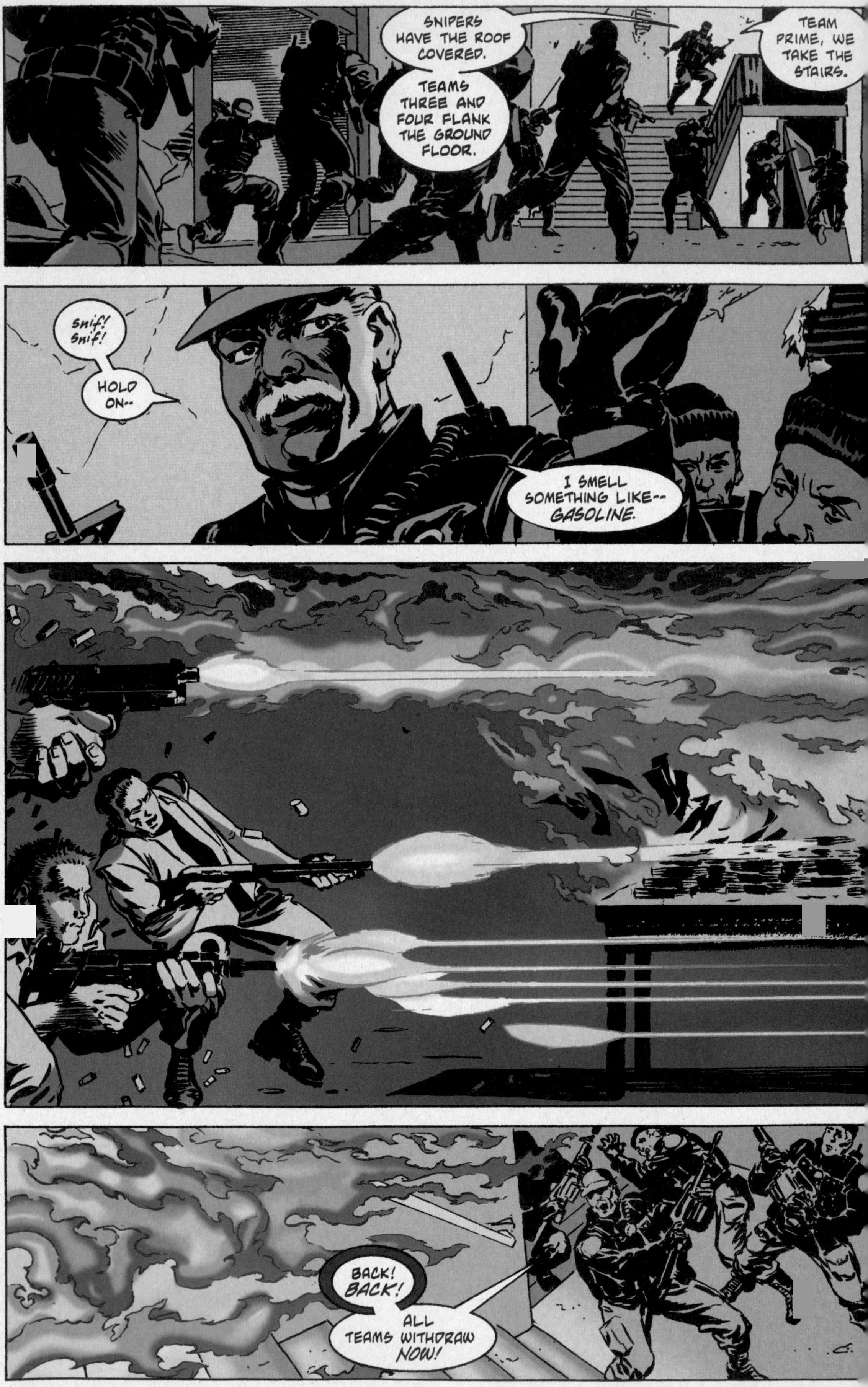
SNIPERS HAVE THE ROOF COVERED.
TEAMS THREE AND FOUR FLANK THE GROUND FLOOR.
TEAM PRIME, WE TAKE THE STAIRS.
snif! snif!
HOLD ON--
I SMELL SOMETHING LIKE-- GASOLINE.
BACK! BACK!
ALL TEAMS WITHDRAW NOW!

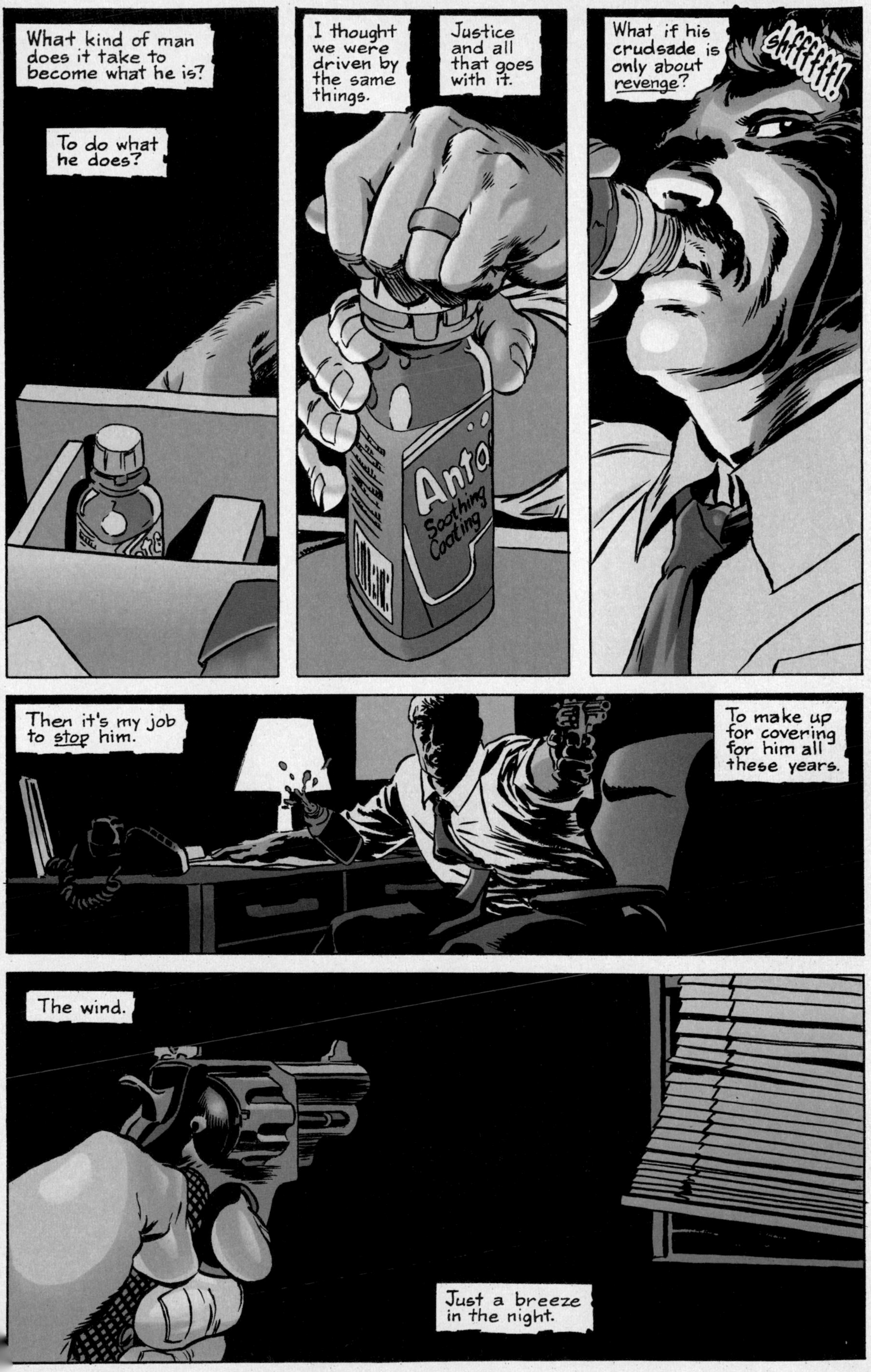
What kind of man does it take to become what he is?
To do what he does?
I thought we were driven by the same things.
Justice and all that goes with it.
Anto
Soothing Coating
What if his crudsade is only about revenge?
shffffft!
Then it's my job to stop him.
To make up for covering for him all these years.
The wind.
Just a breeze in the night.

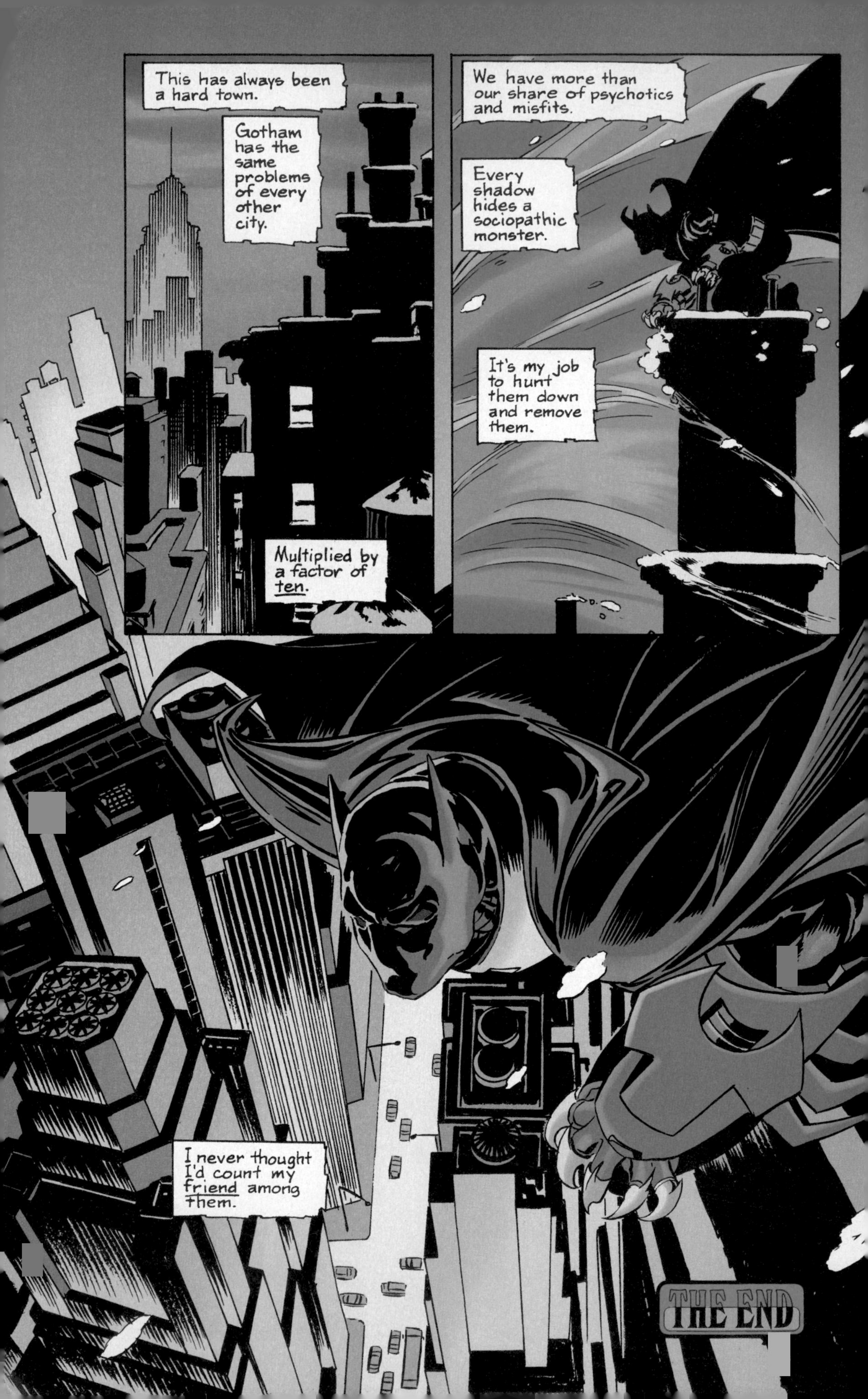
This has always been a hard town.
Gotham has the same problems of every other city.
Multiplied by a factor of ten.
We have more than our share of psychotics and misfits.
Every shadow hides a sociopathic monster.
It's my job to hunt them down and remove them.
I never thought I'd count my friend among them.
THE END

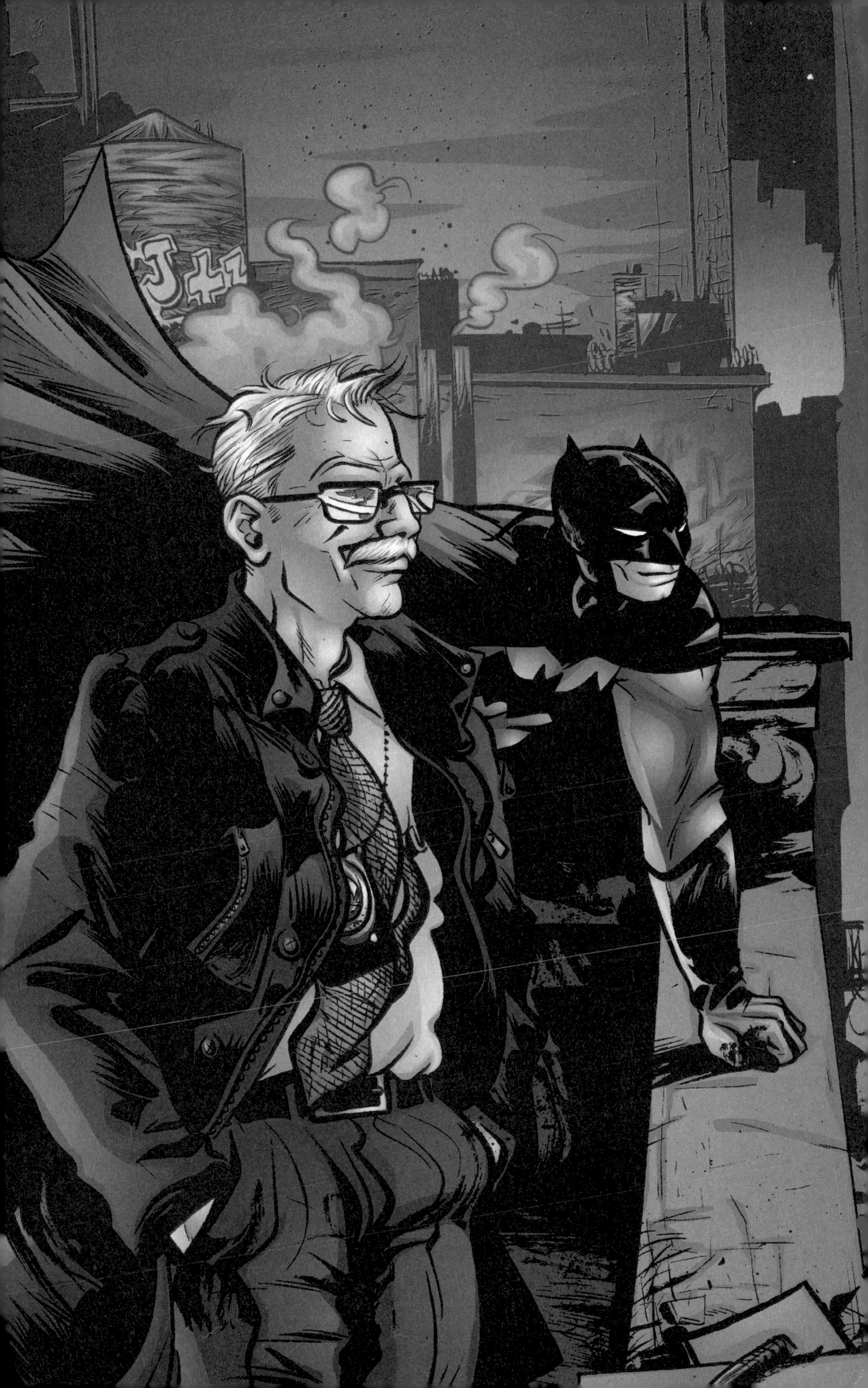

CHAPTER FIVE

COMRADES IN ARMS

Greg Rucka
writer

Paul Pope
penciller

Claude St. Aubin
inker

Paul Pope
cover artist

Patricia Mulvihill
colorist

Willie Schubert
letterer

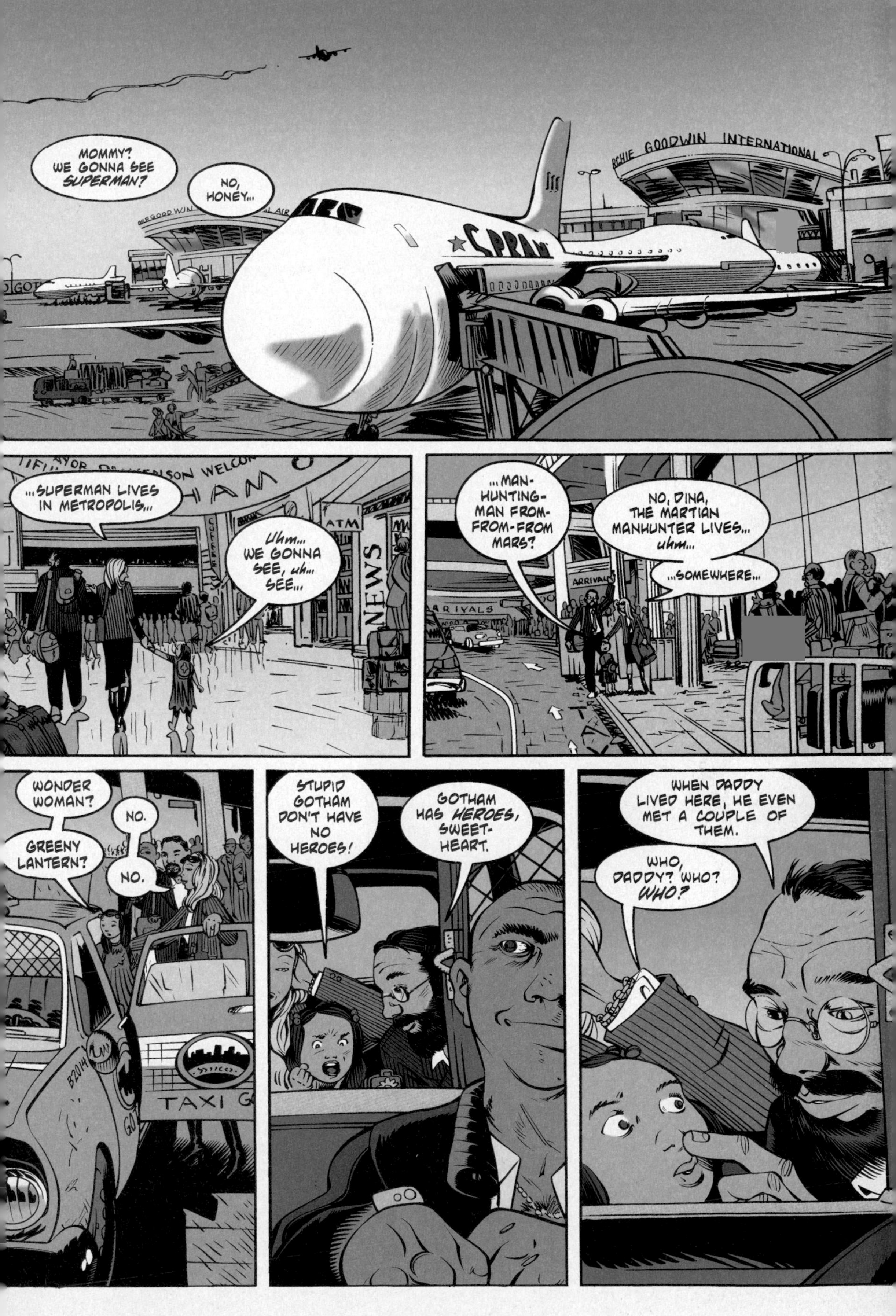
MOMMY? WE GONNA SEE SUPERMAN?
NO, HONEY...
...SUPERMAN LIVES IN METROPOLIS...
Uhm... WE GONNA SEE, uh... SEE...
...MAN-HUNTING-MAN FROM-FROM-FROM MARS?
NO, DINA, THE MARTIAN MANHUNTER LIVES... uhm...
...SOMEWHERE...
WONDER WOMAN?
NO.
GREENY LANTERN?
NO.
STUPID GOTHAM DON'T HAVE NO HEROES!
GOTHAM HAS HEROES, SWEET-HEART.
WHEN DADDY LIVED HERE, HE EVEN MET A COUPLE OF THEM.
WHO, DADDY? WHO? WHO?

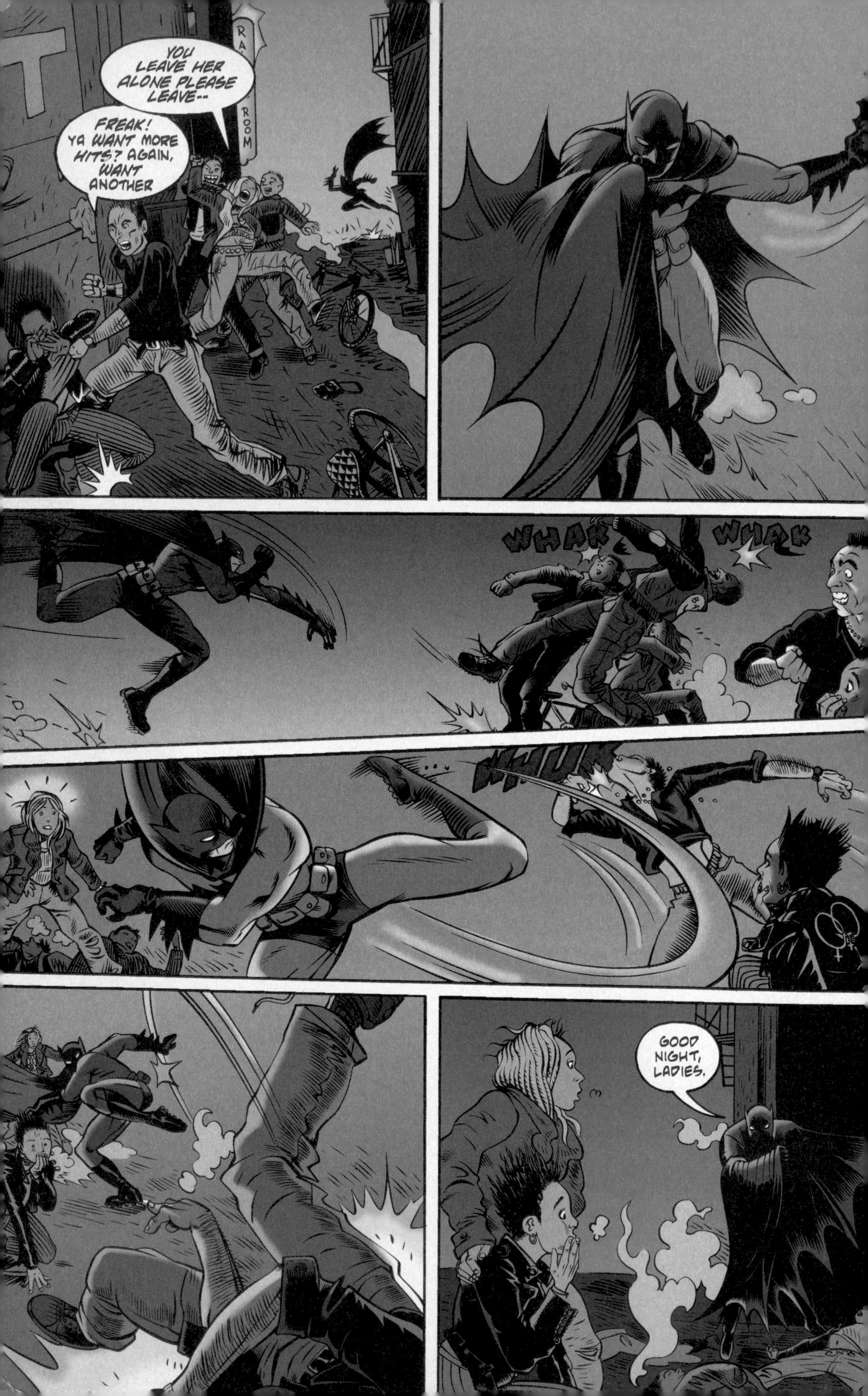
YOU LEAVE HER ALONE PLEASE LEAVE--
FREAK! YA WANT MORE HITS? AGAIN, WANT ANOTHER
WHAK
WHAK
GOOD NIGHT, LADIES.

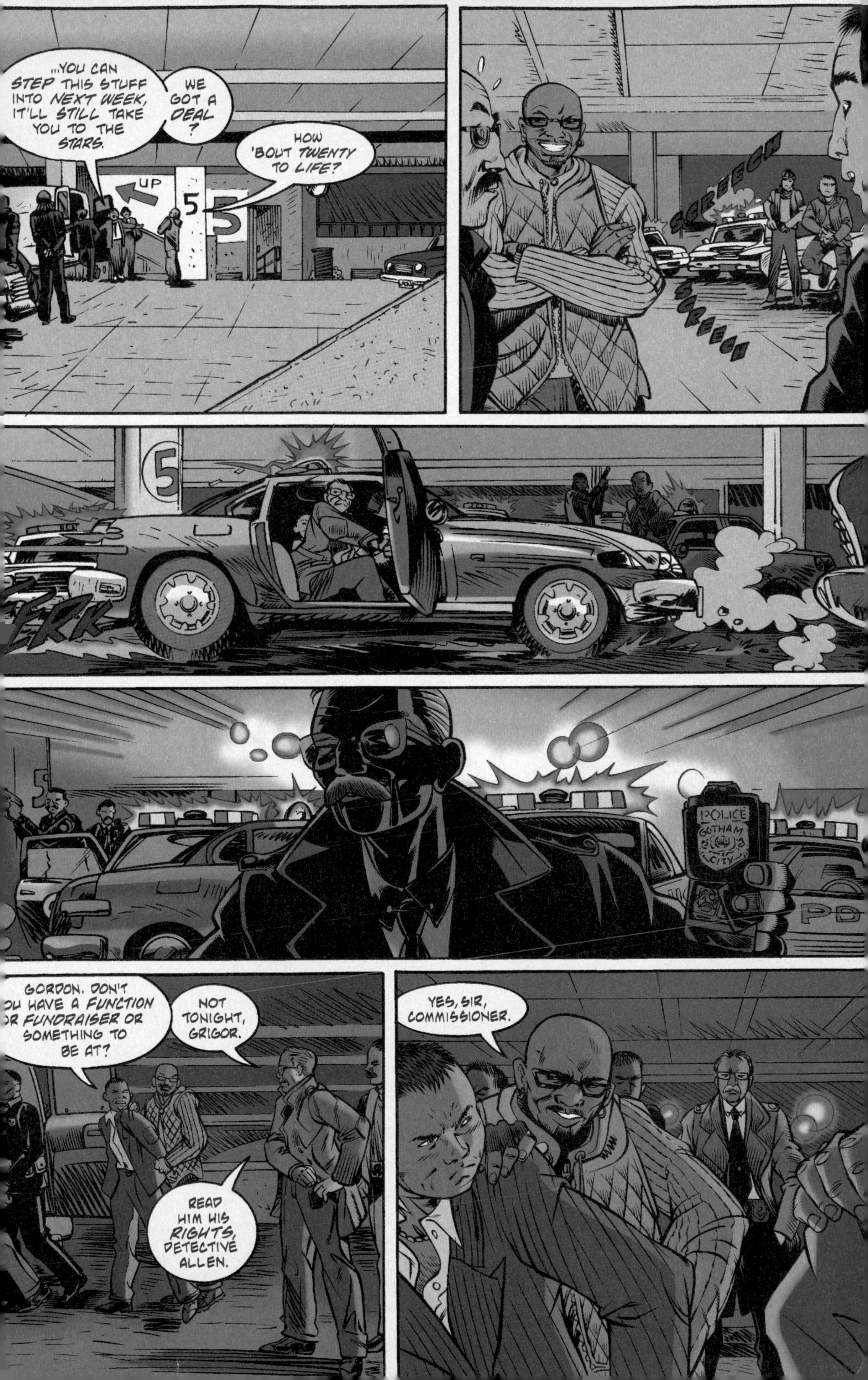
...YOU CAN STEP THIS STUFF INTO NEXT WEEK, IT'LL STILL TAKE YOU TO THE STARS.
WE GOT A DEAL?
HOW 'BOUT TWENTY TO LIFE?
UP
5
SCREEECH
SCREECH
ERRK
POLICE GOTHAM CITY
PD
GORDON. DON'T OU HAVE A FUNCTION R FUNDRAISER OR SOMETHING TO BE AT?
NOT TONIGHT, GRIGOR.
READ HIM HIS RIGHTS, DETECTIVE ALLEN.
YES, SIR, COMMISSIONER.

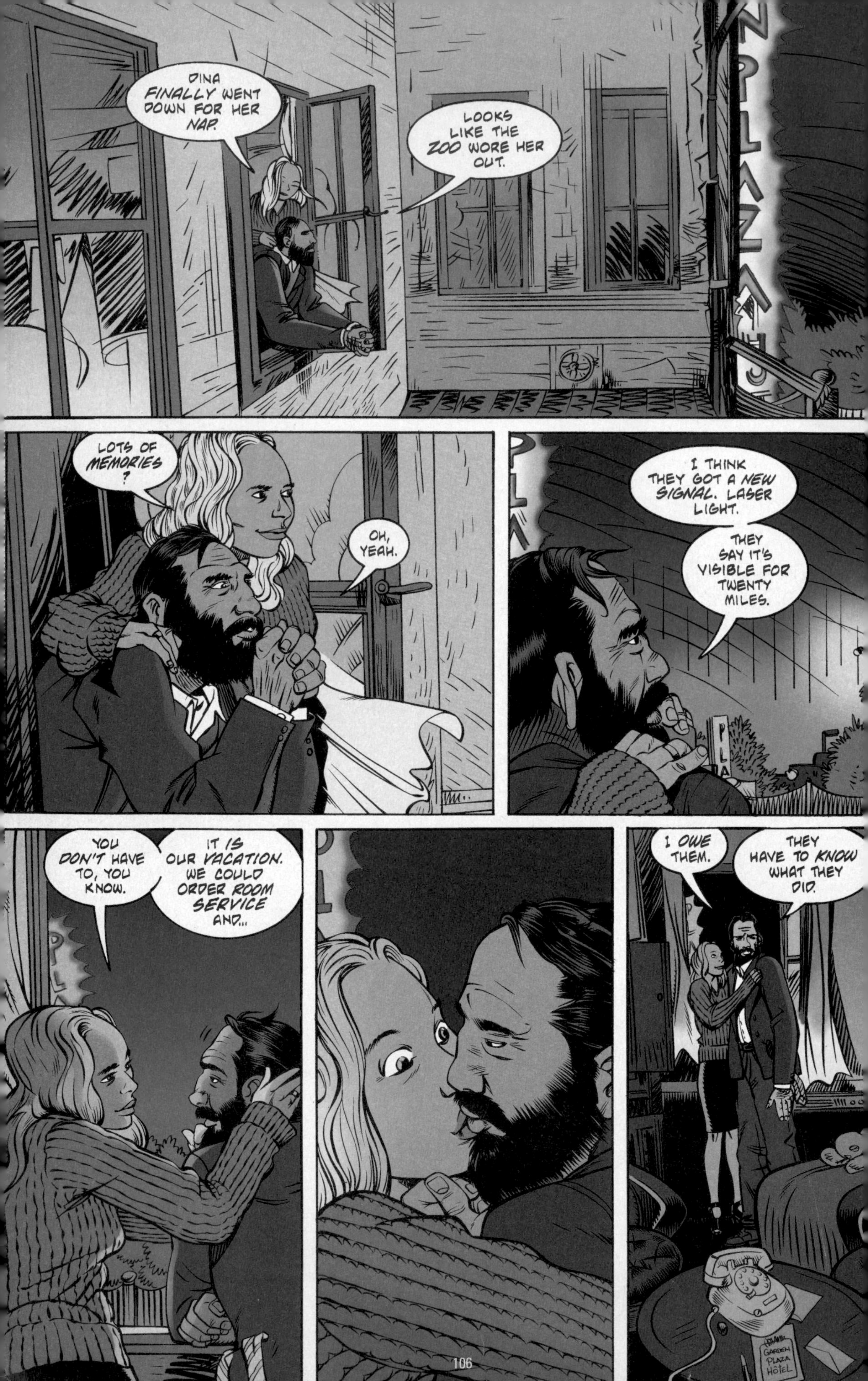
DINA FINALLY WENT DOWN FOR HER NAP.
LOOKS LIKE THE ZOO WORE HER OUT.
PLAZA
LOTS OF MEMORIES?
OH, YEAH.
I THINK THEY GOT A NEW SIGNAL. LASER LIGHT.
THEY SAY IT'S VISIBLE FOR TWENTY MILES.
YOU DON'T HAVE TO, YOU KNOW.
IT IS OUR VACATION. WE COULD ORDER ROOM SERVICE AND...
I OWE THEM.
THEY HAVE TO KNOW WHAT THEY DID.
GARDEN PLAZA HÔTEL

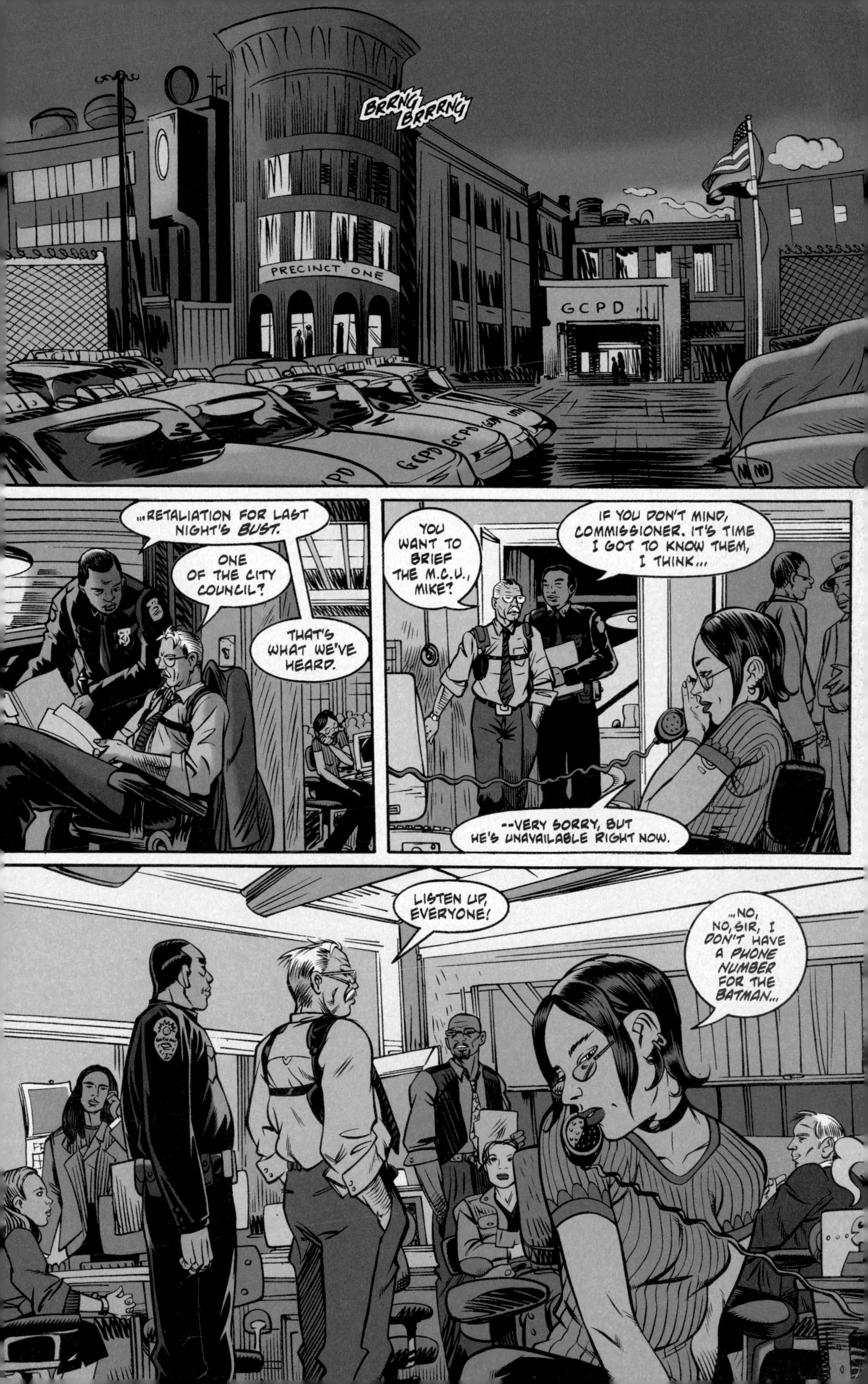
BRRNG BRRRNG
PRECINCT ONE
GCPD
...RETALIATION FOR LAST NIGHT'S BUST.
ONE OF THE CITY COUNCIL?
THAT'S WHAT WE'VE HEARD.
YOU WANT TO BRIEF THE M.C.U., MIKE?
IF YOU DON'T MIND, COMMISSIONER. IT'S TIME I GOT TO KNOW THEM, I THINK...
--VERY SORRY, BUT HE'S UNAVAILABLE RIGHT NOW.
LISTEN UP, EVERYONE!
...NO, NO, SIR, I DON'T HAVE A PHONE NUMBER FOR THE BATMAN...

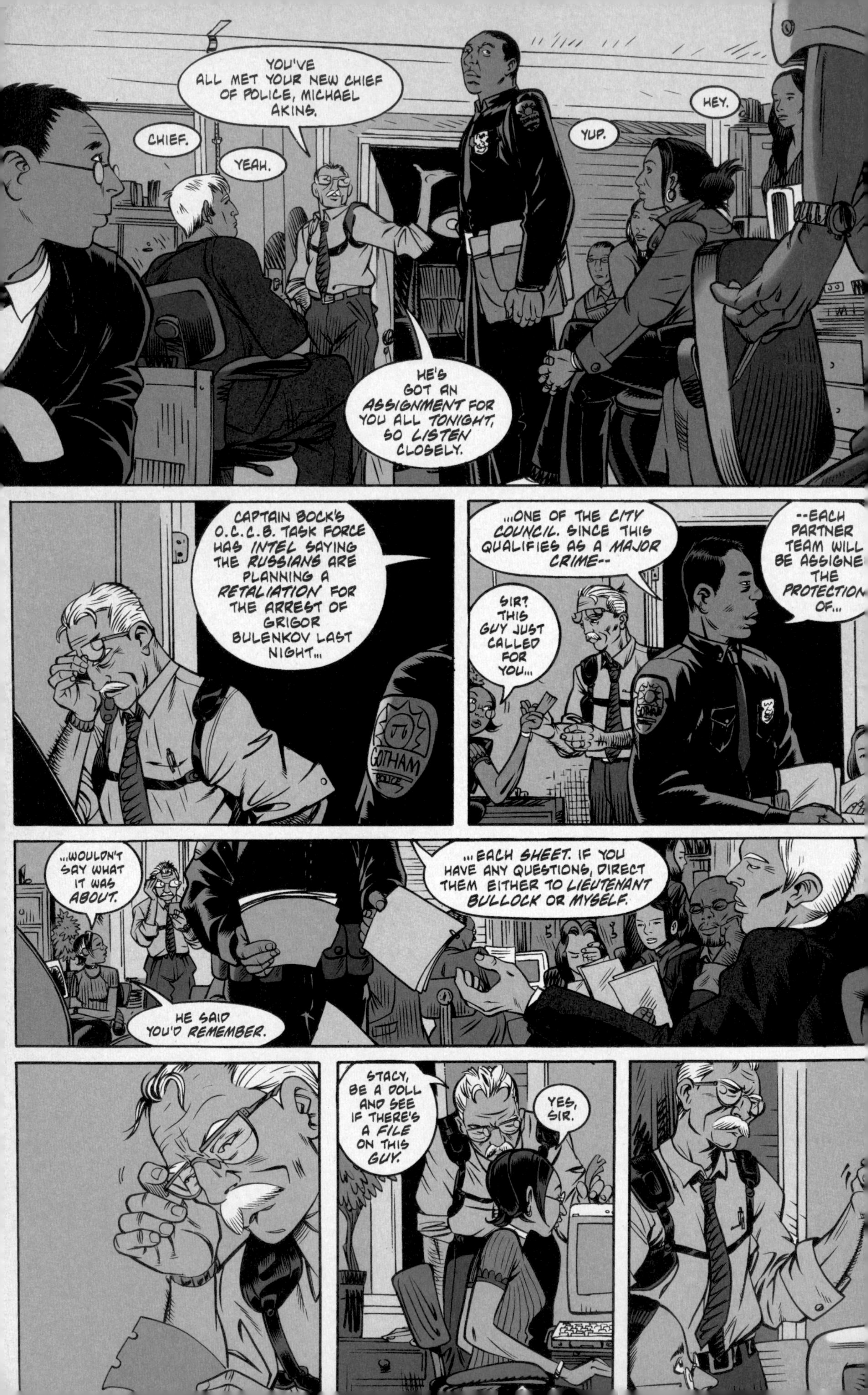
YOU'VE ALL MET YOUR NEW CHIEF OF POLICE, MICHAEL AKINS.
CHIEF.
YEAH.
YUP.
HEY.
HE'S GOT AN ASSIGNMENT FOR YOU ALL TONIGHT, SO LISTEN CLOSELY.
CAPTAIN BOCK'S O.C.C.B. TASK FORCE HAS INTEL SAYING THE RUSSIANS ARE PLANNING A RETALIATION FOR THE ARREST OF GRIGOR BULENKOV LAST NIGHT...
GOTHAM POLICE
...ONE OF THE CITY COUNCIL. SINCE THIS QUALIFIES AS A MAJOR CRIME--
--EACH PARTNER TEAM WILL BE ASSIGNE THE PROTECTION OF...
SIR? THIS GUY JUST CALLED FOR YOU...
...WOULDN'T SAY WHAT IT WAS ABOUT.
...EACH SHEET. IF YOU HAVE ANY QUESTIONS, DIRECT THEM EITHER TO LIEUTENANT BULLOCK OR MYSELF.
HE SAID YOU'D REMEMBER.
STACY, BE A DOLL AND SEE IF THERE'S A FILE ON THIS GUY.
YES, SIR.

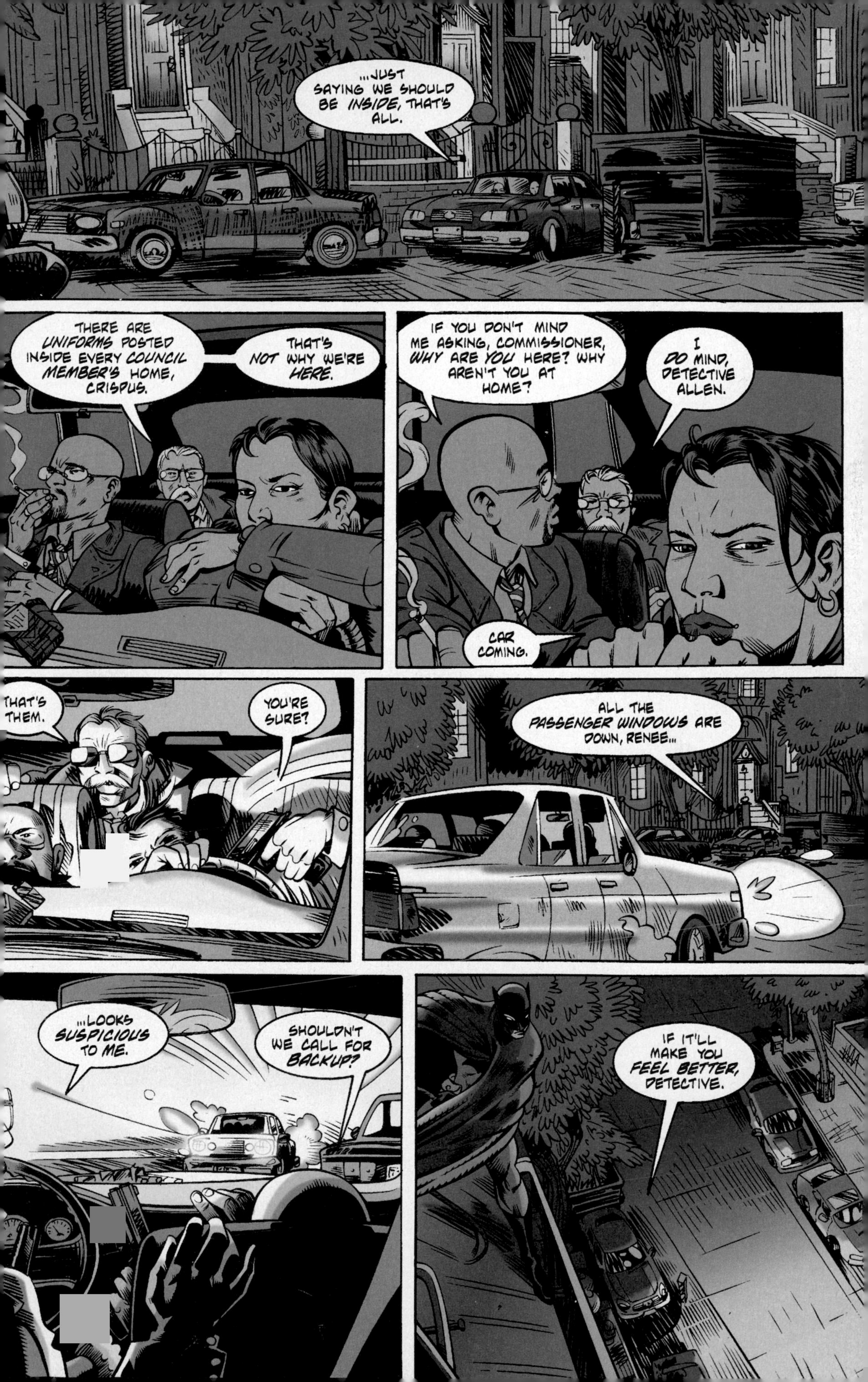
...JUST SAYING WE SHOULD BE INSIDE, THAT'S ALL.
THERE ARE UNIFORMS POSTED INSIDE EVERY COUNCIL MEMBER'S HOME, CRISPUS.
THAT'S NOT WHY WE'RE HERE.
IF YOU DON'T MIND ME ASKING, COMMISSIONER, WHY ARE YOU HERE? WHY AREN'T YOU AT HOME?
I DO MIND, DETECTIVE ALLEN.
CAR COMING.
THAT'S THEM.
YOU'RE SURE?
ALL THE PASSENGER WINDOWS ARE DOWN, RENEE...
...LOOKS SUSPICIOUS TO ME.
SHOULDN'T WE CALL FOR BACKUP?
IF IT'LL MAKE YOU FEEL BETTER, DETECTIVE.

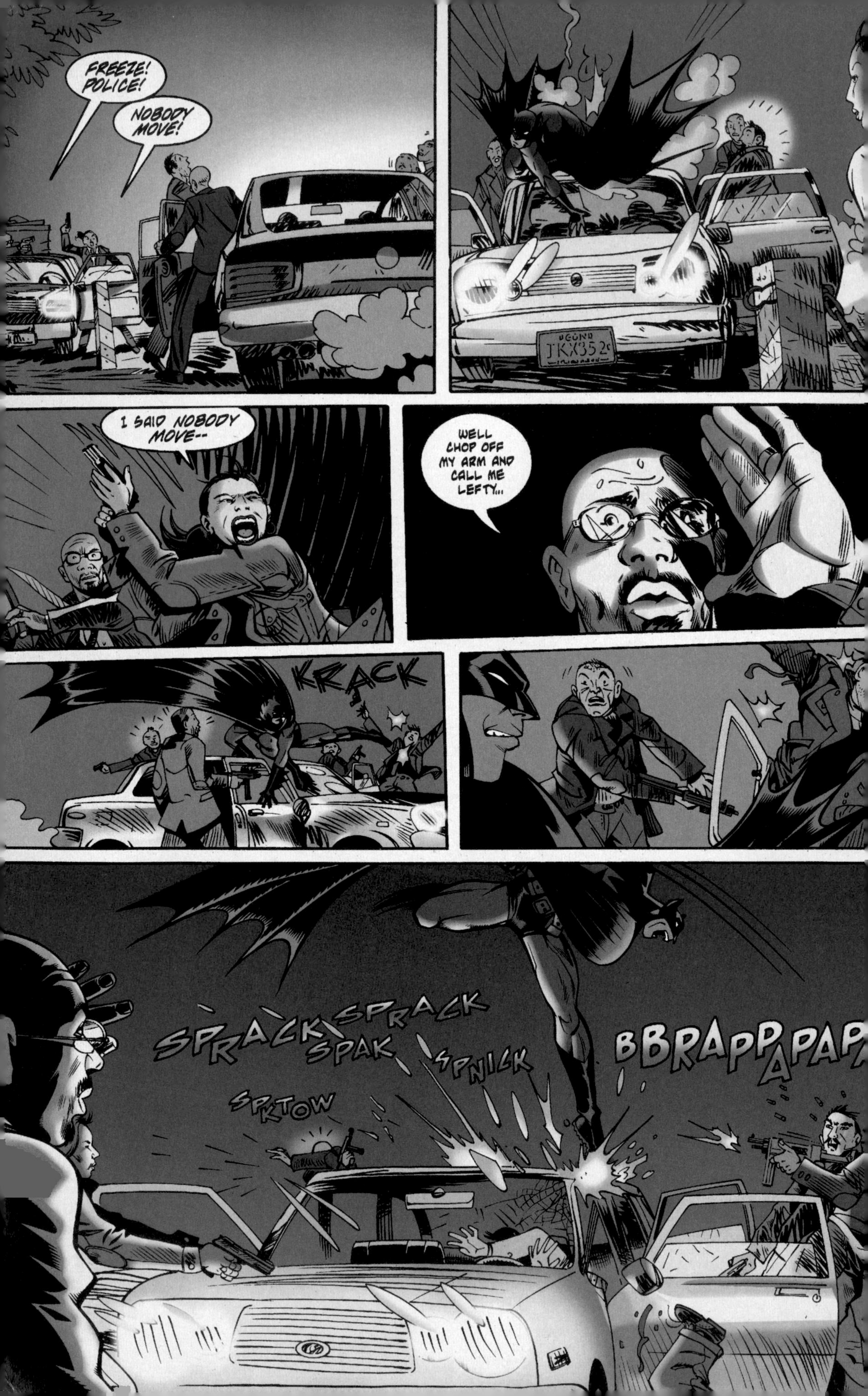
FREEZE! POLICE!
NOBODY MOVE!
I SAID NOBODY MOVE--
WELL CHOP OFF MY ARM AND CALL ME LEFTY...
KRACK
SPRACK SPRACK
SPAK
SPNICK
SPKTOW
BBRAPPAPAP

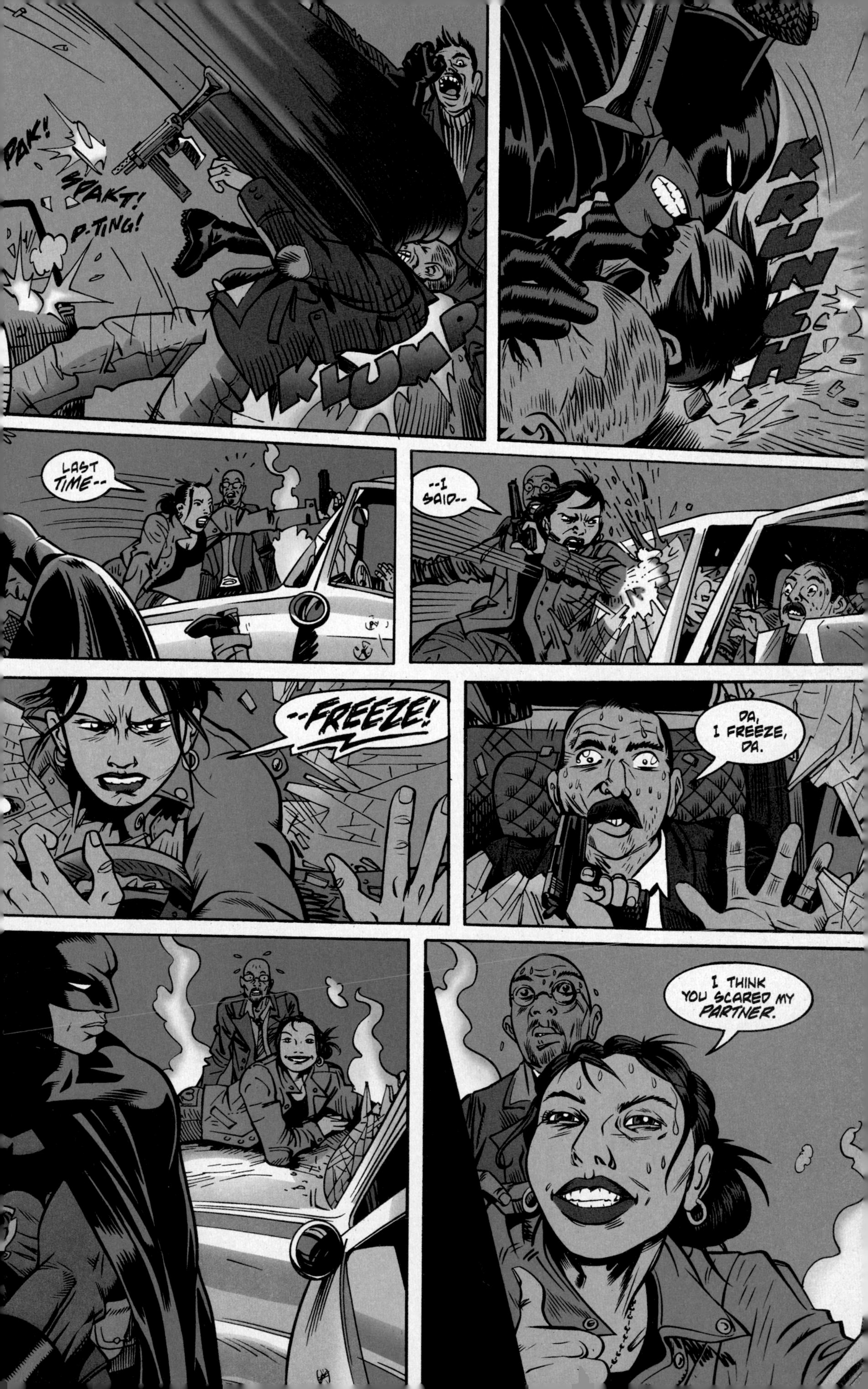
PAK!
SPAKT!
P-TING!
KLUMP
KRUNCH!
LAST TIME--
--I SAID--
--FREEZE!
DA, I FREEZE, DA.
I THINK YOU SCARED MY PARTNER.

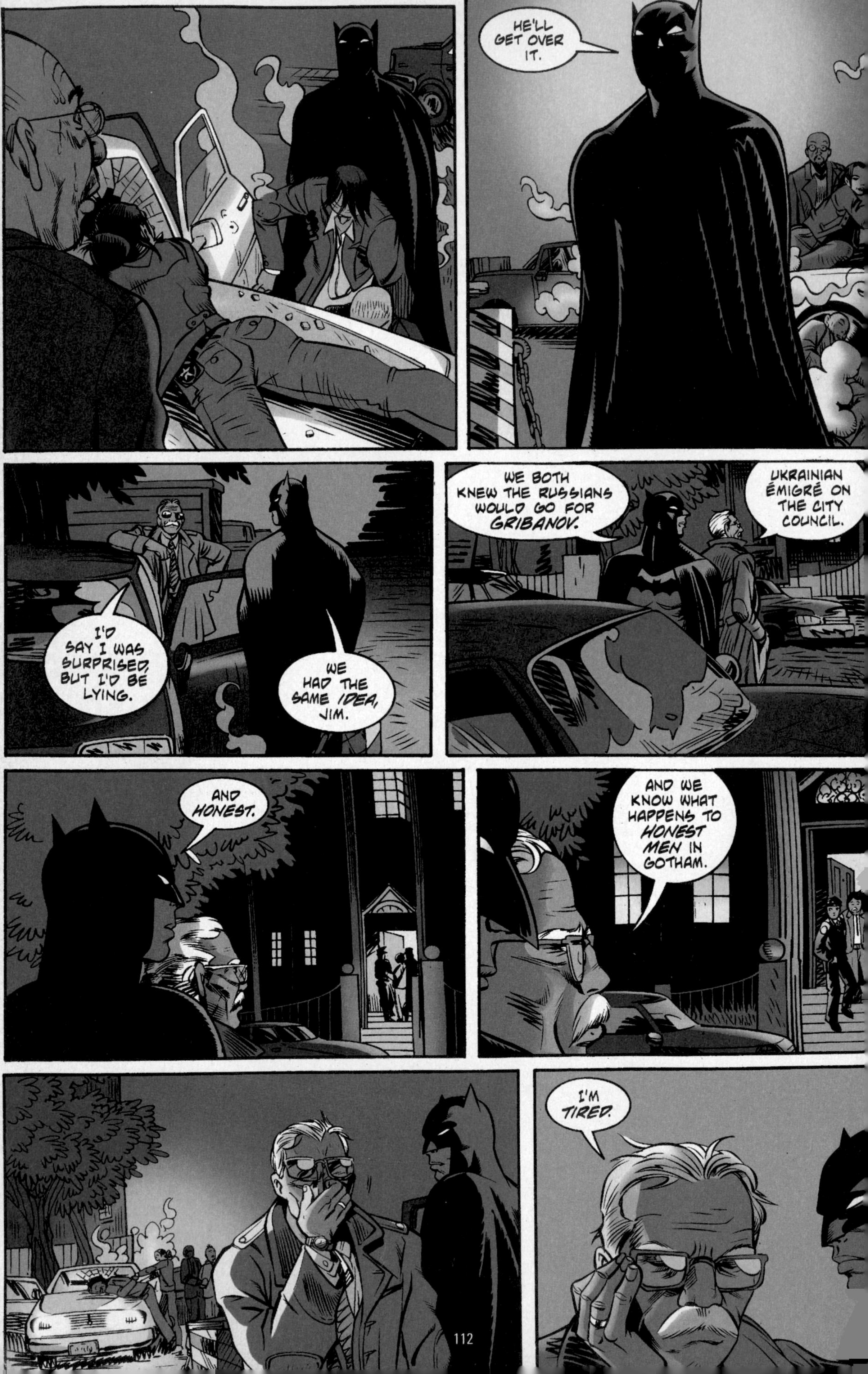
HE'LL GET OVER IT.
I'D SAY I WAS SURPRISED, BUT I'D BE LYING.
WE HAD THE SAME IDEA, JIM.
WE BOTH KNEW THE RUSSIANS WOULD GO FOR GRIBANOV.
UKRAINIAN ÉMIGRÉ ON THE CITY COUNCIL.
AND HONEST.
AND WE KNOW WHAT HAPPENS TO HONEST MEN IN GOTHAM.
I'M TIRED.

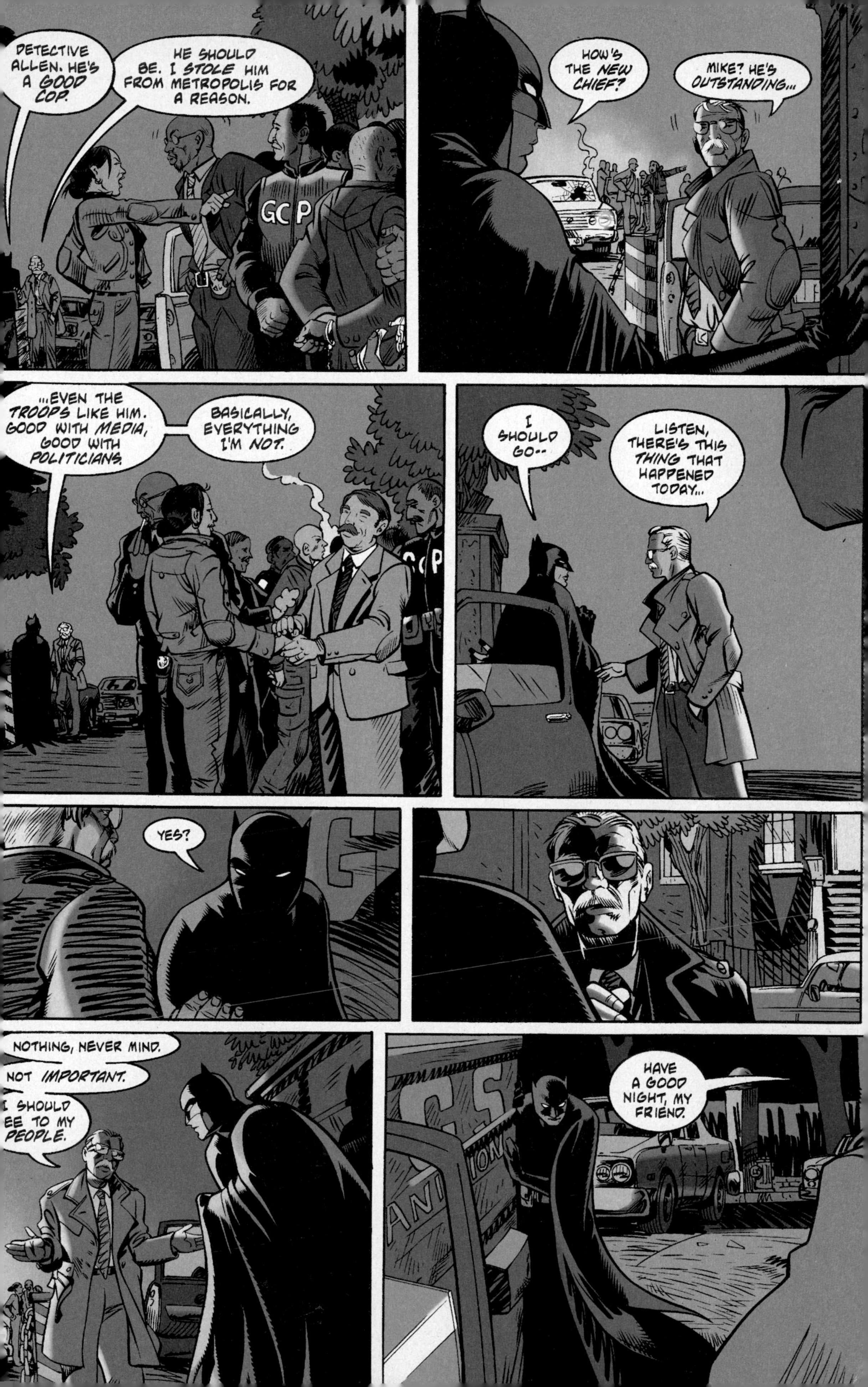
DETECTIVE ALLEN. HE'S A GOOD COP.
HE SHOULD BE. I STOLE HIM FROM METROPOLIS FOR A REASON.
HOW'S THE NEW CHIEF?
MIKE? HE'S OUTSTANDING...
...EVEN THE TROOPS LIKE HIM. GOOD WITH MEDIA, GOOD WITH POLITICIANS.
BASICALLY, EVERYTHING I'M NOT.
I SHOULD GO--
LISTEN, THERE'S THIS THING THAT HAPPENED TODAY...
YES?
NOTHING, NEVER MIND.
NOT IMPORTANT.
I SHOULD SEE TO MY PEOPLE.
HAVE A GOOD NIGHT, MY FRIEND.

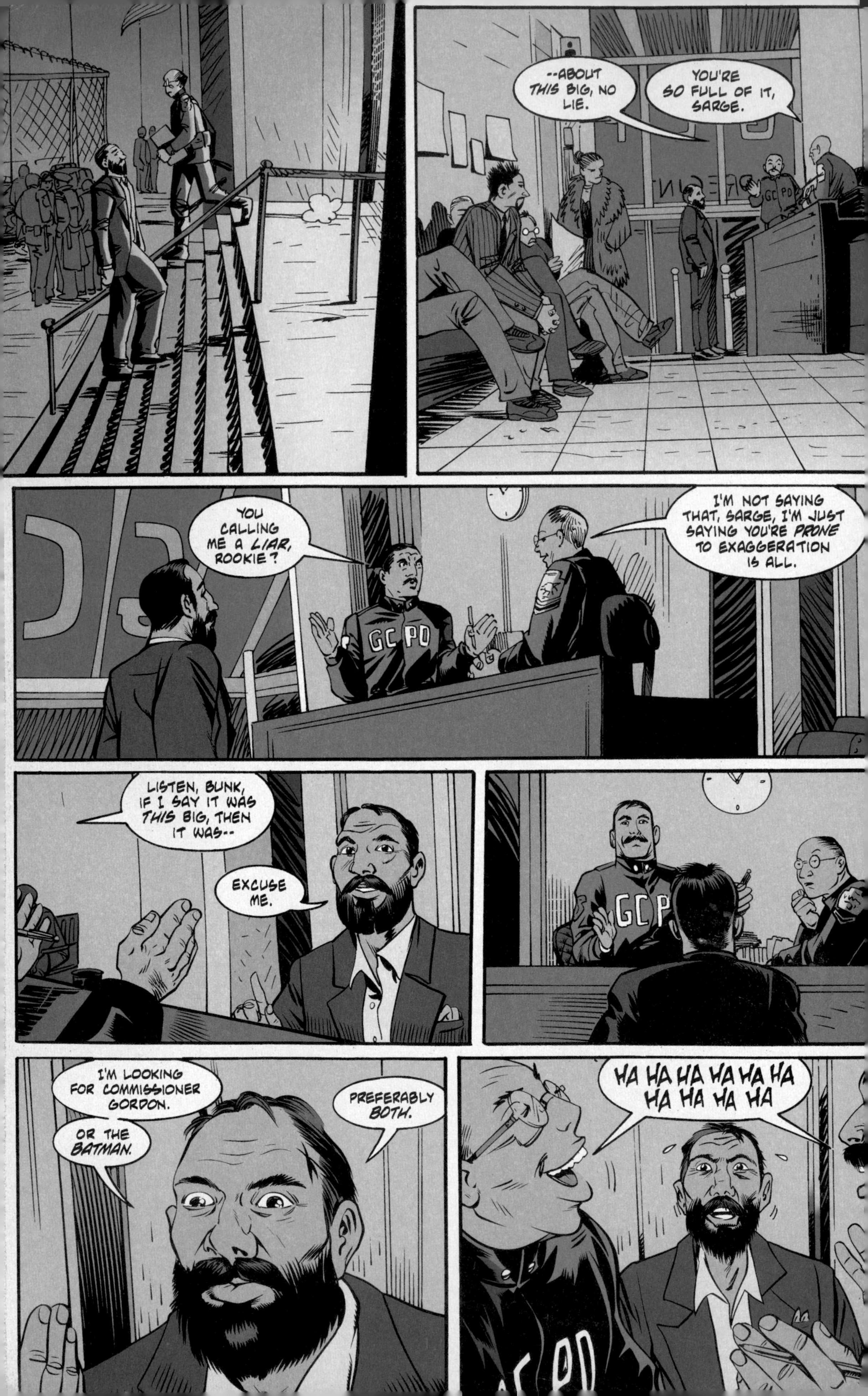
--ABOUT THIS BIG, NO LIE.
YOU'RE SO FULL OF IT, SARGE.
YOU CALLING ME A LIAR, ROOKIE?
I'M NOT SAYING THAT, SARGE, I'M JUST SAYING YOU'RE PRONE TO EXAGGERATION IS ALL.
LISTEN, BUNK, IF I SAY IT WAS THIS BIG, THEN IT WAS--
EXCUSE ME.
I'M LOOKING FOR COMMISSIONER GORDON.
OR THE BATMAN.
PREFERABLY BOTH.
HA HA HA HA HA HA HA HA HA HA

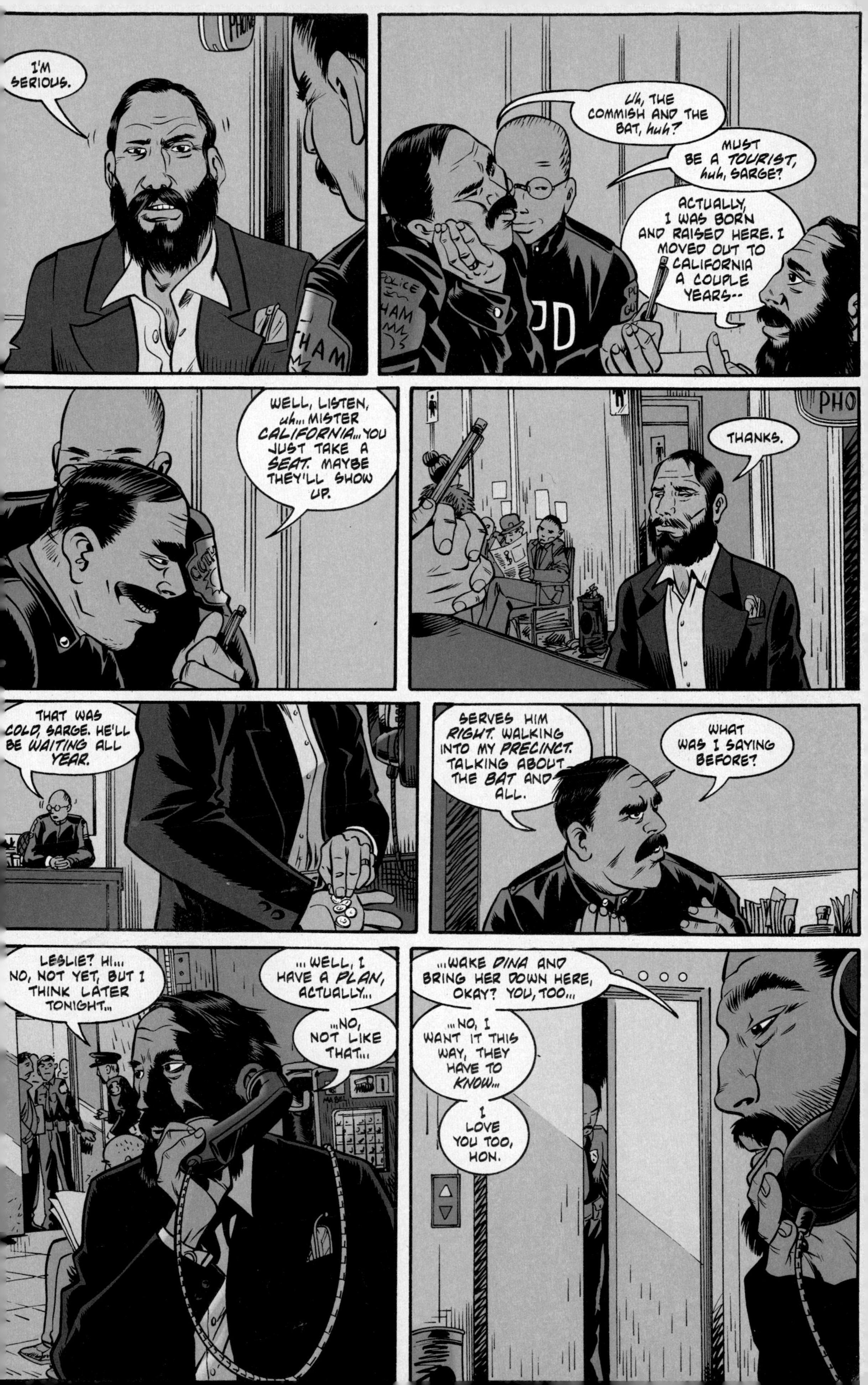
I'M SERIOUS.
UH, THE COMMISH AND THE BAT, HUH?
MUST BE A TOURIST, HUH, SARGE?
ACTUALLY, I WAS BORN AND RAISED HERE. I MOVED OUT TO CALIFORNIA A COUPLE YEARS--
WELL, LISTEN, UH... MISTER CALIFORNIA... YOU JUST TAKE A SEAT. MAYBE THEY'LL SHOW UP.
THANKS.
THAT WAS COLD, SARGE. HE'LL BE WAITING ALL YEAR.
SERVES HIM RIGHT. WALKING INTO MY PRECINCT. TALKING ABOUT THE BAT AND ALL.
WHAT WAS I SAYING BEFORE?
LESLIE? HI... NO, NOT YET, BUT I THINK LATER TONIGHT...
...WELL, I HAVE A PLAN, ACTUALLY...
...NO, NOT LIKE THAT...
...WAKE DINA AND BRING HER DOWN HERE, OKAY? YOU, TOO...
...NO, I WANT IT THIS WAY, THEY HAVE TO KNOW...
I LOVE YOU TOO, HON.

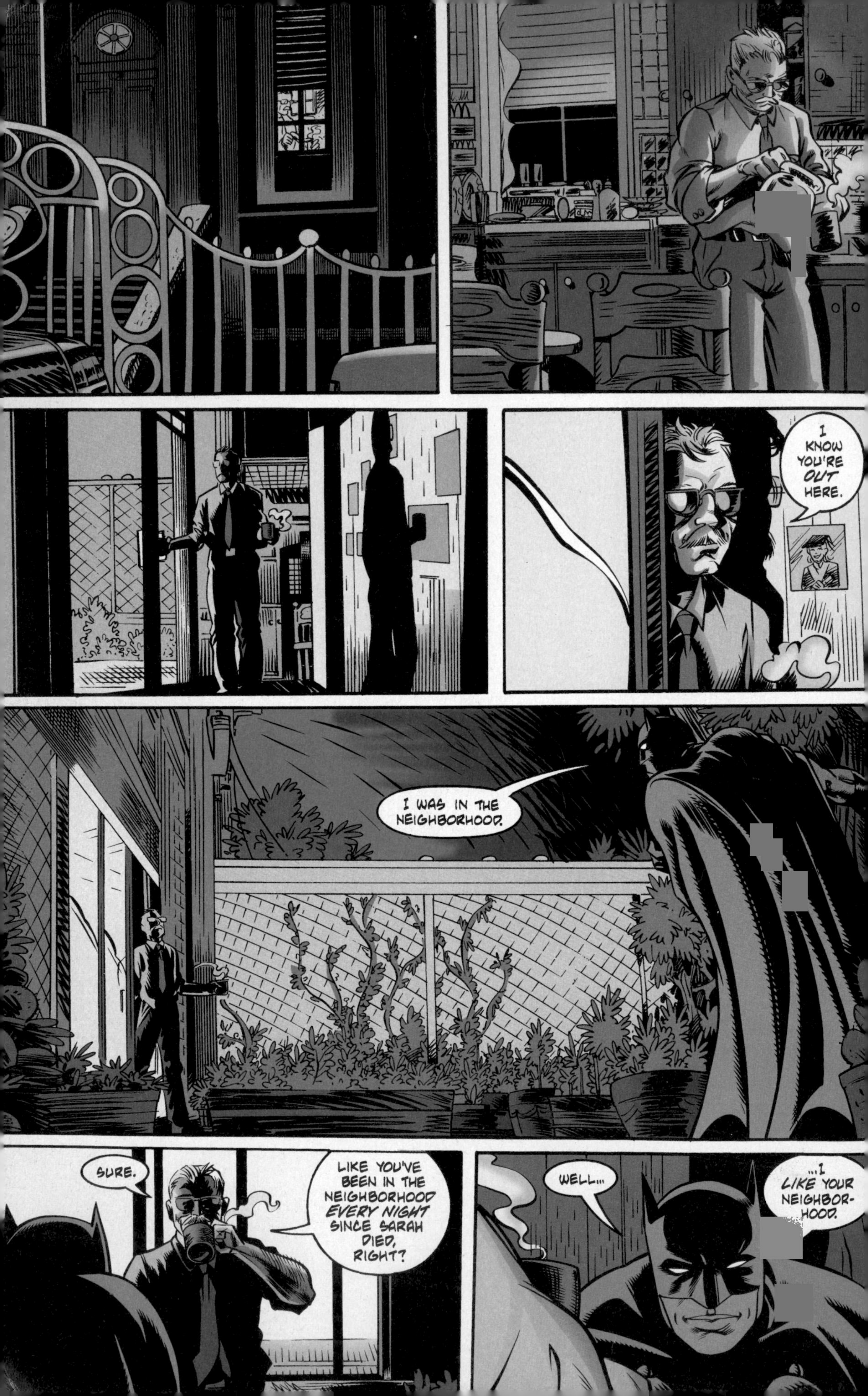
I KNOW YOU'RE OUT HERE.
I WAS IN THE NEIGHBORHOOD.
SURE.
LIKE YOU'VE BEEN IN THE NEIGHBORHOOD EVERY NIGHT SINCE SARAH DIED, RIGHT?
WELL...
...I LIKE YOUR NEIGHBOR-HOOD.

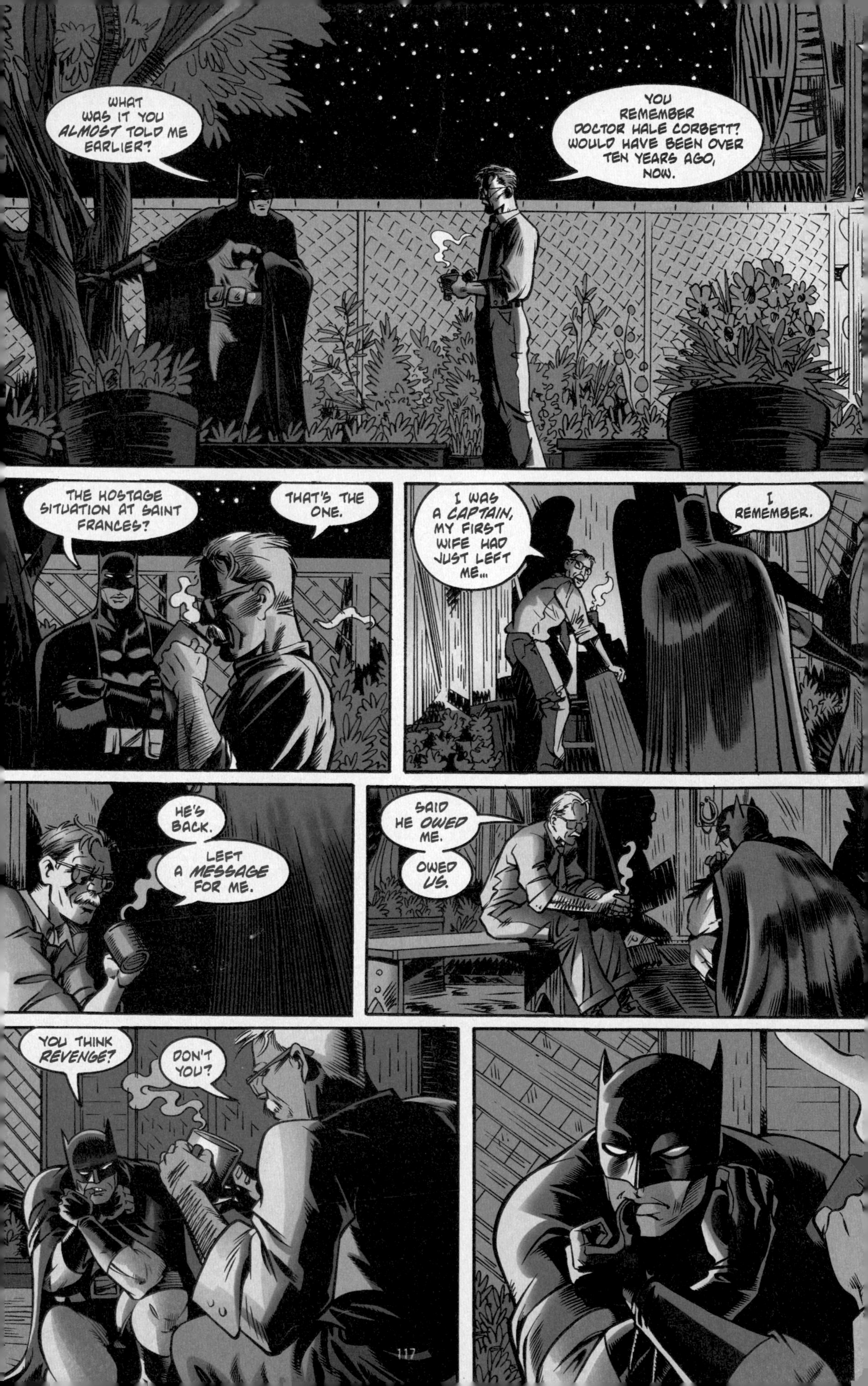
WHAT WAS IT YOU ALMOST TOLD ME EARLIER?
YOU REMEMBER DOCTOR HALE CORBETT? WOULD HAVE BEEN OVER TEN YEARS AGO, NOW.
THE HOSTAGE SITUATION AT SAINT FRANCES?
THAT'S THE ONE.
I WAS A CAPTAIN, MY FIRST WIFE HAD JUST LEFT ME...
I REMEMBER.
HE'S BACK.
LEFT A MESSAGE FOR ME.
SAID HE OWED ME.
OWED US.
YOU THINK REVENGE?
DON'T YOU?

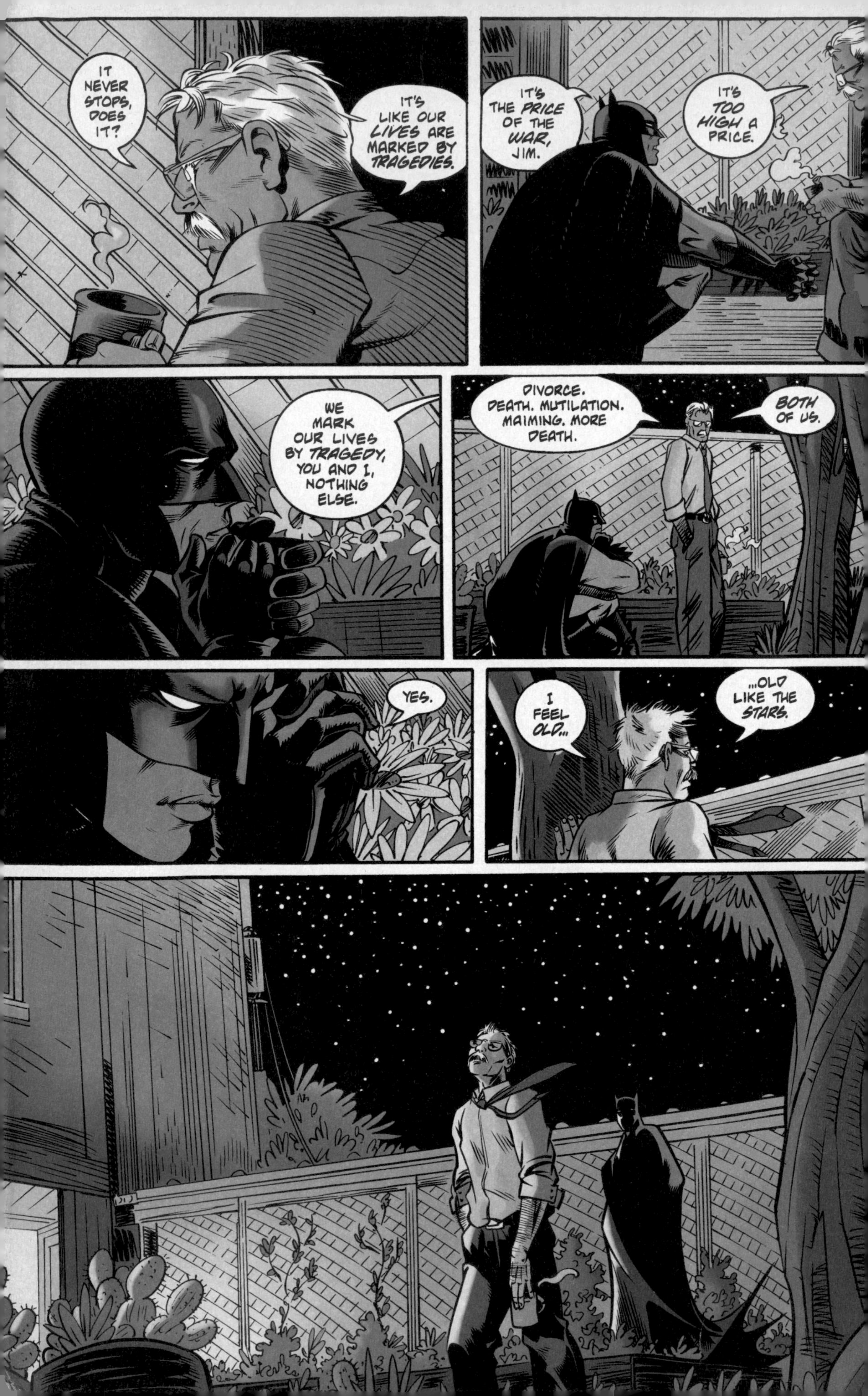
IT NEVER STOPS, DOES IT?
IT'S LIKE OUR LIVES ARE MARKED BY TRAGEDIES.
IT'S THE PRICE OF THE WAR, JIM.
IT'S TOO HIGH A PRICE.
WE MARK OUR LIVES BY TRAGEDY, YOU AND I, NOTHING ELSE.
DIVORCE. DEATH. MUTILATION. MAIMING. MORE DEATH.
BOTH OF US.
YES.
I FEEL OLD...
...OLD LIKE THE STARS.

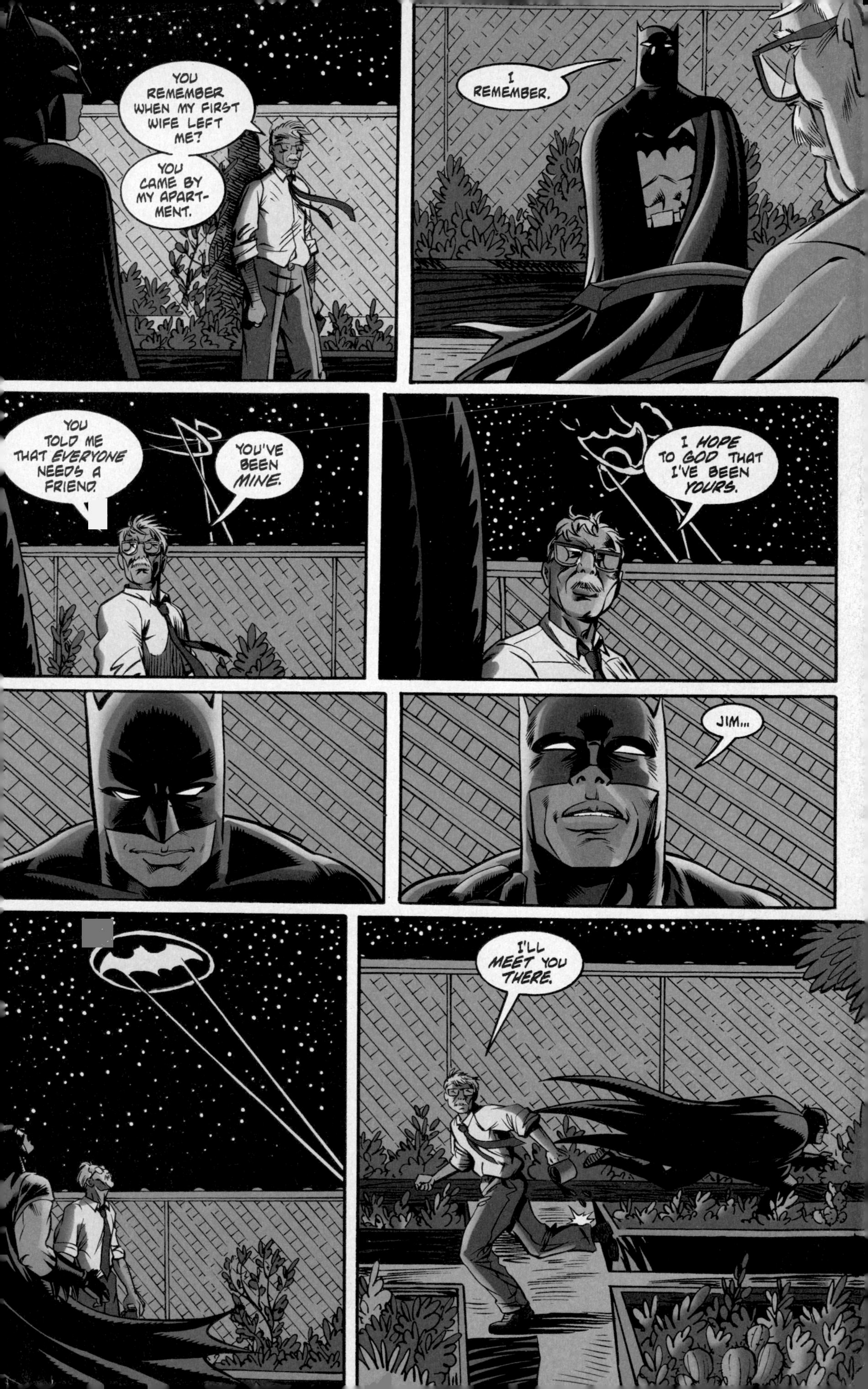
YOU REMEMBER WHEN MY FIRST WIFE LEFT ME?
YOU CAME BY MY APARTMENT.
I REMEMBER.
YOU TOLD ME THAT *EVERYONE* NEEDS A FRIEND.
YOU'VE BEEN *MINE*.
I *HOPE* TO *GOD* THAT I'VE BEEN *YOURS*.
JIM...
I'LL *MEET* YOU *THERE*.

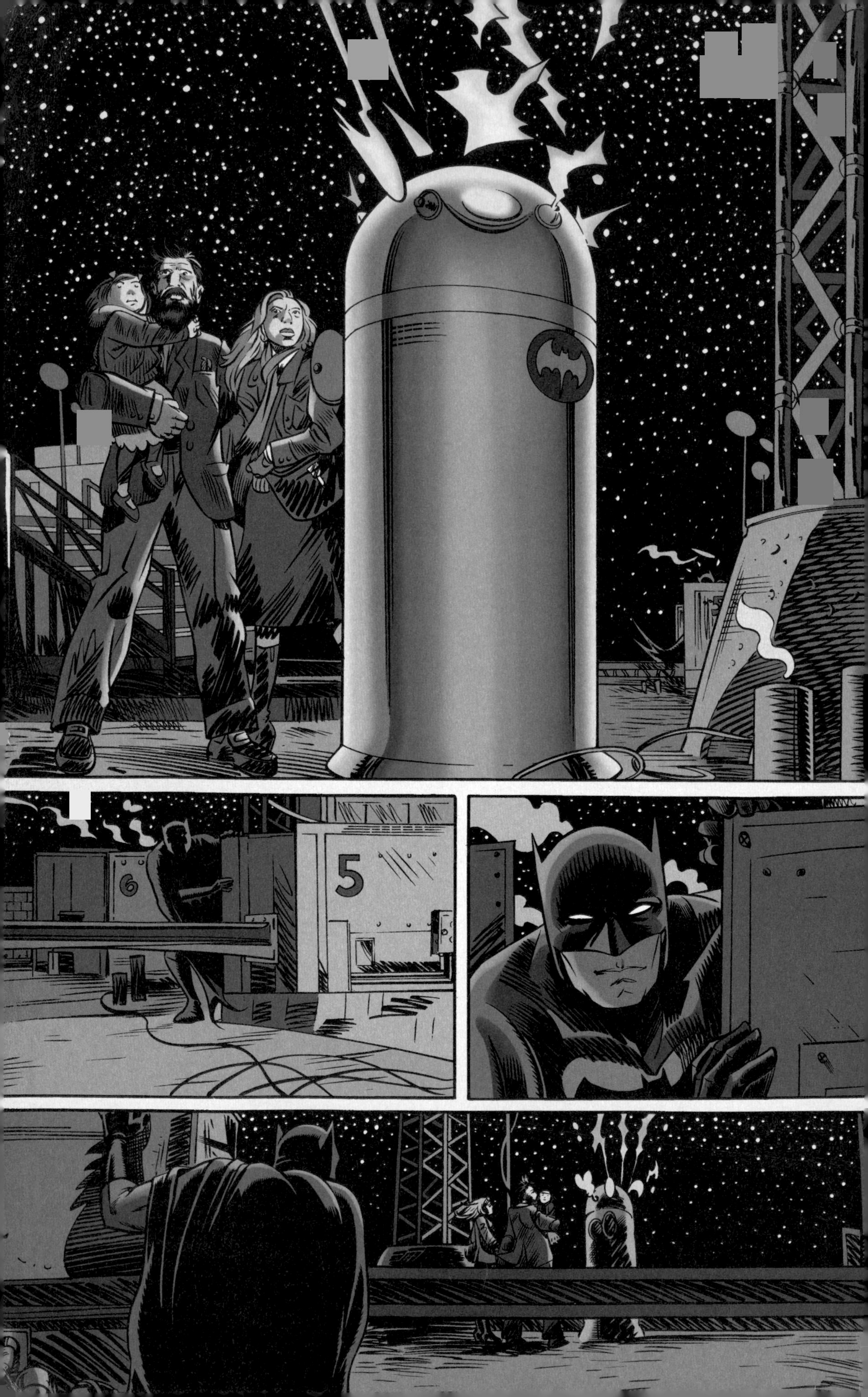
6
5

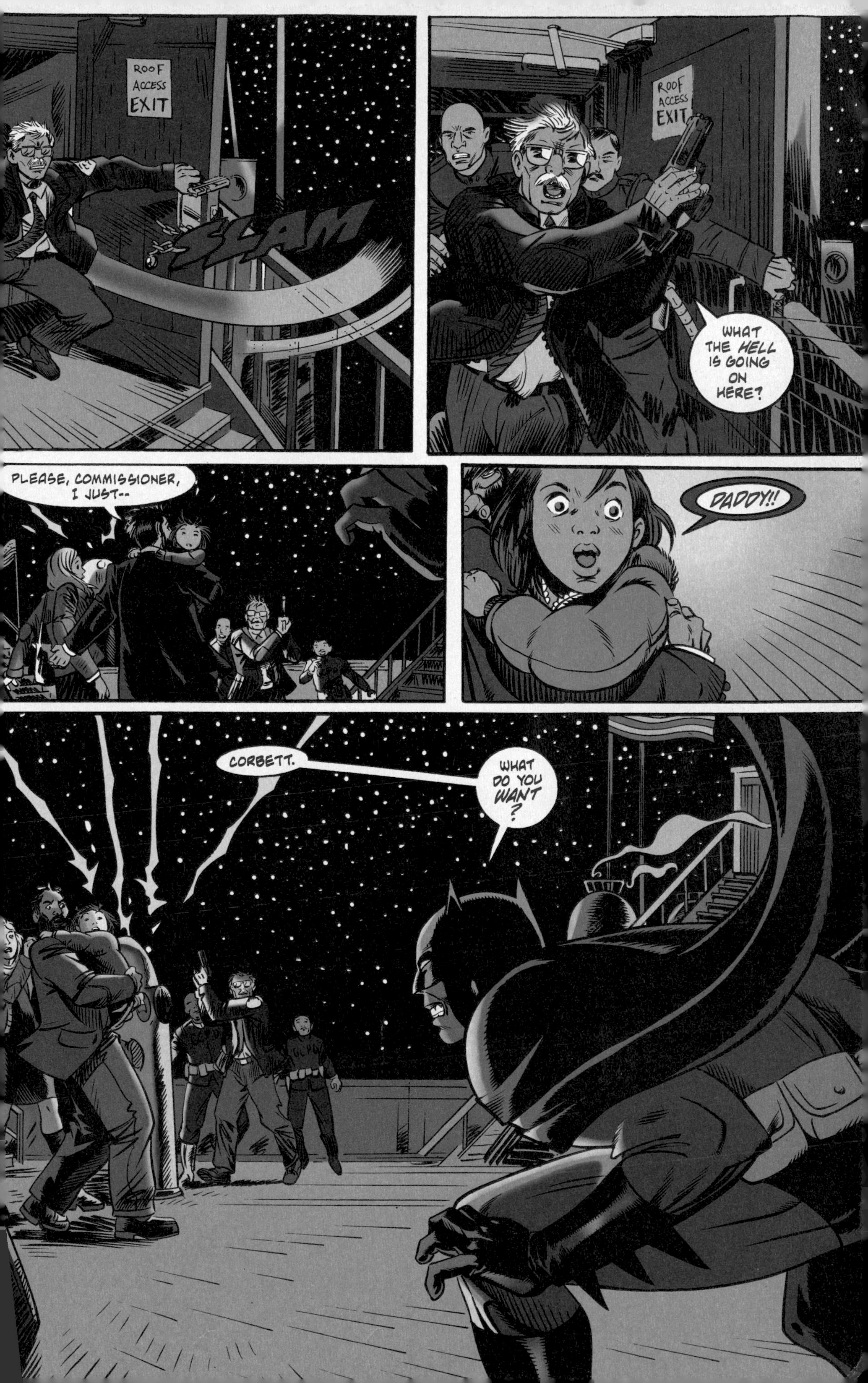
ROOF ACCESS EXIT
SLAM
ROOF ACCESS EXIT
WHAT THE *HELL* IS GOING ON HERE?
PLEASE, COMMISSIONER, I JUST--
DADDY!!
CORBETT.
WHAT DO YOU *WANT*?

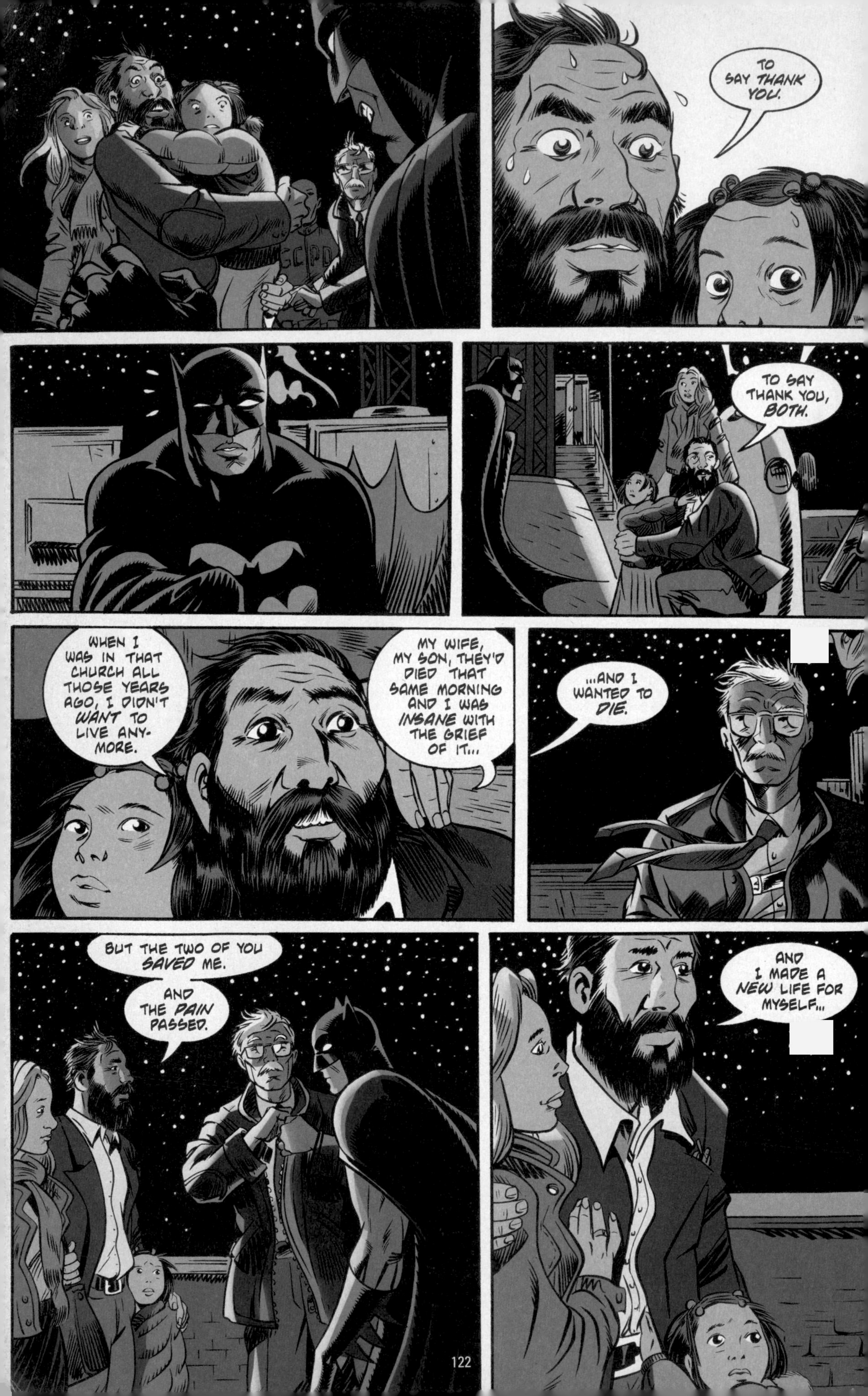
TO SAY THANK YOU.
TO SAY THANK YOU, BOTH.
WHEN I WAS IN THAT CHURCH ALL THOSE YEARS AGO, I DIDN'T WANT TO LIVE ANY-MORE.
MY WIFE, MY SON, THEY'D DIED THAT SAME MORNING AND I WAS INSANE WITH THE GRIEF OF IT...
...AND I WANTED TO DIE.
BUT THE TWO OF YOU SAVED ME.
AND THE PAIN PASSED.
AND I MADE A NEW LIFE FOR MYSELF...

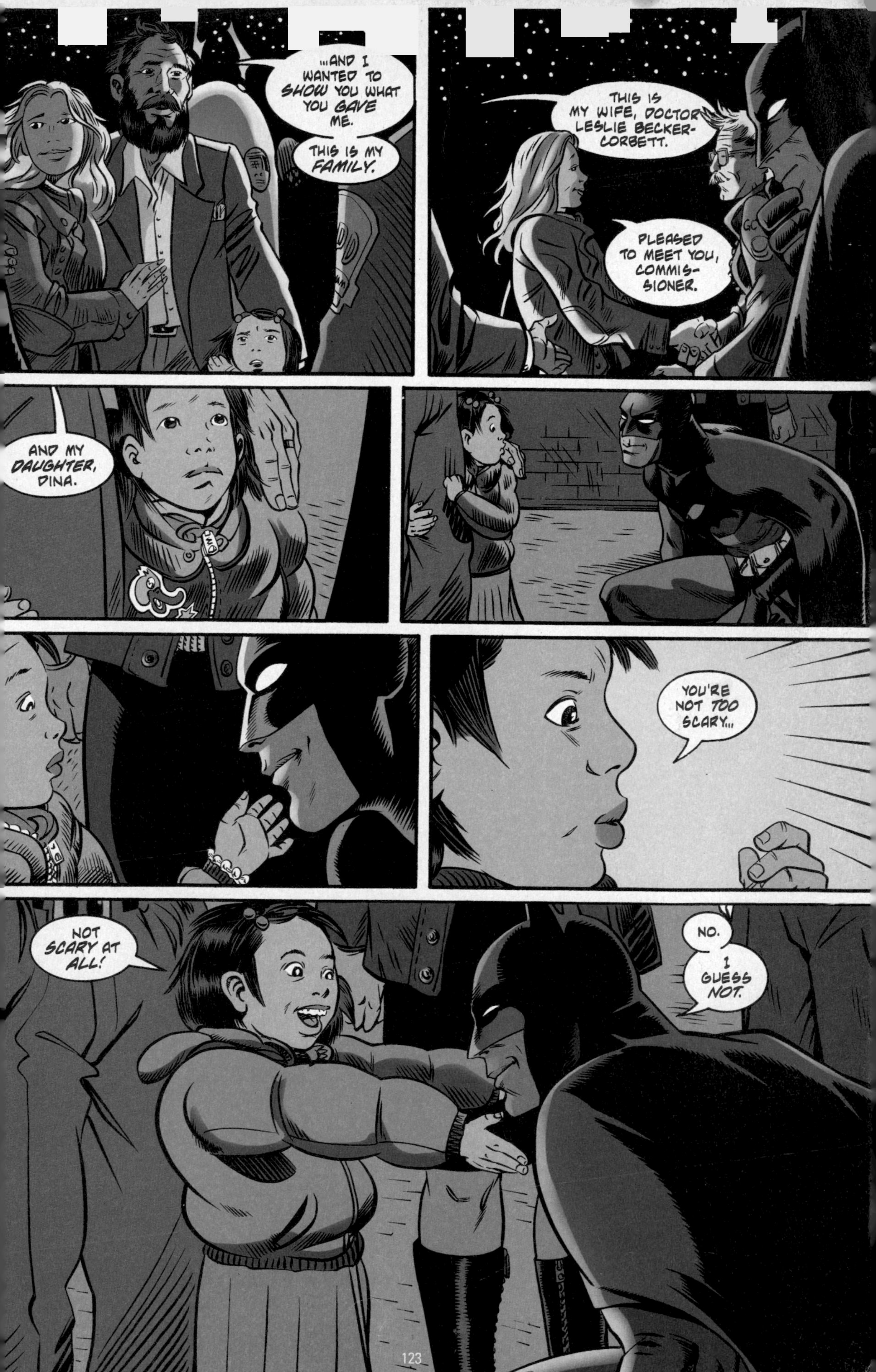
...AND I WANTED TO SHOW YOU WHAT YOU GAVE ME.
THIS IS MY FAMILY.
THIS IS MY WIFE, DOCTOR LESLIE BECKER-CORBETT.
PLEASED TO MEET YOU, COMMISSIONER.
AND MY DAUGHTER, DINA.
YOU'RE NOT TOO SCARY...
NOT SCARY AT ALL!
NO.
I GUESS NOT.

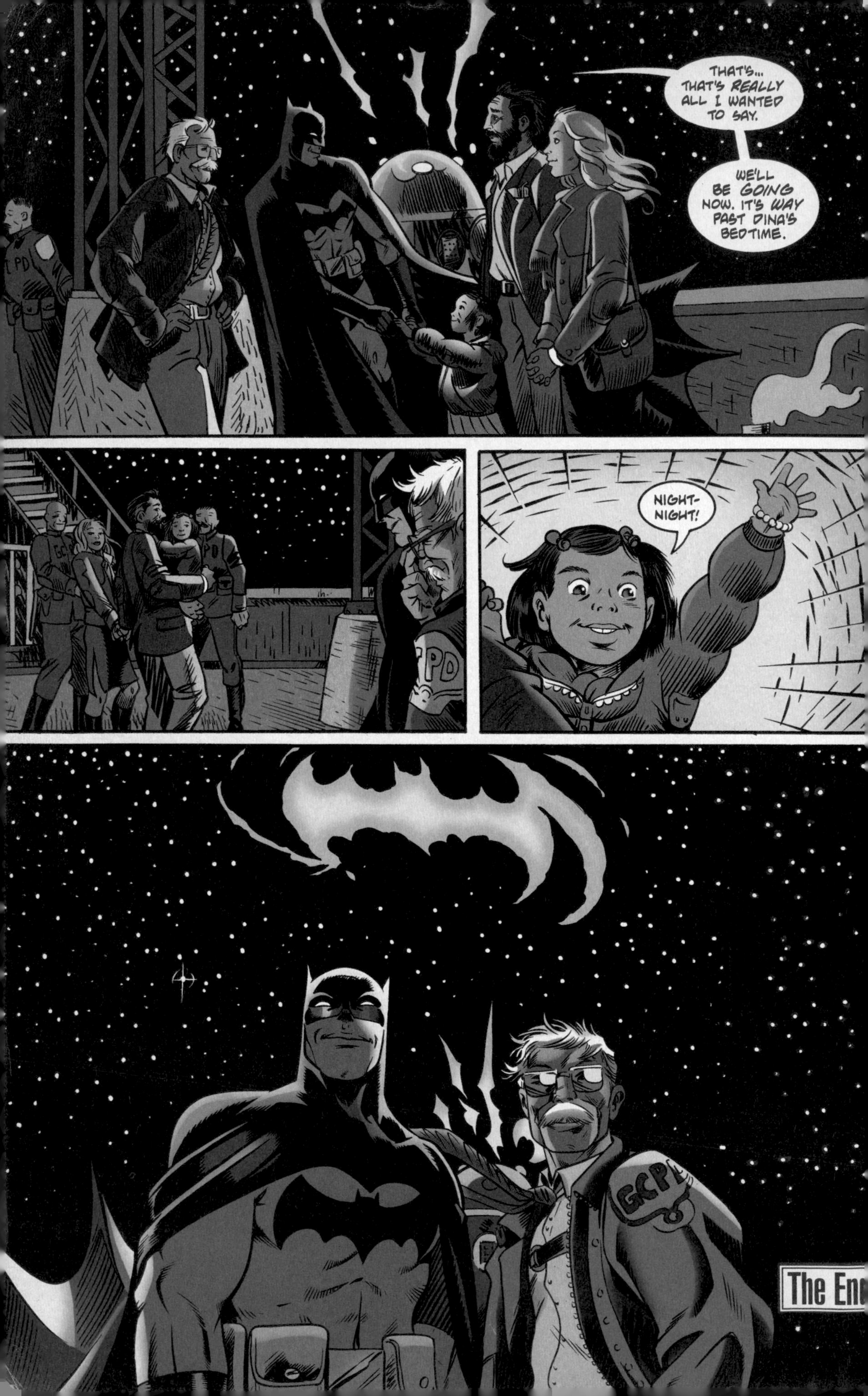
THAT'S... THAT'S REALLY ALL I WANTED TO SAY.
WE'LL BE GOING NOW. IT'S WAY PAST DINA'S BEDTIME.
NIGHT-NIGHT!
The End

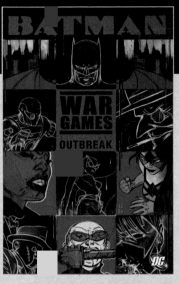

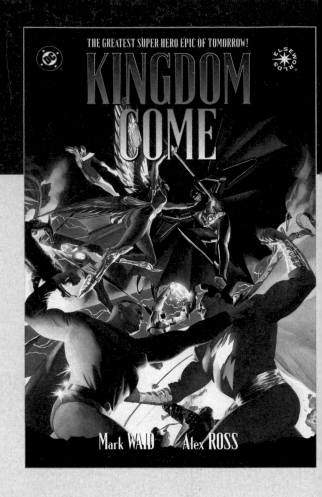
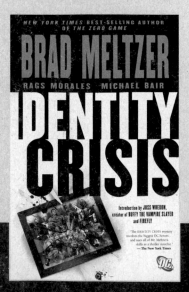